THESE VOLUMES ARE DEDICATED

TO THE MEN AND WOMEN
OF OUR TIME AND COUNTRY WHO BY WISE AND GENEROUS GIVING
HAVE ENCOURAGED THE SEARCH AFTER TRUTH
IN ALL DEPARTMENTS OF KNOWLEDGE

THE MESSIANIC HOPE IN THE NEW TESTAMENT

THE MESSIANIC HOPE IN THE NEW TESTAMENT

BY

SHAILER MATHEWS

OF THE DEPARTMENT OF SYSTEMATIC THEOLOGY

THE DECENNIAL PUBLICATIONS
SECOND SERIES   VOLUME XII

CHICAGO
THE UNIVERSITY OF CHICAGO PRESS
1905

Copyright 1904
BY THE UNIVERSITY OF CHICAGO

TO ERNEST DE WITT BURTON

TABLE OF CONTENTS

xi

INTRODUCTION

THEOLOGICAL reconstruction that shall in any true measure be based upon the New Testament is dependent, not only upon strictly philological exegesis, but also upon that larger historical exegetical process that endeavors to separate the content of a correctly apprehended teaching from the historical form in which it is cast. It is only when this form is resolved that the content stands clear, and it is in the content of biblical teaching alone that men of today can feel more than an antiquarian interest. To make the form co-ordinate with the content is to perpetuate an outgrown method and vocabulary. Theological teachers cannot hope to have modern significance if they force their followers first of all to think as did men of the past and to express truth as did men of the past. Theologians, of all men, should not be anachronistic.

How generally recognized this view has become in practical teaching may be seen in the abandonment of some of the most explicit directions of the New Testament on the ground that they were intended primarily and exclusively for Christians in some city like Corinth. Thus, for instance, few teachers would today assert that women should not speak in meetings, or that there was any divine regulation concerning the length of a Christian's hair. At the same time, these same teachers would assert that the general principles of orderly conduct and modest deportment which found expression in the apostle's directions to Græco-Roman Christians are as applicable to the Christians of today as to those of nineteen hundred years ago. In a much larger way the same statement applies to the Mosaic legislation. The teacher of today must endeavor to main-

tain such of its underlying principles as are not outgrown
by a Christian civilization, while distinguishing and rejecting
their particular and historical embodiment.

All this, the outcome of the practical considerations of
Christian experience, is, however, but one phase of a very
inclusive matter, viz., such a treatment of the Scriptures,
and especially of the New Testament, as will enable one
easily and with reasonable accuracy to distinguish between
the truth and its biblical expression. Or, to put the matter
a little differently, the presupposition of all theological
reconstruction is the existence of criteria which shall enable
one to distinguish the concepts and processes which conditioned the biblical writers from the religious experience
and truth which admittedly constitute the real substance of
what we call revelation.

Such criteria will be found among the thoughts and concepts current in the biblical period. Not that all such
thoughts and concepts were consciously used as merely
formal. More probably many, if not all, of them were
believed to embody as well as to typify realities. There
can be no doubt, for instance, that the ancient world actually
believed that the earth is flat, and that the sun actually
moves across the heavens. Such a cosmology has far-
reaching effects in biblical theology, and must be allowed for
in every case. There are many passages in both Testaments
which a man under the influence of today's cosmic truths
must have great difficulty in understanding. Similarly,
many religious concepts, which to later ages have seemed
very crude and naïve, were regarded as essential truth
by the men of the first Christian century. The criterion is,
therefore, not the valuation accorded a given concept by
those who used it, but the actual existence of that concept.
If it be urged that such current concepts may be essentially
as well as formally true, the only reply for the historical inter-

preter can be an assent to the possibility. Such concepts may be essential; they may be formal; they may conceivably be both. Yet periods which may care to reproduce the truths embodied in these concepts cannot be content to remain in such uncertainty, and will attempt, at least, to distinguish between the two possible valuations of the current beliefs of the past. The first step in the historical process, however, is not this distinction, which in fact is apologetic rather than historical, but is a formulation and an exact estimate of the place any concept holds in a given system of thought. After such an estimate is gained, one may well decide as to its formal or essential character. By that time the decision should have become reasonably easy. If the concept appears to be wholly *a priori*, in no clear way expressive of facts of experience, but is rather the outgrowth of rhetoric, faith, hope, and other emotions; and if it appears chiefly as interpretative and appreciative of what is obviously experience and personality; and especially if the concept in question be one that obviously is derived from a cosmogony or a theology that does not square with historical and scientific facts and processes; it will not be difficult to give it its true value and significance for the constructive and systematizing processes. But the historical process can never be overlooked. We must discover what a concept actually was, and then discover whether it is present in the documents under consideration.

Among all the concepts that appear in the New Testament none is more frequently met than that of messianism. Nor is there one more obviously local and ethnic. The hope of a divine deliverance from misery was not a product of classical religion or of Græco-Roman eclecticism. In the form current in the first century of our era it was not even Hebrew. It was Jewish, and, in its most elaborate form, pharisaic. That it should appear in New Testament literature was inevitable, for it was the medium through which his followers looked at Jesus, the form in which they expressed their appreciation of him, and the warp of all their speculation as to his and their own future. What, then, is its actual place in the teaching of the early church? How far is it formal, how far is it essential, Christianity?

In attempting to answer these inquiries, the method which will be followed will be that of historical exegesis. We shall first of all attempt to discover and formulate the elements of eschatological messianism as it is found in the literature of Judaism; in the second place, we shall examine the New Testament to see how much or how little of this element is to be found on its pages; and, in the third place, we shall attempt to determine the influence of such an element in Christian thought, and as far as possible to discover what would be the result upon historical Christianity if it were removed or, more properly speaking, allowed for.

PART I

THE MESSIANISM OF JUDAISM

CHAPTER I

THE SOCIAL AND NATIONAL MESSIANISM OF THE PROPHETS

MESSIANISM—or, if only the expression has not assumed the too distinct connotation of an expected personal Messiah, the messianic hope—is that fixed social belief of the Jewish people that Jehovah would deliver Israel and erect it into a glorious empire to which a conquered world would be subject. It sometimes, indeed frequently, involved the hope of a personal king—the Messiah, the Anointed One of God— but such an element is far less essential[1] than is implied by the term itself or its synonym, "the messianic hope." The central and ever-present element of the "messianic hope" was that of a divinely established deliverance and kingdom. The king was but an accessory, and, as will appear later, might not figure, except by implication, in one's hope for the nation's future.[2] Nor, even with this limitation as to its elements, was messianism any fixed concept. Rather it was ever developing. The child of the prophet's faith in Jehovah's care for an oppressed Israel, it soon ceased to share in the peculiar spirit of its parent, and, like nomism, the other great characteristic of Judaism, passed far beyond

---

[1] A personal Messiah is lacking, or at the best very indistinct, for instance, in Joel; Wisdom of Sirach, chap. 33; Isaiah, chaps. 24-7; Daniel; in much of Ethiopic *Enoch; Book of Jubilees; Assumption of Moses.* Other Jewish literature might be quoted. The list given by BOUSSET, *Die Religion des Judentums im neutestamentlichen Zeitalter*, p. 209, possibly overemphasizes the absence of the personal element.

[2] This discrimination is vital for an understanding of the rôle played by messianism as a socialized concept. The statement of WENDT (*Teaching of Jesus*, Vol. I, p. 69) is true only with this modification: "The expectation of the Messiah was without doubt widely prevalent among the Jews in the time of Jesus, but it was not quite universal and free from doubt." The remainder of the paragraph in question puts the matter more precisely. So, too (*ibid.*, p. 180), he says truly: "The Messiah was always conceived as the means whereby the kingdom of God was to be set up."

3

the limits set by precedent and experience. To understand
the original form taken by Christianity, it is necessary to
sketch this development and to distinguish between those
elements of faith common to all expressions of the hope, and
the fancies or teachings peculiar to the various writings in
which it has been preserved.

From the time that the first Hebrew dared to speak forth
in Jehovah's name and promise his downtrodden fellow-
countrymen divine deliverance from all their complaints, the
Jewish race mitigated political oppression with ideal utopias.
Primitive enough were these hopes in some of their aspects,
fit products of a cruel and barbarous age. A conquering
Israel, a Davidic king, a suppliant, terrorized, tortured
world—these were the dreams which Jehovah was to make
real. But, as prophecy advanced in its religious and ethical
content, there was associated with this elemental optimism an ever-growing sense of Israel's moral and religious
isolation. As a consequence, although barbarity still displayed itself in all forecasts of the future of heathendom,
ethical ideals were infused into the hopes for the triumph of
Israel. As the Hebrew religion grew moral, so the Hebrew
utopias grew religious. Compared with the hopes of New
Testament times, it is true, they were lacking in those transcendental elements that are commonly associated with messianism, but they were none the less of the same general
nature. That they were full of social content is clear from
the Hebrew literature,[1] even if many elements in early literature be attributed to the prophetic spirit of later editors.
The historical basis of the messianic ideal was the glorious
reign of David and Solomon, and in the pictures of the ideal
kings given in the "royal" psalms[2] there beats the inextin-

---

[1] For the collection of these sayings see GOODSPEED, *Israel's Messianic Hope*
(with good bibliography); DELITZSCH, *Messianic Prophecies;* HÜHN, *Die messianischen Weissagungen.*

[2] Pss. 2:2–4;7–10; 45; 72; 110. *Cf.* GOODSPEED, *op. cit.*, pp. 72, 73.

guishable optimism of a nation's faith in a divinely assured future. Early prophets, like Elijah and Elisha, saw in the religious and political crises resulting from the division of the kingdom of Solomon an opportunity to urge higher national ideals upon both the masses and the court. The calamities that threatened Israel, even during the brilliant reign of Jeroboam II., served as texts, not only for the dark forebodings of Amos, but for Hosea's prophecies of prosperity and peace that would come to the remnant of the nation when once it turned from idols and foreign alliances to a forgiving Jehovah.[1] In the disasters and miseries that came to both kingdoms during the days of Tiglath-pileser III., Sargon, and Sennacherib, Isaiah unfolded to Judah a religio-international policy that promised national deliverance and prosperity under a divinely appointed king,[2] and, as if to guarantee the certainty of the new nation, he set about the preparation of a "remnant" which should be its nucleus.[3] Micah also promised an empire to a faithful nation.[4] That Judah refused to listen to the words of these prophets makes all the more evident the social and political elements in their discourses. In fact, even if one should overlook the elaborate social provisions of Deuteronomy, prophetism, as a whole, was concerned with a regenerate Hebrew nation and a righteous king. That against which it cried out was such matters as the oppression of the poor, the formation of great landed estates, luxury, avarice, international policies, and national bad faith. Yet in denunciation there is the persistent trust in the nation's God. Even after the fading of Isaiah's promised future, Jeremiah, convinced though he was that Judah must certainly fall before the Chaldeans, yet

---

[1] For instance, Hos. 2:19-23; 14:1-8.

[2] Isa. 2:2-4; 4:2-6; 9:2-7; 11:1-9; 19:19-25.   [3] Isa. 8:16-18.

[4] Mic. 4:1-5. The relevancy of these passages will depend upon one's acceptance of them as pre-exilic. If they are post-exilic, the appropriate passages in the text should naturally be expunged.

looked beyond the approaching captivity to a restoration of the nation. Jehovah had made a new covenant with his people,[1] and his law was to be planted deep in their hearts as an inward guide. While it is true that the prophet does not describe in detail ideal institutions, it is clear from his denunciation of economic oppression[2] that just social conditions must have figured largely in his conception of the new covenant and the restored state.

With the exile this religio-political messianic hope, thus far so general and impersonal, passed into a new stage. The misery suffered by the Jews deported to Babylon, and the wonder that Jehovah could permit so great national and individual suffering, resulted in the formation of that pious remnant which Isaiah and Jeremiah had foreseen. Out from the misery there sprang fresh faith in a rapidly approaching divine deliverance. Ezekiel in Babylon planned a new commonwealth centered about a temple rebuilt with extravagant splendor. Religious as the hope of the exile was, and formally non-messianic as the Priestly Code undoubtedly is,[3] each was none the less social,[4] and never more so than when the sorrows of the good men of the nation were distinctly made vicarious[5] for the nation itself. In no

[1] Jer. 31:31-34; 33:17-22.
[2] Jer. 7:1-15.
[3] MONTEFIORE, Hibbert Lectures, p. 319.
[4] Ezek. 11:14-20; 37:21-28.

[5] Isa. 52:13—53:12. The interpretation of this passage, so generally considered by Christians as applicable to Jesus, in Jewish literature is social; the sufferer is not the Christ, but Israel, either a nation or the pious scribes (Bab. Siphré, 48b; Bab. Berach., 5a and 57b; Sota, 14a; Jer. Shekualim, 48c; Bereshith Rabba, 20, 1) in Israel (cf. JUSTIN, Dial. Trypho.,122, 123; ORIGEN, Ag. Celsus, I, 55). The reference of San., 98b, according to EDERSHEIM (Jesus the Messiah, Vol. II, p. 741), is to the Messiah as the "leprous one of the house of Rabbi." But this is from the second or third century, and represents the opinion of only a school of rabbis. See DALMAN, Der leidende und der sterbende Messias, pp. 28 f. Cf. also BUDDE, "The So-called 'Ebed-Yahweh Songs' and the Meaning of the Term 'Servant of Yahweh' in Isaiah, Chaps. 40-55," Amer. Journal of Theology, Vol. III, pp. 499 f.; MONTEFIORE, Hibbert Lectures, pp. 278 f.; CHEYNE, Prophecies of Isaiah, Vol. II, Essays iii-v; WRIGHT, "Pre-Christian Jewish Interpretation of Isa. lii-liv," Expositor, June, 1888; NEUBAUER-DRIVER, Catena of Jewish Interpretations of Isa. liii. There is at present a considerable tendency (e. g., Duhm, Sellin) toward an individualistic, or at least non-social, interpretation. The Servant is the typical good man whose sufferings are inexplicable from the point of view of nomism, unless they are vicarious. On the other hand, GIESEBRECHT, Der Knecht Jahves des Deuterojesaia, holds that the Servant is Israel as a nation.

other literature has the problem of national and communal suffering been more nobly faced and answered.

Throughout this period of prophetic optimism there ran a developing social theory that at last was to be incorporated in an actual society. At the outset the prophets had thought of the nation as a whole; Isaiah saw that the "remnant" alone carried with it the future; Jeremiah, though still hoping for the "remnant," saw also the religious and social importance of the individual; Ezekiel, appreciating as perhaps no other Hebrew the value of the individual, began a new process of national reconstruction. No longer looking to the nation, or even the remnant, as the unit, he attempted to bring all godly individuals into the godly remnant, and this, in turn, into a glorious nation under holy priests and a Davidic king. Thus the cycle of ideals was completed. Nothing remained except to bring these ideals of Ezekiel and the pious men of the exile into an actual commonwealth. And that it attempted this is perhaps the greatest significance of the event known as the Return.

When, through the favor of the Persian Cyrus, Judea again took something like its old place in the world, it was with the determination on the part of its reconstructors to found a theocratic state in which a completed Thorah was to regulate all matters of social life. But this was simply to embody the formulation of prophetic ideals; and this is only to say that the Return was an attempt to institutionalize prophetic messianism. Such an attempt was, in fact, all but inevitable. The prophets had expected that the divine deliverance would consist in the establishment of a Hebrew nation as untranscendental as Assyria and Egypt, its confederates,[1] and through the agency of no more miraculous intervention than would be involved in any political readjustment like the triumph of Assyria[2] or of Cyrus.[3]

[1] Isa. 19:19–25. [2] Isa. 10:5. [3] Isa. 44:28; 45:1.

The righteousness that was to characterize this new Israel was that elaborated in the later code, and obviously was thought of as involving all social relations. How else can one estimate the appearance of the Levitical code, the covenant not only to maintain the temple and its worship, but also to avoid mixed marriages, not to trade with "the people of the land" on the sabbath or a holy day, to let the land periodically lie fallow, to observe the sabbatical year, and not to exact payment of certain debts?[1] Throughout the entire course of this early legalism there runs the same idealism in hope and practice.

But we are not limited to such evidence of an attempt to institutionalize messianism. In the prophecies that may reasonably be assigned to this period the significance of the new commonwealth is described in messianic colors. In no other prophets is the certainty of national deliverance and prosperity through Jehovah's presence more emphasized. The one prerequisite is the observance of the Thorah by the individual and the maintenance of the temple by the nation.[2] Then, too, appeared that hope which was to play so great a rôle in early Christianity, that in those days so soon to dawn Jehovah would send his spirit upon a pious Israel to inspire new prophetic zeal and visions.[3] The coronation of Zerubbabel seemed to Haggai and Zechariah the fulfilment of the promise of a prince from the house of David,[4] and thus one more feature in the messianic kingdom. The Judah of the Return was to be the fulfilment of the prophets' promises. A state was to be founded in which all social life was to be regulated by the divine Thorah.

Of the history of the ineffectual ideal commonwealth

---

[1] Neh. 10:29-31. Possibly this is also the thought of the Pharisee who wrote the *Assumption of Moses*. See especially chaps. 3-5.

[2] Hag. 1:13; 2:6-9; Zech. 2:1-5, 10-13; 8:1-8, 12, 20-23; and especially Isa. 60:1-22.

[3] Joel 2:28, 29.   [4] Hag. 2:23; Zech. 3:8; 4:6-10; see also 6:11, 12.

which grew out of this hope it is not necessary to speak. Nor indeed are we in a position to trace its career with any certainty. Early Judaism is all but hidden in its own literatureless career. The few facts preserved by Josephus do not enable us to picture satisfactorily any of its phases, and we are forced to be content with conjecture and ingenious reconstructions.[1] If we were to judge of the time only by the "Wisdom" literature which may fairly be ascribed to it, we should be led to believe that the Jewish spirit had become philosophical, without enthusiasm for revealed law, and, with all its moral earnestness, callous as to religious idealism. Yet such a judgment would be one-sided. The transition from a renascent Hebraism to the new Judaism was marked by tendencies quite other than those toward philosophical Hellenism. These obscure years were in truth critical, for in them were developed tendencies that later were to result in the new Jewish world of the New Testament epoch. It was then that the new Hellenizing aristocracy of wealth, later to be known as the Sadducees, was founded in the family of that extraordinary adventurer, Joseph.[2] Then, too, began that scrupulous devotion to the Thorah which was later to give religious history one of its most interesting figures, the Pharisee.

Yet, as regards materials for tracing the development of messianism, these years are sadly deficient. Indeed, it is hard to discover that there was any such hope in a glorious future for Judea as would merit being called messianic. Doubtless, if it were possible to picture the faith that survived among the humble folk that afterward were known as the Pious, it would appear that the idealism which brought about the Return was by no means dead. It is impossible to believe that the outburst of messianic literature that followed the persecution of Antiochus Epiphanes would have

[1] For instance, CHEYNE, *Jewish Religious Life after the Exile.*   [2] *Ant.*, xii, 4.

been possible without some widespread religious hope. Certainly, the new Judaism that rose when once the party of the Pharisees had differentiated itself from the Pious and the Sadducees, found ready to its hand all the elements of later messianism. There were (1) the ineradicable belief that Jehovah would re-establish the Jewish nation in indescribable glory, and (2) under a "legitimate" monarch, a son of David; (3) the equally fixed belief that he would judge the world and punish with indescribable sufferings the enemies of his chosen nation, and, though this is less clear, the wicked generally, whether gentiles or Jews. (4) A fourth element, the belief in a resurrection of the dead, indistinctly associated with the establishment of a regenerate Israel, can easily be overemphasized, but was undoubtedly present, at first in a somewhat figurative sense—the resurrection of a defunct state. It was this hope that later was to develop into an entire eschatology.

Such a catalogue of elements subsequently synthesized it would have been impossible to find in any other nation than that of the Jews. The fact that none of them was novel in the last pre-Christian century argues the persistence, so far as Palestine itself is concerned, of the prophetic idealism across these years of almost unbroken literary barrenness. And this idealism was, in the New Testament period, to follow two lines of development. There was, first, the revolutionary messianism of the masses; and, second, the ecshatological messianism of the literary classes, notably the Pharisees. Both hopes were implicit in the prophetic messianism of the pre-Maccabean age, but the former, alone following more closely the spirit of earlier prophetism, constituted something like a genuinely religio-social movement. The messianism of the Pharisees, on the other hand, following rather the apocalyptic tendency first really distinct in the Maccabean period, grew scholastically religious and quite without social content.

CHAPTER II

THE POLITICO-SOCIAL PROGRAM OF REVOLUTIONARY MESSIANISM

WHILE it is true that under the pressure of political misery both transcendental and revolutionary messianism differentiated themselves simultaneously in Judaism, it was the latter that remained the more conservative. Development is limitless within the region of such speculation as went to constitute the pseudepigraphic literature of apocalyptic, but in social movements hopes are tempered by experience. Further, the thoughts and hopes of the masses are always difficult to trace, but doubly so when, as among the Jews, they are all but unexpressed in literature and must generally be inferred from references in an unfriendly historian like Josephus. None the less, popular messianism deserves more attention than could be accorded it as long as no distinction was made between messianism as a regulative social concept and as a hope for a personal Messiah. It is difficult to show that the latter was universally cherished in the time of Jesus, but the hope for a new Israel, delivered and ruled by God, was always and everywhere in evidence. Throughout the entire period from Judas Maccabæus to the fall of Jerusalem, this hope of a new Israel was never suppressed, and at last became utterly uncontrollable. But revolution was not in the program of the literati or the well-to-do classes. It is, indeed, no unstriking parallelism that might be drawn between the different effects produced by English philosophy upon the literary circles and the masses of France during the eighteenth century, and the two manifestations of messianism among the scribes and the despised

11

'*am haarets* of Judaism during New Testament times. In both these pre-revolutionary epochs the radicalism of the literary circles, quite content with a policy of *laissez-faire*, was opposed to struggle, while the discontent of the masses, when once it had appropriated the watchwords and philosophy of the literary world, undertook to bring into actual existence a future which the comfortable middle class was quite ready to intrust to providence. Only, unlike the philosophers of France, in Judea the Pharisees had no keen interest even in reform, and the masses had no need to wait for the slow infiltration of ideas which they, as well as the Pharisees, had received as a common inheritance from their past.

It is commonly held that the messianic hope is wanting in 1 Maccabees, and this is true if one looks only for distinct references to an expected messianic king. The only approach to such a hope is to be seen in expectation of the prophet who was to come and solve riddles;[1] but, as is now pretty generally held, this prophet is certainly not the Messiah, but one like those of the old Hebrew days who was expected to appear and give a perplexed people infallible directions for conduct.[2] None the less, it is not improbable that the author of 1 Maccabees, like the authors of Judith, Tobit, and Baruch, expected a divine deliverance of Israel as well as a punishment of the heathen, and it is very probable that, in the spirit of the approximately contemporary portions of the *Sibylline Oracles*, though regarding David's dynasty as perpetual,[3] he saw in the Asmonean house something more than a family of successful adventurers. In fact, he expressly gives them a messianic significance in the general sense of playing a part in the divine program for regenerating Israel, when he

---

[1] For example, the disposition of the stones of the polluted altar of burnt-sacrifice (1 Macc. 4:46) and the adjustment of the new Asmonean priestly dynasty with the claims of the house of Zadok (1 Macc. 14:41. *Cf.* also 1 Macc. 9:27).

[2] *Cf.* Mark 6:15; 8:28, where the prophet is sharply distinguished from the Christ.

[3] 1 Macc. 2:57.

explains the defeat of certain emulators of Judas. They were "not of the seed of the men by whose hand deliverance was given unto Israel."[1]   As has already been said, there is certainly nothing improbable in the conjecture that the pre-suppositions lying back of such a comment are near akin to that hope and faith that found expression in the con-temporary literature of Daniel and *Enoch*. Doubtless the disappointment over the later Asmoneans felt by the pharisaic author of the *Psalms of Solomon*[2] was due in no small degree to the striking contrast between hopes cherished by his party in its earlier stages and the actual history of the descendants of John Hyrcanus. In this experience, as may later appear, is one very probable explanation for the subse-quent refusal of the Pharisees to place confidence in any-thing less than superhuman catastrophic messianism. Cer-tainly this is the dominant teaching of 2 Maccabees, itself a sort of pharisaic reply to the realism of 1 Maccabees. God is sure to render judgment upon the oppressors of Israel, and assures eternal life at least to pious Hebrews.[3]

The reign of Herod I. was not conducive to even apocalyp-tic messianic hopes, much less to any attempt to establish a new kingdom, whether of man or God, in Judea. We are, indeed, quite without any distinct literary reference to messianism during his reign — a fact that argues, not only repression, but also tolerable content on the part of the literary classes.[4] Yet, possibly, revolutionary messianism is to be seen in the robber bands which Herod was forced to reduce. Such scanty evidence as exists concerning these men makes it probable that they were akin to nationalists rather than to

[1] 1 Macc. 5:62.   [2] *Cf*. Pss. 1:5–9; 2:3, 5, 8; 4:5; 7:2; 8:9–14.

[3] 2 Macc. 7:9, 11, 14, 19, 23, 29, 35–37; 12:43, 44. The second of the two letters pre-fixed to 2 Maccabees has a hope of a re-established nation and cult.

[4] The plot of the Pharisees described in *Ant*., xvii, 2:4, can hardly be messianic, since they are said to have promised the kingdom to Pheroras. Josephus's descrip-tion of this party is doubtless taken from Nicholas of Damascus. It hardly reads like the opinion of one who was himself a Pharisee.

brigands.[1]   The conspiracy of the ten men,[2] and the revolt
of the people under the rabbis Judas and Mattathias,[3] were
also an exhibition of a nationalism which, though not to be
very clearly described, certainly had its origin in the religious sensibilities of the masses.[4]

It was with the death of Herod that revolutionary messianism entered upon its uncontrollable career.   From that
time it is possible to trace its history in a series of more or
less successful revolts, a succession of not always abortive
popular movements, and the formation of sects.   Indeed,
the entire course of rebellion, which culminated in the
triumph of the Zealots and the war of 66–70 A. D., is best
understood as an ever-increasing revolutionary messianism—
an attempt on the part of popular leaders to hasten that
divine deliverance of their nation which the prophets had
foretold, and which every Jew believed was sure to come.
The words of Josephus[5] describing the motive of the
rebellion give us the only true point of view: "What
most stirred them up to the war was an ambiguous oracle
that was found also in their sacred writings, that about
that time one from their country should become ruler of
the world."   To adopt this point of view is, however, not
to say that all revolts were messianic.   Several of them,
as, for instance, those that followed the death of Herod,
were clearly without any such significance.[6]   Nor is the

---

[1] For example, Hezekiah and his band (JOSEPHUS, *Ant.*, xiv, 9:2), though this
case is less probable than the other (*Ant.*, xiv, 15:4, 5).   The robbers he restrained
in Trachonitis by settling colonists from Idumæa (*Ant.*, xvi, 9:1, 2) were of quite
another type.

[2] *Ant.*, xv, 8:3, 4.   [3] *Ant.*, xvii, 6:2-4.

[4] JOSEPHUS, *Ant.*, xv, 10:4, explains Herod's remission of a third of the taxes as
an effort to regain the good-will of an outraged people.   Josephus also in this connection notes Herod's use of spies and his forbidding meetings of all sorts except
those of the Essenes.

[5] *War*, vi, 5:4.   *Cf.* TACITUS, *Hist.*, v, 13; SUETONIUS, *Cæsars*, Vespasian, 4.

[6] For instance, that of the slave Simon and the shepherd Athrongæus (*War*, ii,
4:2, 3), and various other outbreaks, as those of *War*, ii, 5:1 ff.

revolt of 66–70 to be unreservedly called messianic. Many men, then, like Justus[1] were doubtless nothing more than rebels of a purely political sort. Those disturbances alone are to be considered messianic which are the work of a peculiar religious sect or, in particular, are evidently connected with the great Zealot movement of the middle of the century.

The emergence of this revolutionary messianism as a distinct political factor was at the taxing which succeeded the erection of Judea into a procuratorial province at the banishment of Archelaus in 6 A. D. At that time Judas[2] of Gamala in Gaulanitis and a Pharisee named Zadduk organized a fourth sect, especially influential among the younger Jews, co-ordinate with the Pharisees, Sadducees, and Essenes, and encouraged the people to revolt against the new foreign ruler.[3] Its character is clearly set forth in the description of Josephus: "Its disciples agree in all other things with the pharisaic notions, but they have an inviolable attachment to liberty, and say that God is their only ruler and lord." The share of this sect, so clearly that of the Zealots, with its "kingdom of God," in the downfall of the Jewish state is emphatically declared by Josephus.[4] To trace the rise of the Jewish revolt is hardly anything else than to trace the growth of the messianic propaganda. Nor was its spirit wholly confined to Judea. For, though anything like complete information is wanting, it is difficult not to see something akin to Zealot fanaticism in the gathering of armed Samaritans near Gerizim in order to discover the

[1] JOSEPHUS, Life, 65.

[2] A Galilean (War, ii, 8:1; Ant., xviii, 1:1, 6). According to GUTHE (art. "Israel," Ency. Bib.), he was probably the son of the "robber" Ezekias executed by Herod (Ant., xvii, 10:5; xiv, 9:3 f.).

[3] Ant., xviii, 8:1, 6. His sons, like those of Mattathias under Antiochus Epiphanes, apparently continued the movement begun by their father, for they were crucified by Alexander the procurator (Ant., xx, 5:2).

[4] Ant., xviii, 1:1, 6.

sacred vessels buried in the mountains by Moses.[1] But it
was in Judea and Galilee that the leaven worked most effect-
ively.   The prophet Theudas, who, in 45 or 46 A. D., induced
a great multitude to follow him toward Jordan, which, like
another Moses, he promised to divide, evidently appealed to
the messianic hopes of the masses.   That his career produced no results was due to the promptness of the procurator
Fadus.[2]   Under Felix, Judea and Galilee were alive with
robbers and impostors, some of whom, like Eleazar, who for
twenty years had led a band of outlaws,[3] the procurator executed; and some of whom, like the newly appearing Sicarii,
he seems to have used to further his own plans.[4] Along
with the Sicarii were men like Theudas urging the masses
to follow them into the wilderness, there to see miracles.
One of these impostors—if it is fair to use quite so harsh
a term—was an Egyptian who promised his followers
from the *'am haarets* to stand on the Mount of Olives
and cause the walls of Jerusalem to fall.[5]   More significant, however, are the obscure words of Josephus[6] in
which he describes a body of "wicked men, cleaner in their
hands, but more wicked in their intentions, who destroyed
the peace of the city no less than did these murderers [the
Sicarii].   For they were deceivers and deluders of the
people, and under pretense of divine illumination were for

1 *Ant.*, xviii, 4:1. If this should have been by any chance connected also with
the work of John and Jesus in the vicinity, it would have been one element in a piece
of poetic justice. For it was his dispersion of this gathering that brought Pilate
into exile.

2 *Ant.*, xx, 5:1; *cf.* Mark 13:22; Matt. 24:11, 24. The disturbances under
Cumanus (*Ant.*, xx, 5:3, 4; *War*, ii, 12:1, 2) were due to religious fanaticism, though
hardly to messianic currents.

3 *Ant.*, xx, 8:5; *War*, ii, 13:2, 3.

4 These Sicarii were a group of fanatical Zealots, and hence messianists (*cf. Ant.*,
xviii, 1:1), who turned to assassination as a means of hurrying in the kingdom of
God. Their share in the revolt of 66–70 A. D. was not considerable, but they held
Masada, and perished there by their own hands (*War*, ii, 17:6; iv, 7:2, 9:5;
vii, 8:1 f., 10:1, 11:1).

5 *Ant.*, xx, 8:6; *War*, ii, 13:5; *cf.* Acts 21:38.   6 *War*, ii, 13:4.

innovations and changes." It is not difficult to see in these men a body of fanatics bound upon assisting God[1] to bring in the deliverance for which their nation was passionately hoping.[2]

Under Felix there began to appear in this seething messianism of the masses elements of social as well as political revolution. Several of the bodies of fanatics who were urging the masses to revolt were also plundering and burning the houses of the well-to-do people and killing their owners.[3] How far the "innovating party at Jerusalem," which, according to Josephus,[4] under Albinus became a combination of "arch-robbers," and their "satellites" is to be identified with these emulators of the early Maccabeans it is impossible to say. The times were breeding anarchy quite as much as revolutionary idealism. Yet one cannot doubt that the messianism of the Zealots included some wild schemes for reorganizing the Jewish state. Peasant utopias are always hard to reconstruct, so completely is one at the mercy of hostile chroniclers and historians; but if one comes to the history of the Zealots from that of the German and English Peasant Wars, and especially from the strikingly analogous movements among the French peasantry and proletarians just before and during the Revolution of 1789, it will be easy to see, back of the violence Josephus delights in char-

---

1 They believed that "God would show them signs of liberty " in the desert.

2 This hope of the Zealots has also been seen (e. g., SCHÜRER, Vol. III[3], p. 219; MATHEWS, New Testament Times in Palestine, p. 168) in Assumption of Moses, 10:8, which has sometimes been translated, "Thou shalt tread upon the neck and the wing of the eagle," the reference certainly suggesting Rome, and breathing thus the spirit of Zealotism. The translation, however, of the evidently mutilated verse should probably be, " Thou shalt mount up on the neck and the wings of the eagle," i. e., toward heaven, a thought immediately expressed in 10:9, 10. The entire fragment seems to express quietism and the non-resistance of the Chasidim as well as the unwarlike transcendentalism of early pharisaism. See especially 9:4–7, with which compare 1 Macc. 1:53; 2:31–38; 2 Macc. 6:11; 10:6; Ant., xii, 6:2. That the author was a Pharisee is now held by CHARLES, Assumption of Moses; CLEMEN, in KAUTZSCH, Apokryphen und Pseudepigraphen, Vol. II, pp. 314 f. The fragment was probably written during the first quarter of the first Christian century.

3 War, ii, 13:6.   4 War, ii, 14:1.

ging upon them, a determined effort on the part of men like John of Gischala and Eleazar to establish a new Jewish state in which there should be not only liberty,[1] but also equality. This purpose it is that explains, at least partially, that cleavage between the wealthy, learned, and official classes and the masses, which characterized the entire revolutionary period. Such cleavage was no new phenomenon, for the *'am haarets* had always been despised by the Pharisees and high-priests,[2] but with the first resistance to the procurator Gessius Florus it became a source of civil war. From the outset the Pharisees and high-priests as a class opposed the revolt. Singularly enough, however, the radical who first proposed that the sacrifices for the emperor cease was Eleazar, the son of the high-priest Ananias, at that time governor of the temple; and, despite the opposition of the class to which he belonged, he was able to carry his plan into action.[3] The conservative element in Jerusalem was, indeed, with the greatest difficulty induced to abandon the non-political[4] attitude of apocalyptic messianism. It undertook the organization of the revolt only as the less of two evils, and doubtless with the purpose of making peace as soon as possible with Rome[5]—a fact that gives special significance to the labors of that enemy of dilettante revolutionists, John of Gischala.[6] But even such adjustment of the "classes" and "masses" was short-lived. The moment the Zealots and their sympathizers among the masses gained

---

[1] *Cf. War*, iv, 4:1, 5; 5:5.

[2] That this contempt should have grown under the later rabbis is very likely due in part to the events of the civil war, 66–70 A. D. For illustration of what this feeling was, see quotations in SCHÜRER, *Jewish People, etc.*, Div. II, ii, 8(*b*), especially *Demai*, ii, 3. On some more shocking expressions (*e. g.*, "a member of the *'am haarets* may be slit up," *Pesachim*, 49*b*) see some very sensible words in LAZARUS, *Ethics of Judaism*, Vol. I, pp. 258 f.

[3] *War*, ii, 17:2.   [4] *Ant.*, xvii, 11:1, 2.

[5] JOSEPHUS, *Life*, 7; *War*, ii, 17:4; iv, 5:2. See also *War*, ii, 20:1–3.

[6] *War*, ii, 21:1, 2; *Life*, 13.

any advantage, their policy of economic as well as political revolution emerged. Thus in the first excitement of the attempt to establish the ideal state they set fire to the public archives,[1] burned all records of indebtedness, and massacred the high-priest Ananias.[2] This anti-aristocratic spirit developed rapidly after the collapse of the attempt of the *bourgeois* party to organize a successful revolt in Galilee, and, thanks to the enthusiasm of the younger Jews, throughout the fearful days of civil war it grew even more extreme. A band of fanatical Idumean patriots was introduced as the means of establishing a veritable reign of terror, in the midst of which many wealthy men were killed, including the noble high-priest Ananus.[3]   The effort to force the hand of Jehovah and to compel him to hasten the deliverance of an abortive messianic state had become, like so many a later revolution, a carnival of blood. Yet through all this struggle one can see the persistent, though ever-diminishing, idealism of the Zealots. They would have a peasant high-priest, a new state, a new people, and no king but God.[4]   The ancient prophets in whose words they trusted could not be seen to foretell anything but triumph for such an ambition,[5] and during the miseries of the last days of the capital the later prophets were urging the people to await deliverance from God.[6]

Their mad hope of deliverance included, as has already been said, a conqueror, whose appearance was assured by the "ambiguous oracle" (χρησμὸς ἀμφίβολος) of which Josephus speaks, and which can be no other than that of Daniel.[7]

[1] Yet, *cf. War*, vi, 6:3.

[2] *War*, ii, 17:6, 9. That they were seeking after some ideal state is clear from Eleazar's execution of the would-be tyrant Menahem.

[3] *War*, iv, 5:1-3.   [4] *Cf. War*, iv, 3:6-8; 5:4, 5; 6:1.   [5] *War*, iv, 6:3.

[6] *War*, vi, 5:2. Many portents are described by JOSEPHUS, *War*, vi, 5:3.

[7] That Josephus himself regarded this prophecy as foretelling the destruction of Rome seems implied by his refusal to interpret the "stone" of Dan. 2:45 in *Ant.*, x, 10:4.

Here in this hope the *motif* of the entire Zealot movement may be seen: its members believed that, if once they could organize an independent republic, during its struggle with Rome the Messiah himself would come to its aid.[1] It is even possible to see in the desperate faith of the Jerusalem prophets[2] a faith born of Dan. 9 : 25, that the very destruction of Jerusalem would in God's own time — "seven weeks and three score and two weeks" — be followed by the appearance of the Messiah.[3]

In very truth, the Jews who had rejected Jesus as Messiah paid terribly for their rejection of "the things that pertained to peace" and their choice of another hope. The Jewish state fell, the victim of an ever-developing fanaticism, born of a faith in a coming kingdom and king. In the attempt made by the Zealots to hasten God's time there is to be seen a hope for an actual commonwealth, which, however we may admit our lack of information, was clearly to embrace new social institutions. How vain was their dream is apparent, but it was no less dreamed. Nor did messianism of this type perish with the temple. A half-century later it again blazed out, but with its champions no longer separated from the party of the Pharisees. In its new form revolutionary messianism was guided and inspired by no less a person than the great rabbi Akiba.

[1] The rôle played by the prophecies of Daniel throughout this period of the Jewish state is great. Chief reliance was undoubtedly laid upon the vision of the "stone cut without hands from the mountain" (Dan. 2:45) and the vision of the "Son of man" (7:13), the Messiah (9:25), and the apocalypse of chaps. 11 and 12. The "ambiguity" in these oracles can have been only whether the new prince was to be a native Jew of Palestine or a foreigner. JOSEPHUS interprets it in the latter sense (so GERLACH, *Die Weissagungen d. A. T. in den Schriften d. Fl. Jo.*, p. 73), apparently thereby giving up all further expectation of a coming Messiah — a conclusion, however, hard to accept in the light of *Ant.*, x, 10:4, and his treatment of the prophecy of Balaam (*Ant.*, iv, 6:5). It is perhaps worth noticing that this familiarity of the people at large with the prophecies of Daniel is an important element in judging the meaning Jesus conveyed by speaking of himself as ὁ υἱὸς τοῦ ἀνθρώπου.

[2] *War*, vi, 5:2. [3] GERLACH, p. 84.

CHAPTER III

THE APOCALYPTIC MESSIANISM OF THE PHARISEES

SECTION I. THE RISE OF APOCALYPTIC

As THE legalism of pharisaism was the outgrowth of the Codes, so the idealism of its apocalyptic was the outgrowth of prophetism. The forerunner of apocalyptic must be sought in what had been a regulative thought of the prophets, the Day of Jehovah—that time when the God of Israel would exercise his right and inflict terrible punishment upon all those who had not kept his law. What this Day had been to Israel before Amos may be conjectured from the national belief in Jehovah as a God certain to defeat all rivals; it was to be a day of joy and peace for a conquering Hebrew nation.[1] With Amos and the great prophets who succeeded him the Day became one in which Israel was to be punished by Jehovah for its sins. Instead of glory there was to be frightful suffering. The luxury of the nation, springing as it did from economic oppression, had grown hateful to the prophet and his God,[2] and the degenerate people was to be destroyed as a vindication of Jehovah's righteousness.

Ever after Amos the Day had the same religious coloring. Yet it was no longer to be a punishment merely of a wicked Israel, but of a wicked world. Zephaniah saw an all but universal judgment day, for Jews as well as heathen.[3]

[1] See the discussion by J. M. P. SMITH, "The Day of Yahweh," *American Journal of Theology*, July, 1901, pp. 505 f.

[2] Amos 2:6-8; 3:9-15; 5:10-13; 6:4-8. HARPER, "The Prophecies of Amos Strophically Arranged," *Biblical World*, 1898. *Cf.* McCURDY, *History, Prophecy and the Monuments*, Vol. I, pp. 308 f.

[3] Zeph. 3:8, 14-20, however, argue the exception of Judah. If this is late, 1:2-18; 2:4-15, present the Day with sufficient distinctness.

21

Ezekiel conceived of it as a day of battle in which Jehovah would conquer all of Israel's foes.[1] Later prophets, like Malachi, foretold the fearful punishment to be then meted out upon the wicked, Jew and gentile alike. Whatever hope of deliverance the Day might contain was for the pious remnant.

After the exile this thought of deliverance from their enemies naturally grew stronger among a people consciously striving to keep Jehovah's law, and thus the Day became assimilated with the new messianic hope. All its terrors were believed to be reserved for the enemies of the new Judah.[2] Religious faith lost itself in visions, and revenge found earthly warfare insufficient for its purposes. A new rhetoric was demanded, in which the extremes of pessimism as to the present and the wildest optimism for the future might be properly exhibited. And then arose the apocalypse.[3]

One cannot be far from the truth if he considers the apocalypse the exposition of the Day of Jehovah in a literary form resulting from the Hellenistic influences under which the Jews lived even from before the days of Alexander. This influence was both philosophical and æsthetic. Of philosophy was born Wisdom, and of æsthetics was born apocalyptic. Greek influence always prompted a people to some form of æsthetic expression, but the new art, in so far as it was not simply imitative, was determined by a people's past. As the Greek turned to marble and bronze and canvas as the media in which to perpetuate his anthropomorphic symbols of truth and hopes, the Jew, fearing to make to himself any graven image, used language for his statues and his paintings. Utterly lacking in a knowledge of technique,[4] hardly ven-

---

[1] Ezek. 30: 2 f.; 34:12; 39:8 f.   [2] Cf. Joel 2:18–27.

[3] Cf. CHARLES, art. "Apocalyptic," HASTINGS's Dictionary of the Bible; TORREY, "Apocalypse," Jewish Encyclopædia, Vol. I, and literature cited there.

[4] Cf., for instance, the bas-relief decoration in the castle of Hyrcanus, east of Jordan, in 'Arak el-Emir (JOSEPHUS, Ant., xii, 4:11).

turing to look at a Greek god or goddess, deficient in the very elements of art, he painted his word-pictures as he had seen the uncouth monsters of Egypt and Assyria.[1] His symbols became strange creatures with eagles' wings and lions' bodies, legs of brass, and feet of clay. Unity was as lacking in the composition of his pictures as in their units. Bulls and buffaloes and sheep and goats and birds and shepherds jostled each other in his visions, and the fixed order of nature was unhesitatingly reversed. Yet in all these inartistic, confused symbols stands the one great thought of the prophetic Day of Jehovah. God will judge mankind, will gloriously deliver a righteous Israel from oppression, will indescribably punish the wicked and the heathen, and will establish a regenerate Judah at the head of the entire world.

It is not to our purpose to discuss how far these composite pictures of pessimism and extravagant hope were also influenced by the creation myths of Babylon.[2] That there was such influence is clear, not alone from the characters and scheme of each apocalypse,[3] but from the fact of the appearance of this bastard prophetism among those who had been subjected to the influences of the exile. Yet the apocalypse really belongs to the Greek period of Jewish history. While visions were not unknown to genuine prophetism, it is not until the post-exilic second Zechariah[4] that a true apocalypse is met in Hebrew literature. As might have been expected, this first apocalypse deals, however interruptedly, with the Day of Jehovah, although "that day" is preferred to this precise term. There, as always, its chief content is that of punishment, but along with threats there are

---

[1] *Cf.* for a popular statement F. DELITZSCH, *Babel und Bibel.*

[2] The question as to whether the apocalyptic pictures are mythological or products of their times " scheint mir vielfach ein Streit um des Kaisers Bart zu sein," says PREUSCHEN, *Zeitschrift für die neutestamentliche Wissenschaft*, 1901, p. 169, note

[3] See GUNKEL, *Schöpfung und Chaos*, pp. 286–93, for summary.

[4] Zech., chaps. 9–14.

the promises of blessings; for Israel was to be repentant, and out of its sorrow was to come deliverance. But wild as are the figures with which these complementary thoughts are set forth, it would be untrue to the general spirit inspiring the early apocalyptic writing to think of its visions as in the strictest sense eschatological.[1] A complete eschatology was possible only when to other hopes there was joined some recognition of the resurrection of the dead. In a general sense, it is true, one might call these forecastings of the future eschatological, but only in the sense that the apocalypses looked across the culmination of one "age" into the events of another. Farther than this it is impossible to go. The synthesis of the nation's and the individual's future attempted by Ezekiel had been wholly within this mortal life. It would be impossible to deny that the Jews throughout his period, when the material of later messianism was developing, had some belief in immortality, but there is no evidence that this hope had become in any way connected with messianism. Yet after the Return such a union could not long be postponed. The influence of Ezekiel's nationalism and of the later prophetic individualism was too strong. With Isa. 26:1–19, that is, probably in the fourth century B. C.,[2] immortality appears with distinctness, but only as limited to pious Hebrews. The son of Sirach seldom ventures to forecast the future, and then generally[3] in the spirit of prophecy, but by the time of Daniel[4] the belief in the resurrection has come to include others than Hebrews, and

---

[1] The limitation of the term "eschatological in the strict sense" to forecasts of the future involving a resurrection of the dead may appear somewhat arbitrary, but seems necessary for clear thinking. Some word like "neo-eschatological" might possibly be used to distinguish the eschatology of pharisaism from that of prophetism.

[2] CHEYNE, *Introduction to Isaiah*, pp. 145 f., and art. "Isaiah" in *Encyclopædia Biblica*; DRIVER, *Introduction* (6th ed.), favors a date early in the fifth century B. C.

[3] Ecclus. 35:18, 19; 47:11; 48:10, 11; 50:23, 24.

[4] Dan. 12:1 f. On this matter in general see CHARLES, *Eschatology*, and his articles in the *Encyclopædia Biblica* and HASTINGS's *Dictionary of the Bible*. Unfortunately, he has not fully treated this particular phase of the subject.

is joined with the messianic hope. Although this union concerns only the consummation of deliverance, like so much
else in Daniel, it was the beginning of that which was to
prove so potent a supplement of the social messianism of
the prophets, the new eschatology of later apocalyptic.

SECTION II. THE APOCALYPSE AS A MEANS OF TRANSITION
FROM POLITICAL TO TRANSCENDENTAL MESSIANISM

While the messianism of the masses, following, though
but blindly, in the path of the older prophetic nationalism,
was seeking to establish a regenerate Israel as the precursor
of the kingdom of God, that of the literary classes, and of
the Pharisees in particular, advanced in the line of apocalyptic. This fact was a natural outcome of the difference
between the comfortable and the distressed elements in the
Jewish state. The masses wished for a new kingdom in
which an end should be made of the actually felt misery
born of poverty and social inequality quite as certainly as of
the national dishonor of subjection to a heathen power. The
Pharisees, enjoying personal comfort and respect, were
naturally concerned rather with the more impersonal, if not
paradoxical, matter of the establishment of a new Jewish
state without revolution or social regeneration. Their hope
was in consequence more joined with patience. God, and
not man, would bring in the new age. Throughout the
three centuries in which the apocalyptic suggestions of
Daniel were developed into new doctrines, pharisaic messianism became increasingly transcendental. A literary bour-
geoisie could well afford to discountenance revolution and
await the fulfilment of academic dreams.

Yet the Pharisees, in their early days, were by no means
indifferent to politics. The great scribal movement from
which they sprang had crystallized first in the party of the
Chasidim, and the society of Pharisees had differentiated

itself from the older party largely because it saw in national affairs the need of applying its principle of separation. The break between John Hyrcanus and those who had been his family's truest supporters doubtless came from the refusal of the Pharisees to have further share in the traditional Asmonean policy of immersing Judea in international politics. The bitter war which the Pharisees had waged with Alexander Jannæus was due to their opposition to the growing monarchy. Under Alexandra and Simon ben Shetach the Pharisees had supported the government, and had brought great prosperity to the nation. Later they had taken sides in the unhappy struggles between Aristobulus and Hyrcanus II., and had thus been involved in the new political life resulting from the conquest of Judea by Pompey.

But with the rise of the house of Antipater the political interests of pharisaism had weakened. The awakening from the dream of an ideal Israel administered by a Sanhedrin devoted to the oral law, to the rough-and-ready government of a foreigner supported by a heathen power, was too rude even for their political idealism, and they attempted to reduce Jewish political life to the minimum. Confronted with the alternative of revolt or of submission to such rulers, at first they chose neither. Twice at least did they endeavor to induce the Romans to govern Judea through a provincial official and local Jewish councils rather than through a *rex socius*,[1] and then, when these requests had been repeatedly refused, the leaders of the society advised submission to rulers, whoever they might be.[2] Yet even then many of them refused to take a formal oath of allegiance to Herod.[3]

[1] Thus in the appeal to Pompey (though the Pharisees are not mentioned) (*Ant* xiv, 3:2) and at the probating of Herod's will (*Ant.*, xvii, 11:1, 2). *Cf.* also the desires of the high-priest for peace (*War*, iv, 5:2) and the attitude of Josephus and his party at the outbreak of the revolt of 66 A. D. (JOSEPHUS, *Life*, §§ 5, 7, 13).

[2] Thus Pollio and Sameas counseled submission to Herod (*Ant.*, xiv, 9:4; xv, 1:1).

[3] With the Essenes, they were excused by that monarch (*Ant.*, xv, 10:4; xvii, 2:4), though fined.

With political hopes thus destroyed, the Pharisees turned with an ever-increasing faith to Jehovah and his law. In his good time deliverance would come to his people. In the meantime his people might well await the divine plan. Throughout the period in which revolutionary messianism was developing, the Pharisees, as well as the Sadducees, constituted a party of law and order. Revolution was farthest possible from their plans, and it is their spirit that breathes in the unceasing denunciation of the Zealots in Josephus. That body, though agreeing with the Pharisees in matters of general belief,[1] differed from them radically in all matters pertaining to the kingdom of God. The one attempted to hasten, the other awaited, God's deliverance.[2]

Yet with the Pharisees, as with the Zealots, messianism was grounded in a sense of misery so abject as to be hopeless except for Jehovah; only in their minds this misery was given a purely religious explanation. The world, though originally created for Israel,[3] seemed too miserable and wicked for Jehovah's immediate presence, and pharisaism became half deistic and thoroughly dualistic. God had abandoned the evil world. It was his *Memra*, his Word, that was present,[4] and his law rather than the Shekinah was the sign of his regard for men. The misery which the righteous suffered, though a punishment for the sins of Israel,[5] was in no way interpreted as evidence of an approaching

---

[1] *Ant.*, xviii, 1:1, 6; *War*, ii, 8:1.

[2] So far from correct is the undiscriminating statement of EATON, art. "Pharisees," HASTINGS's *Dict. of the Bible*, that the Zealots "simply carried out the pharisaic principles to their logical conclusion." The logical conclusions of pharisaic messianism were precisely those exemplified in pharisaism itself — a peaceful awaiting of the coming of the eschatological kingdom of God and the Messiah. For the relations of the two parties see, for instance, *Ant.*, xviii, 1:1; *War*, iv, 3:9 ff. GUTHE (art. "Israel," *Ency. Bib.*) has distinguished between the two parties.

[3] *Assumption of Moses*, 1:12; *cf.* 1:14–17; 4 Ezra 6:55, 59; 7:11; *cf.* CHARLES's note, *Assum. Mos.*, 1:12; *Apoc. Bar.*, 14:18.

[4] *Enoch*, 40:7. See, for a somewhat extreme presentation of this entire matter, BALDENSPERGER, *Das Selbstbewusstsein Jesu*, chaps. 1, 2.

[5] *Enoch*, 89 f. See also the *Psalms of Solomon, passim*.

deliverance.   On the contrary, misfortunes were evidence of the existence of a "Prince of the World," of a Satan,[1] or of an Antichrist, the great opponent of God and the future Christ, who was allowed for a time to torment Jehovah's people. Even when not conceived of as transcendent, this opposing personality was ever present in the mind of the pious Pharisee.   Antiochus Epiphanes; the dread figure of Daniel and the *Assumption of Moses;*[2] the kings of the Medes and Parthians;[3] the world of demons with its prince Beelzebub—all seemed to explain Israel's misfortune and to stimulate new faith.[4]   The very indefiniteness of this present evil ruler must have made the Pharisee discountenance revolution and look the more eagerly for the interference of Jehovah.   The arm of flesh would have been weak indeed against the Prince of the power of the air.   Thus there grew up the dualistic belief in two opposing kingdoms, that of God and that of Satan; the one peopled with good angels, the other with demons[5] and evil angels.   Humanity itself was the prize for which they strove.   Small, indeed, as was the joy to be expected by the righteous in the present age, Satan with all his demoniacal host was to be punished,[6] and God's kingdom with all its blessings would certainly come.   If for the present Satan seemed supreme, his triumph was but temporary.   Fearful as was to be the struggle

---

[1] *Assumption of Moses*, 10:1; *Enoch*, 53:3.

[2] Chap. 8.   [3] *Enoch*, 53:1 f.; 56:1 f.; 90:1 f.

[4] On Antichrist see BOUSSET, *Der Antichrist;* PREUSCHEN, " Paulus als Antichrist," *Zeitschrift für die neutestamentliche Wissenschaft*, 1901, pp. 169-201.

[5] According to *Enoch*, 15: 8–12, the demons are the children of angels and women. *Cf.* Gen. 6: 2. Yet in 19:1 apparently the demons were in existence prior to this event.

[6] See, for instance, *Enoch*, 10:6, 12 f.; 14:5; 16:1–4; 21:10; 41:9; 54:5 f.; 55:4; chaps. 64, 68, 88; 90:15, 21–24; *Book of Jubilees*, 5:10; 10:8. *Cf.* also 23:29. According to BOUSSET, *Die Religion des Judentums*, p. 242, this dualism seems to disappear from Jewish literature.   It certainly is present in rabbinical, even if it be not prominent or present in 4 Esdras; and BACHER, *Agada der Tannaiten*, gives but three references.   Orthodox Judaism today, at least in Palestine, is a firm believer in demons as the authors of misfortune.

between him and God (or Christ),[1] there was no question as
to its outcome. Righteousness, not sin, was the eternal
element in the universe.[2]

The passage from the religio-political messianism of the
earlier Asmonean days to that of the passive resistance of
the first Christian century was due to the increasing influence of this magnificent moral optimism, and is easily to be
traced in the literature of pharisaism. In its early writings,
the kingdom is still superior to the Messiah, and patriotism
is still of this world. Only gradually did the images of the
apocalypse cease to be political symbols and become literal
figures. None the less, from the first the certainty of the
triumph of God's kingdom and the establishment of the
long-expected world-judgment forbade appeal to arms.
Even before the development of apocalyptic in the Enoch
literature, Elijah was to come as the forerunner[3] of the
glorious, though still hardly individualized, son of David[4]
and the eternal kingdom of Israel.[5] Judith[6] and Tobit[7]
expect an approaching judgment of God upon the enemies
of Israel which clearly echoes the prophecies of the Day of
Jehovah. The triumph and glory of Israel are vividly
promised by Baruch,[8] and immortality is predicated of those
alone who were to share in the messianic kingdom.[9] The

---

[1] *Test. XII Pat.*, Levi, 18; Dan., chap. 5; Naph., 8; *Assum. Moses*, 10:1.

[2] The ease with which men turned to apocalypse as a means of stimulating their
despairing countrymen is seen in the sudden transition, both in style and contents,
that marks *Assumption of Moses*, chap. 10.

[3] Mal. 3:23, 24; Ecclus. 48:10 The rôle played by Elijah in later messianism
will be considered below.

[4] Ecclus. 47:11; 1 Macc. 2:57.   [5] Ecclus. 37:25; 44:13; 2 Macc. 14:15.

[6] Judith 16:17.   [7] Tobit 13:11-13, 16-18.

[8] *Baruch*, 2:34, 35; 5:1-9. Possibly, however, these passages are as late as the
fall of Jerusalem.

[9] 2 Macc. 6:26; 7:9, 11, 14, 20, 23, 29, 33, 36; 12:42-45. As to the fate of the wicked
see especially 7:14. There is, of course, a fair critical question as to whether these
passages belong to the early Asmonean time. See NIESE, *Die Krtik der beiden
Makkabäerbücher*. *Cf.* Tobit 14:6, 7.

Sibylline Oracles[1] show even in their most elevated passages that political hopes had not been entirely abandoned by those who readily adopted the apocalypse as a literary form. The misery suffered under the Seleucidæ was quite too recent to be forgotten even by a Jew of the dispersion. The judgment was still national rather than individual, the messianic age the day of a Jewish empire, and the king who was to be sent by God from the east—or sun—to "make all the world cease from cruel war, killing some and making faithful treaties with others," was doubtless an idealized John Hyrcanus. Yet even here the writer could not stop with mere political supremacy. The earthly representatives of Satan's kingdom, the enemies of Israel, were to perish, the righteous Jews were to be eternally blessed, and at last "he who formally gave the Law to the pious would take the kingdom forever over all men."[2]

The line of development of messianism for a considerable period does not seem to have followed the resurrection of the dead already noted in Dan. 12:2, fruitful as it was later to become, but kept true to its uneschatological and mundane limitations. The passage from glowing visions of a triumphant, re-established Israel to the Pharisees' belief in the literal character of the apocalyptic drapery is long, if easy, and one must look beyond Daniel to find it accomplished. For the early apocalyptic movement extraordinary word-paintings were intended to portray actual political and social regeneration. The Day of Jehovah itself involved the re-establishment of Jerusalem and certain institutions modeled on the strong lines of the older prophetism.[3]

---

[1] Metrical translation by TERRY, *The Sibylline Oracles;* German translation of essential portions by BLASS, in KAUTZSCH, *Apok. und Pseud.*, Vol. II, pp. 177-217; Greek text, RZACH, *Oracula Sibyllina;* GEFFCKEN, *Oracula Sibyllina.*

[2] *Sib. Or.*, iii, 655-97, and especially 710-42, 755-60, 766-72, 930.

[3] *Cf.* Zech. 12:5-9, and also the extraordinary readjustment of the topography of Judea in Zech., chap. 14.

Apocalyptic itself, in its first portrayal of the emergence of an exulting nation from bitterest anguish, had a social content. Its figures were truly figurative. The new Judah was not to be in the sky or composed of imaginary beings, but was to be geographical and political.[1]

The perception of a concrete and, so to speak, historical phenomenon in the messianic community is to be seen clearly in the great parent of later apocalyptic, Daniel. How thoroughly this writing is prophecy *post eventum* has been apparent to most recent interpreters. Nor can exegesis find within it forecasts of a dim future. The various beasts represent, not world-epochs, but kingdoms which had been all too real in the affairs of the Jews. Three times over is the history of Israel's international relations traced. The lion, the bear, the leopard, and the fourth beast of chap. 7 are almost obviously the Babylonian, the Median, the Persian, and the Macedonian empires. The same is true of the visions of chaps. 2 and 8.[2] This historical horizon, however, is bounded by the career of Antiochus Epiphanes, so strikingly pictured in the visions,[3] and with the death of that king upon his expedition to the East the writer passes at once to the glories of the messianic days. Yet here his vision is still national. The "son of man," or human being,[4] pictured the coming and triumph of a very real kingdom of the saints. From the point of view of this prophecy, in

[1] Zech. 9:9, 10.

[2] The historical difficulties connected with finding a Median empire between the Chaldean and the Persian are considerable, but affect the historical worth of the book rather than this interpretation. Dan. 6:1; 8:3, 20; 9:1 can hardly mean anything else than that the Median empire of Darius really was the second world-power. See commentaries by DRIVER, BEVAN, MARTI, BEHRMANN; the general *Introductions* and the articles in *Encyclopædia Biblica* and HASTINGS'S *Dictionary of the Bible*. Critical scholarship is practically a unit in assigning the book to the Maccabean period.

[3] Dan. 7:8, 20–26; 8:23–25; 11:21–45.

[4] Dan. 7:13. It is impossible to see in כבר אנש any other meaning. The contrast is clearly between beastlike and human symbols. No personal Messiah is suggested. As the beasts stood for heathen empires, so a man symbolized the new Israel.

fact, the early Maccabean uprising must have appeared a part of the divine deliverance promised the oppressed Pious. Yet in the same proportion as it is thus judged messianic must it also be declared social and political. As a revolt it was no mere incident in Jewish, or, indirectly, in universal, history. Until the unexpected uprising of the Pious, the Jewish state was being slowly amalgamated with a classical antiquity. Not only had it lost its independence, it was losing its religion as well. A theocracy whose high-priest was indifferent to the cult that conditioned the very existence of his nation could hardly be expected to resist much longer the pervasive Hellenism of its suzerain. The double rebellion of Mattathias and the Pious was no more the reaction against persecution than it was the child of devotion to the law and of a desperate idealism. The bands of fanatics which ranged through the little state, "smiting sinners in their anger and lawless men in their wrath," pulling down heathen altars, circumcising neglected children, guaranteeing, as far as with them lay, safety in the observance of the Thorah and the developing oral law,[1] certainly regarded themselves as appointed by Jehovah, both for deliverance and for the reconstruction of the state.[2] Apart from their devotion to law, it is to be admitted that evidence of any definite social program is wanting; but back of all the development of the state under the Asmonean house, and inextricably united with the new nomism, there is to be presupposed such hopes as run through the earlier portions of *Enoch*. God was ever more strongly to aid the new theocracy and punish its and his own enemies. With the Maccabean epoch messianism, like scribism, enters upon a new stage.

Nor did success, as so often, prove fatal to the belief of the scribes and their followers that God's kingdom was soon to appear. Even in Hellenistic Judaism the Day of

[1] 1 Macc. 2:42-70.   [2] 1 Macc. 5:55-62.

Jehovah still fills the future. It is impossible to see in the divinely promised king of the *Sibylline Oracles*[1] any other than one of the Asmonean house, Simon, or possibly John Hyrcanus. Under him all war was to cease, and God would send blessings upon the righteous and punishments upon the lawless. Bloody wars and convulsions in nature were to establish a peaceful state, bountifully supported by a miraculously fruitful earth. The nations would come under the law of Jehovah, and all the world become an empire with Jerusalem as its capital. In the other literature of the time may be traced similar expectations. "Wisdom" itself, with all its disillusions, could not quite disbelieve in a judgment of the heathen, a deliverance of God's people, and an everlasting Jewish empire under a Davidic dynasty.[2] The writer of the book of Tobit ventures the hope that when the new Jewish empire is established all the heathen will be converted to God.[3] Such messianism, though expressed in terms of apocalyptic, evidently had not become transcendental, but possessed still the social content of prophetism itself. Its mission was to picture the rise of a triumphant nationality—a new and divinely established world-power.

How truly national the hopes of the Pharisees were appears as we trace the stream of their literature from Daniel onward. If the new Israel was to be the result of miracle rather than of revolution, it was none the less to be a state. Indeed, it is impossible to avoid feeling that at the beginning, behind symbols and visions of vengeance, there is lingering the conviction that possibly war itself may be the duty of a holy people. But this conviction, if it were

---

[1] *Sibylline Oracles*, III, 652-794.

[2] Ecclus. 32:18, 19; 33:1 f.; 37:25; 47:11; 50:24; with the first of these references *cf.* Judith 16:17.

[3] Tobit 13:11; 14:6, 7. How far this hope ran through the Dispersion can hardly be said because of lack of data. But *cf.* BERTHOLET, *Die Stellung der Israeliten und der Juden zu den Fremden*, pp. 257-302, 337; and FRIEDLÄNDER, *Das Judenthum in der vorchristlichen griechischen Welt.*

really present, is sedulously concealed.   Saints were to be delivered; they were not to achieve deliverance.

SECTION III.   THE MESSIANISM OF THE EARLIER APOCALYPTIC

The stream of literature to which we have just referred is always pseudepigraphic, and consists of the visions of the future granted to great men of the past, like Enoch, the patriarchs, Moses, Baruch, and Ezra.   These saints are represented as bequeathing in the way of admonition and encouragement to their descendants.   Of the entire literature the canonical Daniel is by far the most typical.   Its method, its range of vision, in many ways its symbols, repeatedly reappear in its successors.   All portray history symbolically in terms of explained mysteries and prophecy, only to pass into apocalyptic poetry when describing the future; all are unconcerned about historical accuracy; all represent nations and persons under the forms of animals.   What is even more important, all the pseudepigraphic literature like Daniel was written for the purpose of arousing faith and courage by insisting upon the certain destruction of those who had brought misery upon Israel, and the equally certain deliverance and supremacy of the Hebrew people.   It is this confidence that lies at the foundation of whatever genuinely ethical teaching there may be contained in its interminable and commonplace visions.

Most important of this uncanonical pseudepigraphic literature is that which bears the name of Enoch.   It is probably not quite accurate to say that Daniel is the progenitor of the Enoch literature as a whole.   The fact that so much of this literature sprang up practically contemporaneously with Daniel would rather argue that both literatures are the outcome of the same literary and spiritual movement.   Within the cycle of visions brought together by some unknown editor is to be clearly seen the passage from political messianism expressed in apocalyptic form to a transcendental messianism in which apocalyptic elements have been literalized and political elements all but removed.[1] In the original groundwork of the present book (Ethiopic) of *Enoch*, chaps. 1–36, 72–104, the messianic element, though expressed in apocalyptic terms, is national. In it, as in Daniel, is to be seen the misery and the faith of an oppressed people. Jehovah had permitted their enemies to crush the pious, but the future was certain to see the punishment of the oppressors. If we neglect the various discussions of nature, and the origin of evil through the wicked angels, chaps. 1–36 consist chiefly of the portrayal of the punishment to be accorded the wicked, both demoniac and human, and the awards awaiting the righteous. Central in the entire portrayal is the day of judgment,[2] when the fate of mankind is fixed. The punishment is all but invariably unquenchable fire, though in a somewhat elaborate chapter[3] sheol is divided into four sections, in two of which are the souls of the righteous, and in the other two, suffering different punishment, are the two classes of dead sinners, those who had and those who had not suffered in their earthly life. The rewards of the righteous are sensuous; they are to live five hundred years,[4] will beget a thousand children, and die in peace.[5] The entire earth will be miracu-

[1] Recent criticism, as represented by Schürer, Beer (in KAUTZSCH, *Apok. u. Pseud.*), Charles, Flemming and Radermacher, Bousset (*Die Religion des Judentums*), is agreed on the main divisions of *Enoch* and the general periods of their composition. The original work, chaps. 1–36, 72–104, barring numerous interpolations, was written before 100 B. C.; chaps. 37–70, before 64 or 37 B. C. Each of these divisions is in no small degree composite, but the precise lines of divisions must in many cases remain a matter of discussion. Compare, *e. g.*, the analysis of Charles (*The Book of Enoch*) and Beers, KAUTSCH, *Apok. und Pseud.*, II, pp. 217–35.

[2] 1: 1, 6–9; 10: 6, 12; 16: 1; 19: 1; 22: 4, 11 f.; 25: 4. A complete list and classification is given by CHARLES, *Book of Enoch*, p. 125, note. According to 1: 4, this judgment is to occur on Mount Sinai, but *cf.* 27: 4.

[3] Chap. 22.

[4] 10: 10. This is called ζωὴ αἰώνιος by the writer. Clearly αἰώνιος refers to the character rather than the endlessness of the life. It is the life of the Age. See also 5: 9; 25: 6.

[5] 10: 17.

lously fruitful, and joy and righteousness will be universal, the heathen being converted.[1]   Jerusalem thus becomes the center of a Jewish empire.[2]

It is difficult to see in these words any hard-and-fast theory as to the future.   Rather are they extravagant picturings of misery and joy.   How poetical rather than transcendental they are appears in the indifference of their author to the resurrection.   It is not explicitly taught, and, though possibly implied,[3] it exerts no influence upon the general messianic picture.[4]   Possibly the joyous life of the righteous follows this indistinctly portrayed resurrection.   If so, nothing is said concerning their future after their second death, and the reader is left in doubt as to whether the wicked are to be annihilated or raised to suffer new punishments.[5]

In the Dream Visions (chaps. 83–90), written during the days of Judas Maccabæus[6] or John Hyrcanus,[7] the interest is still shown in angels as the originators of the sin[8] that compelled Jehovah to send the deluge, but still more in the misfortunes of Israel.[9]   In a series of rapid scenes, in which sheep, rams, and wild beasts are the chief actors, he traces Hebrew history up to the days of the Asmonean revolt. The years of misery are described as under the control of the seventy shepherds, doubtless the angelic[10] representatives of heathen oppressors of Judea, whose reign falls into the four periods[11] in which the sufferings of the little country were

---

[1] 10:20–22.   [2] 25:5.   [3] So Charles on basis of 22:11, 13.

[4] Possibly these sensuous pictures are to be referred to the supposed condition of the world after the deluge. Cf. 10:20 and 12:1. The section, chaps. 6–11, however, seems to be composed of a large number of traditions and legends uncritically joined together. It is probably hopeless to discover consistency in the melange that has resulted, yet its purpose is certainly to some degree messianic.

[5] Cf. 22:10, 11, 13.   [6] Bousset, Charles.

[7] Beer and Dillmann. Schürer places it 166–100 B. C.

[8] 84:4; chaps. 86–88.   [9] Chaps. 89, 90.   [10] So Charles, Schürer, Beer.

[11] (1) Till Cyrus (twelve hours); (2) till Alexander; (3) till conquest of Palestine by Syria about 200 B. C. ; (4) till the messianic period.

divided, the last, as the author trusted, being about to end in the dawn of the messianic age. This new age is introduced by the day of God's judgment,[1] when all evil persons, including the wicked angels and the seventy shepherds, are cast into an abyss of fire.[2] Then the new, and apparently heavenly, Jerusalem is established by God,[3] all surviving humanity is converted, the dead (again by implication) are raised,[4] the Messiah appears, and all men are transformed into his likeness.[5] In all this there is little that is transcendental, and nothing that demands a new earth or a general resurrection. Indeed, the resurrection of the dead is very shadowy. The apocalyptic is still true to the spirit of prophetism. The Messiah, though distinct in the symbolism of the white bull, has no function of either judgment or conquest assigned him. The new kingdom is a gift of God to a suffering Israel.

In the little "Weeks" apocalypse,[6] however, one discovers the transition to a more transcendental hope. A period of peace and joy follows the overthrow of the enemies of Israel, the angels alone are judged, all men repent, and a new heaven appears in which goodness and happiness are eternal. There is no mention of a Messiah, and this fact, as well as the general character of its portrayal of the future, leads one to refer this section to another source than its context.[7]

When one passes to the later chapters of this oldest section of the Enoch literature, there are again met the elements of a triumphant Israel, a day of judgment,[8] and the suffering of the wicked. But there now appear more distinctly

[1] 90:18–20. [2] 90:24–27. [3] 90:28, 29.
[4] 90:30–33. [5] 90:37, 38. [6] 91:12-17; chap. 93.

[7] This, however, in the light of *Enoch*, chaps. 1-36, does not necessitate any radical change in date from that assigned its larger context, but rather argues that in its early years pharisaism was combining its hopes for the appearance of the eschatological kingdom with its political forecasts.

[8] 99:15; chap. 102; 104:5.

some of the characteristics of the new eschatology. The wicked are to be slain in sheol[1] after a fearful struggle with Israel's champion. During this conflict the righteous sleep,[2] to be awakened only that they may share in the resurrection of the spirit.[3] This resurrection, it should be noted, comes at the close, not at the beginning, of the messianic kingdom, and is to be followed by the enthronement of those who enjoy it.[4] The Messiah is referred to only in a general way as "my son,"[5] and his reign is evidently one of struggle rather than of blessedness—a tribute to the systematic tendency already noted. A similar advance over the earlier messianism is seen in the retreat of purely sensuous conceptions. It is obviously impossible to reduce in any sure system these various elements of the hope for the future. It may well be doubted whether the writers of these portions of the Enoch literature had any consistent ideal in their minds. We have doubtless reached the frontier of certainty when we catalogue the elements of divine deliverance for Israel, the day of judgment, the punishment of the wicked in hell, and the resurrection of the righteous. These, at least, are common to the entire literature. A Messiah, a period of struggle before the wicked are subdued, the manner and time of the resurrection, the place and nature of the punishment, the length and degree of sensuousness of the blessings—all these vary with the different writers. The tendency away from the sensuous toward the transcendental is, however, apparent.

From such inconsistent and bizarre[6] pictures as these, in which the imagination shrinks from no extravagant pictures of sensuous and transcendent bliss, the transition was easy

---

[1] 99:11; 100:5; 108:3.   [2] 100:5.

[3] 103:4. There apparently is no resurrection of the body. One cannot help surmising that this singular expectation bespeaks a philosophical tendency not commonly discovered in pharisaism, but clear in Paul. *Cf.* his σῶμα πνευματικόν.

[4] 108:11, 12.   [5] 105:2; *cf.* 4 Ezra 7:28, 29; 14:9.   [6] *Cf.* Isa. 65:20-22; 30:23 f.

to the next group of Enoch visions (chaps. 37–71). In them the literalizing of the apocalypse is clearly begun. To mention only the most important matters, the Messiah is now distinctly individualized with a variety of names — Son of man,[1] the Elect, the Anointed, the Righteous One. He is preexistent[2] and a judge[3] conjointly with God himself. In this judgment all, both good and evil, even though dead,[4] share. Kings and nobles suffer punishment[5] with the evil angels.[6] No sin goes unpunished, though, except in the case of the kings,[7] repentance seems always possible through the mercy of God.[8] Yet even here the scene shifts back to earth. The Jews of the dispersion return to Palestine,[9] and the Messiah reigns[10] over a righteous nation happy in the enjoyment of peace and equality.[11] Heaven joins the earth, and immortal men dwell together with angels in a world forever free from sin.[12]

In these visions it is difficult to see anything but the phantasies of a glowing faith, utterly untrammeled by the conceptions of modern science. They have even less consistent eschatology than cosmogony. Demons, disobedient stars, angels, magical trees, palaces, and mountains of pre-

[1] Unless the sections in which this term is used be held to be post-Christian (see BOUSSET, *Jesu Predigt*, 105 f.; DRUMMOND, *Jewish Messiah*, 61 f.; PFLEIDERER, *Das Urchristentum*, 315 f.; and a good summary of arguments for this position in STALKER, *Christology of Jesus*, App.), a view with which it is difficult to agree. While interpolation is of course not impossible, all indications, especially the utter absence of any reference to the historical Jesus, point against such a hypothesis. See LIETZMANN, *Der Menschensohn*, pp. 42–8; SCHÜRER, *Geschichte des jüdischen Volkes*[3], Vol. III, pp. 200–202; BEER in KAUTSZCH, *Apok. und Pseud.*, Vol. II, pp. 230–32. BOUSSET, in his *Die Religion des Judentums*, pp. 13, 196, has adopted pre-Christian date. According to some texts, in 62:5 and 69:29 the title "that Son of the woman" appears; this reading is rejected, however, by CHARLES, *Book of Enoch*, p. 164.

[2] 46:1, 2; 48:3, 6; 62:7.

[3] 45:3; 47:3; 50:4; 62:2. *Cf.* CHARLES, *Enoch;* BEER in KAUTZSCH, *Apok. und Pseud., in loco.*

[4] 51:1, 2.   [5] Chaps. 62 and 63.   [6] 54:5, 6; chap. 64.   [7] 63:6–9.

[8] The position given men in the heavenly kingdom is apparently determined by the time of their repentance. *Cf.* chap. 50.

[9] Chap. 57.   [10] 45:3–5.   [11] 53:6, 7.

[12] 39:5–12; 41:2; 45:4–6; 49:12; 51:4; 58:3; 71:16.

cious stones chase each other in a *Waldpurgis* night dance of oriental imagery. As for definite ethical concepts, beyond the most general manipulation of the thoughts of sin and punishment, righteousness and reward, they are practically neutral. Symbolism itself has all but ceased to be symbolic and has become literal. Political rulers and parties are with difficulty seen to be the chief actors of the new apocalypse, and the reader is introduced into an eschatology in which the pharisaic dualism reaches a solution in the thin air of transcendentalism.

Far less elaborate than this hope is that of the writer of the Haggadist commentary on Genesis, the *Book of Jubilees*.[1] Indeed, the messianic hope in any precise sense is all but lacking in his book. Like the Ethiopic *Enoch*, its angelology and demonology are well developed, and most important events of the Old Testament history are referred to superhuman personalities. The evil spirits are under "the prince of the Mastêma,"[2] from whose power the good angels protect the righteous, and who at last is to be judged.[3] Yet, writing as he does in the height of Maccabean success, it is not unlikely that the author of *Jubilees* conceived of the messianic age as having already begun.[4] Members were to live a thousand years. The new age apparently was to be inaugurated with a widespread study of the law,[5] and the age was to be free from the influence of Satan.[6] The

---

[1] It is with much hesitation that I place the *Book of Jubilees* in Maccabean times. The arguments of CHARLES, *Book of Jubilees*, Introduction, § 17, fall far short of demonstration, and it is not easy to square all references in the book itself by such a theory of its authorship. At the same time, the weight of probabilities is somewhat in its favor. See also BOUSSET, *Die Religion des Judentums*, p. 13; BOHN, *Studien und Kritiken* (1900), pp. 167-84; LITTMANN in KAUTZSCH, *Apok. und Pseud.*, Vol. II, pp. 31-8. To the contrary, SCHÜRER, *Geschichte d. jüd. Volkes*[3], Vol. III, pp. 274-80.

[2] Or Prince Mastêma, according to the Ethiopic manuscripts.

[3] *Jub.*, 10:8.

[4] Charles thinks that *Enoch*, 83-90, shows the same belief, but it is by no means obvious.

[5] *Jub.*, 23:26, 27; *cf.* 23:15.   [6] *Jub.*, 23:29.

judgment comes at the close of this messianic period, and no resurrection precedes it, the only immortality being that of the spirit.[1] Another passage, however,[2] seems to imply that the judgment is to precede the establishment of the kingdom. But here, as in all Jewish literature, it is impossible to discover absolute chronological consistency in eschatological descriptions. There is no reference to a Messiah, unless it be the very general prophecy concerning Judahs' supremacy.[3] A bloody triumph of a nation that kept Jehovah's law—this was the chief good expected. Terrible suffering was to be endured by Jews before their conversion to a devotion to the Law,[4] but just how the new age is to be ushered in the author nowhere explains. It is probably safe, therefore, to assume that he would not differ from other apocalyptic writers in judging its coming to be cataclysmic.[5] Yet *Jubilees* is too completely legalistic in tone to justify any precise conclusion as to its eschatology, and especially as to its messianic hope. One must be content with saying that, wherever such elements appear, they are clearly akin to the general expectation, as it appears in the contemporary literature we have already considered.

It is not difficult to appreciate the stage reached by this new transcendentalism in the noble group of songs that sprang into use during the last half-century before Christ— the *Psalms of Solomon*. That these songs are of pharisaic origin can hardly be questioned.[6] According to the belief of their author, misfortune never came to a nation except as a punishment for sin. That Judea was suffering, therefore,

---

[1] *Jub.*, 23:31.   [2] 23:11.   [3] 31:18-20.   [4] 23:1-23.

[5] CHARLES, on the basis of *Jub.*, 1:29; 4:26; 23:26-28, says that the author holds to gradual transformation of creation, conditioned ethically by the conduct of Israel. *Book of Jubilees*, p. 9, note. It is impossible to agree with such far-fetched conclusions.

[6] For a general argument see RYLE AND JAMES, *Psalms of Solomon;* KITTEL, in KAUTZSCH, *Apok. und Pseud.*, Vol. II, p. 127. For text see RYLE AND JAMES and GEBHARDT, *Die Psalmen Salamo.*

argued long-continued secret wrong-doing on the part of its rulers.[1]   The Romans, though their leader had experienced God's wrath,[2] were but God's agents of punishment;[3] the real offenders were the degenerate Asmonean high-priests, whose faults seem to have been the change of the kingless theocracy to a monarchy; in case a monarchy was inevitable, their presumption in usurping the throne of the divinely appointed Davidic family; their misuse of their priestly office; and their surrender to Rome.   Yet the writer all but never makes use of the apocalyptic scheme or method. He writes as a good Pharisee, but as a poet rather than a seer.

It should be remembered that the Pharisees, in their Chasidim days, had cheerfully submitted to the high-priesthood of the Asmonean house.   It was not the displacement of the house of Zadok which displeased them, for the Asmoneans were priests,[4] and any technical difficulties the Pharisees, with the people, were content to waive until some prophet should appear to solve them finally.   It was the monarchy as such that the Pharisees opposed.   The ideal Judea, composed of those who were righteous, was impossible as long as "sinners" controlled the state.[5]   A righteous king was therefore the first condition of that righteous and glorious state for which all Jews longed.[6]

From this point of view the messianic portrait of Pss. 17 and 18 is quite intelligible.   In them the apocalyptic element is all but wanting.   The pious are indeed to rise from the dead,[7] but there is no clear correlation of this eschatology with the messianic hope.   Yet there is nothing in the Psalms inconsistent with the apocalyptic messianism.   The picture, however, is more personal than in the older apocalypses.

---

[1] See especially Ps. 1.   [2] Ps. 2:30, 31.   [3] Cf. 2:7, 8, 17.

[4] According to 1 Macc. 7:13, 14, the Chasidim had been ready to submit to the Hellenist Alcimus, since he was of the seed of Aaron.

[5] Cf. 17:26.   [6] 7:9; 9:19.

[7] 3:16; 14:1–3, 7.   For the wicked there is no such hope (3:13–15; 13:10; 14:6; 15:11).

The thought of a kingdom is in marked subordination to that of the Messiah. No picture could be more clearly drawn than his. Neither a sufferer nor a teacher, pre-existent nor miraculously born, a priest like the Asmoneans nor an eschatological wonder like the Son of man of Enoch, he is the mighty king, the vice-gerent of God. In character he is to be sinless,[1] obtaining wisdom from God,[2] and strong through the Holy Sprit.[3] His capital is to be Jerusalem, which is first to be purged of all heathen,[4] and his kingdom is to be composed of sanctified Jews,[5] sons of God, among whom there will never be pride or oppression or unrighteousness of any sort. He is to conquer the entire heathen world, and even the sinners — by whom the Asmonean house may be meant — will be "convicted in the thoughts of their hearts" (vs. 27). The entire earth shall serve him, and he will have mercy only upon those who fear him.

Yet this mighty king is not to be a man of war. He is to put no trust in horses or cavalry or bows or armies. His conquests are to be wrought "with the word of his mouth."[6] The expression is a true echo of pharisaism. The king is certainly not to be a teacher or a preacher or a philosopher, but the author of the psalm does not wish to be understood as counseling war, and therefore falls back on miracle. The Christ is to be so mighty that he does not need to fight.[7]

The *laissez-faire* spirit of pharisaism as regards political evils could hardly be better joined with limitless hope. The world is to be subjected to a pharisaized Israel,[8] over whom a great king is to reign as a representative of God; but the messianic ideal of these psalms is farther from that of the

---

[1] 17: 35, 36. [3] 17: 37, 42. [5] Vss. 26, 32, 33, 36.
[2] 17: 31, 35. [4] 17: 25, 30, 31. [6] 17: 36–39.

[7] There is no need, however, of using this fact as a basis for the view that the Jews had a double conception of the Christ, sometimes thinking of him as a warrior and sometimes as a judge, as in BALDENSPERGER, *Das Selbstbewusstsein Jesu* (3d ed.), pp. 111 f. The two are really two phases of the one conception of the conquering king

[8] Λαὸς ἅγιος, 17: 28.

Zealots than from that of the apocalypses. One sees in it
an attempt to express the spirit of apocalyptic without the
assistance of visions. As the nearest approach made by
pharisaism to picturing a literal Jewish state, it demon-
strates how utterly unworldly even its non-apocalyptic messianism had grown. Social evolution, to say nothing of
revolution, is not thought of. God's Messiah must come
and miraculously establish the new kingdom. In the meantime pious Jews must wait in patience.

SECTION IV. THE TRANSCENDENTAL MESSIANISM OF LATER PHARISAISM

With the final establishment of the Roman suzerainty,
the hope of pharisaism turned unreservedly to apocalypses
in which the judgment is, as might be expected, all-impor-
tant. As if in terror of any revolutionary bias, the *Assumption of Moses*, written during the first years of the Christian
era, mentions no Messiah and distinctly says that God
alone will punish the gentiles.[1] In the same treatise,[2] also,
suffering is made the incentive, not only to repentance[3] and
religious faith, but also to confidence in the ultimate establishment of the kingdom of God. The hostile kingdom of
evil, with its great king, was to be overcome.[4] The condemnation of all heathen, the punishment of enemies of God
in Gehenna, and the surpassing glory of a reunited Israel in
the new dispensation,[5] were to follow. Again the kingdom and
not the Messiah is central, the latter being unmentioned.

[1] 10:7.

[2] CHARLES, *Assumption of Moses;* CLEMEN in KAUTZSCH, *Apok. und Pseud.*

[3] 1:18.

[4] *Assum. Mos.* gives in chap. 8 a striking picture of the persecution of Antiochus
Epiphanes, but does not, as BOUSSET, *Die Religion des Judentums*, p. 243, thinks,
present the king as "the tyrant of the end of the age who rules over the entire
world." The tyrant, when called "king of the kings of the earth," is evidently
viewed historically rather than eschatologically. *Cf.* Ezek. 26:7; Dan. 2:37; Ezra
7:12. As CHARLES, *Assumption of Moses*, p. 30, says, the phrase is a title peculiar to
oriental monarchs.

[5] 10:1–10.

God is a great judge, granting salvation only to the kingdom's members. Even more central is the final judgment of both angels and men in the *Secrets of Enoch,* also written some time near the beginning of the Christian era.[1] After it, there begins for the righteous who have entered the kingdom a new age, endless and blessed, without illness or sorrow of any sort.[2] Of the Messiah or resurrection there is no mention. It is noteworthy also that in this work the doctrine of the millennium is distinctly formulated and derived.[3]

Transcendentalism is seen in its final form in the various cycles of apocalypses that were brought together after the destruction of the Jewish state. As the persecution of Antiochus Epiphanes had given rise to the Daniel and Enoch apocalypses, so the new catastrophe produced the *Apocalypse of Baruch* and *4 Esdras.*[4] Within the former it is perhaps possible to distinguish two sorts of forecasts of the future, the one evidently optimistic, and the other hopeless, as to the future of Israel as a nation. In both alike it is the judgment and the messianic kingdom that fill the seer's horizon. In the one cycle, the future holds a new Jerusalem, already prepared in heaven;[5] a mighty Messiah who should slay all those who had ruled or even known the

---

[1] 46:3; 48:8,9; 19:1-5; 65:6-10; *cf.* also 9:1 ff.; 10:3-6; 18:1-6. MORFILL AND CHARLES, *The Book of the Secrets of Enoch.*

[2] 61:2 f.; 65:8-10. [3] 32-33:2.

[4] Genuinely critical treatment of these two works may be said to have begun with the article by KABISCH, " Die Quellen der Apocalypse Baruchs," *Jahrbücher für protest. Theol.,* 1891, pp. 66-107. He regards *Baruch* as the work of at least four writers, and as consisting of a groundwork (1-23; 31-34; 75-87); two complete visions (36-40 and 53-74)—in which he is supported by DE FAYE, *Les apocalypses juives;* fragments of a third apocalypse (24:3-29); and various material, including editorial passages, like 28:5; 30:1; 32:2-4; 35; 76:1. CHARLES, *Apocalypse of Baruch,* finds three "Messiah apocalypses" (27-30:1; 36-40; 53-74; chap. 85); and two groups of sections (1:1; 43-44.7; 45-46:6; 77-82; 84; 86, 87; and 9-12; 13-25; 30:2-35; 41-42; 44:8-15; 47-52; 75, 76; 83). It is difficult not to feel the force of the arguments for some broad division of the book into constituent material, but one may well reserve an opinion as to such elaborate analysis.

[5] 4:2-6; 32:2-4.

Jewish nation;[1] and a new age in which all evil and physical pain should disappear.[2]   For the other, the future holds no such glory for Israel.   Jerusalem had been destroyed, Israel hopelessly defeated, and the end of the corruptible world seemed the one precondition of permanent happiness.   Not a new nation or even a new age for Israel was to be expected, but a new world-epoch[3] in which the very dead should be raised,[4] and in which the world should become immortal[5] and invisible.[6]   At this conviction even apocalypse halted.   Unlike the earlier writers (unless we except *Sibylline Oracles*, III, 97–807), the author of the *Apocalypse of Baruch* regarded the messianic kingdom itself as but temporary.   It marked the end of "the present age,"[7] was to be followed by a general resurrection, after which was to come the final judgment,[8] and a new age in which corruption should be no more.[9]   When each man has been given his deserts, then begins the everlasting age in which time ceases, the righteous, like angels, dwell in heaven and not on the earth, and the wicked agonize in fire.[10]   In *4 Esdras* the picture is more elaborated, but, with one exception, hardly different in essentials.   The pre-existent Christ[11] rises from the sea in company with Enoch, Moses, and Elijah.[12]   For the first time in Jewish literature — unless we except the questionable instance in *Enoch*, 105 : 2 — he is addressed by God as "My Son, the Messiah."[13]   He destroys the united

---

[1] 72:1-6; *cf.* chaps. 39, 40; 70:7-10.   [2] 44:8-15; chaps. 73; 74.   [3] 32:6.   [4] 50:2.
[5] 51:3; *cf.* 48:50.   [6] 51:8.   [7] 40:3; 74:3.   [8] Chap. 30.
[9] 44:12; *cf.* 85:5.   [10] 51:1-12.   [11] 12:32; 13:26, 52; 14:9.

[12] *4 Esdras*, 6:26 ("they shall see the men who have been taken up, who have not tasted death from their birth," *i. e.*, Enoch, Moses, Elijah) ; 13:2, 3, 5, 25, 52.

[13] *4 Esdras*, 7:28, 29; *cf.* 13:32, 37, 52; 14:9.   DALMAN, *Words of Jesus* (Eng. trans.), pp. 268–74, is doubtless correct in arguing that Ps. 2:7 is the ancestor of the Christian use of the term ὁ υἱὸς τοῦ θεοῦ in a messianic sense.   At the same time he recognizes the surprising lack of evidence tending to establish a general use of the term in that sense in Jewish literature.   So far as lexicography goes, it is difficult to show that the term comes over into the New Testament from any source whatsoever.   Obviously this is to prove too much, for it is impossible to account for the term in the New Testament literature on ontological grounds.   Were it otherwise,

enemies of Israel[1] without war, but with fire that proceeds from his mouth.[2] The ten tribes of Israel return to dwell with their brethren in a new Jerusalem, not made with hands, but which had come down from heaven.[3] At this point, however, appears a new element which one cannot help believing is in some measure due to Christian influences. The Messiah and all mankind die, the world being for an entire week locked in death.[4] Then comes the general resurrection, and God establishes the judgment[5] in which the endless destiny of every man is fixed. The rewards and punishments of life have already been experienced in some degree,[6] but now the righteous go to an eternal paradise and the wicked to eternal hunger and pain.[7] Thereafter God is supreme.

It is not necessary to trace the development farther. The alleged[8] two cycles of conceptions in *Baruch*, and to some extent in *4 Esdras*, in which the historical and the transcendental element are apparently interwoven, are not to be too readily treated as documentary. Quite as likely are they but

there would certainly be some use of the ontological concept. The case is, however, not so anomalous as might appear. The idea of sonship of God is by no means uncommon in the Old Testament. Thus of Israel as the special object of Jehovah's love (Exod. 4:22, 23; Deut. 14:1, 2; Hos. 11:1); of some individual who may be conceived of holding a peculiar relation to God (2 Sam. 7:14; 1 Chron. 17:13, 14; 22:10; Pss. 2:7; 89:20-37.) Somewhat similarly in Philo, God is figuratively said to be the father of innumerable virtues, graces, persons, and even the Logos. In all Philo uses the analogy, occasionally with startling explanations, something like 300 times. I wish to express my indebtedness to an as yet unpublished paper by A. S. CARMAN. More particularly, the υἱοὶ θεοῦ seems to have acquired a somewhat technical force: "those who are (or are to be) members of the kingdom of God" (*Pss. Sol.*, 17:27; *cf.* Luke 20:36). In the light of this usage, both of the analogy and of the term, it is not difficult to see how, as in *4 Esdras* and the interpolations of *Enoch*, the Messiah should have been regarded as ὁ υἱὸς τοῦ θεοῦ, or simply υἱὸς θεοῦ, *par excellence.* See BARTON, *Journal of Biblical Literature*, 1902, Part I, pp. 78-91; for an attempt to connect the term with current Roman usage see DEISSMANN, *Bible Studies* (Eng. trans.), pp. 166 f.

[1] 12:31-34.

[2] 13:37, 38, an echo of *Pss. Sol.*, 17:39, perhaps in its turn derived from Isa. 11:4.

[3] 13:39-47; 7:26; 10:55; 13:36.   [4] 7:29, 30.   [5] 7:31-35.

[6] 6:5 f., though these verses are not beyond question.   [7] 8:52-59.

[8] See CHARLES, *Apoc. Bar.*, Intro.

two hemispheres of the same hope. To a modern, the material already presented from the earlier apocalypses is hardly less an inconsistent combination of political hope and religious imagery. The fact seems to be that the Jew could not distinguish between the supremacy of God and the supremacy of his people Israel.[1] For teachers surrounded by heathenism such a point of view was inevitable. It was inconceivable that God should not finally be supreme; but it was just as inconceivable that his people should not be supreme as well. Inevitably the mind of a seer would thus waver between the two descriptions. One moment he would picture in non-political words the triumph of God, and the next, with precisely the same *dénouement* in mind, he would picture the triumph and imperial supremacy of the Jew.

Similarly, in these apocalypses appears another contradiction to be noticed in all literature of the class: the dualism as regards the enemy to be overcome. Repeatedly the reader is confused by the sudden transition from an obviously political enemy—at first Antiochus Epiphanes and afterward the Roman empire—to Satan or evil angels. Here again a modern mind is sure to be confused and tempted to appeal to the ever ready *deus ex machina* of analytic criticism. But from the point of view of the Jew there was no difficulty in such identification of politics and demonology. If the kingdom of God was to be in practice the kingdom of the Jews, so the enemy of God was in practice some political oppressor. It was as easy to identify the one set of parallels as the other. Middle terms like Edom[2] or the visions of Daniel[3] or Nero as Antichrist[4] were always at hand.

---

1 BOUSSET, *Die Religion des Judenthums*, pp. 201-3.

2 *4 Esdras*, 6:8–10; *Targ. Jon. Lev.*, 26:44. *Cf.* BACHER, *Agada*, Vol. I, p. 292.

3 *4 Esdras*, 12:11; 5:3, 11, 12; *Baruch*, 39; JOSEPHUS, *Ant.*, x, 11:7.

4 *Ascension of Isaiah*, 3:13—5:1. Cf. CHARLES, *Ascension of Isaiah*, LI–LXXIII, and in general on this point BOUSSET, *Religion des Judenthums*, pp. 204-6.

Even when such process of identification was not utilized, the Jewish mind would find no difficulty in demanding the punishment of both sets of enemies. Indeed, it is to be noticed that the punishment of wicked men—who must certainly be heathen—was made the same as that of the devil and his angels.[1]

Another inconsistency for the modern mind lies in the expected resurrection. It is apparent that by the time the messianic hope had reached this stage of its development, immortality, at least of the righteous, had become one of its integral parts. The passage from the age of present misery to the age of glory and joy logically involved an emphasis upon the continuance of human life, not only in its national, but in its individual form. The *Wisdom of Solomon* presents this hope in perhaps its most perfect form:

> "The souls of the righteous are in the hand of God;
> And no torment shall touch them."

> "For even if in the sight of men they be punished,
> Their hope is full of immortality." [2]

This hope of immortality, as has already appeared, was by no means the child of messianism. Before the hope of the prophets had finally been transformed by the apocalyptic tendency, the pious Jew had reached a clear faith in a life after death. Not to trace the earlier stages of this hope, in which there are few elements that do not appear in most primitive religions,[3] it will be necessary only to call attention to the general silence as regards the conditions of the wicked dead. That they are annihilated it would be hardly safe to affirm, although the *Wisdom of Solomon*[4] distinctly

[1] *Enoch*, chaps. 62, 63, especially 63:6; *cf.* Matt. 25:41.

[2] *Wis. Sol.*, 3:1-3.

[3] Thus shades, the pit, the upper and the under world. For a general summary of the Hebrew belief see Charles, *A Critical History of Eschatology*, etc., pp. 152 f.; but one needs to be constantly on guard as regards the author's exegesis.

[4] 3:9, 17:14; 15:2, 3.

limits immortality to the righteous. More probable is it that pharisaism and Essenism, as described by Josephus,[1] represented the current religious belief in these particulars, and that the Sadducees were exceptional in holding that "souls die with the body." Yet the further statements of Josephus in this connection are well substantiated by the entire literature of the Pharisees. "They believe," he says, "that there will be under the earth rewards and punishments, according as men have lived virtuously or viciously in this life; and the latter souls are to be detained in an everlasting prison, but the former will have power to live again." In the *Jewish War*[2] he says expressly that the Pharisees believe that "the souls of good men only are removed into other bodies, while the souls of bad men are punished with eternal punishment." This limitation of the resurrection to the righteous is in keeping with the entire pharisaic literature, and reappears in the silence of Paul and the other New Testament writers concerning the resurrection of the wicked.

These words of Josephus enable us also to see clearly the force of the references already noted in the literature to the place and nature of the punishment which, according to pharisaism, awaited the unrighteous. Sheol was originally simply "the pit" under the earth to which all dead persons were supposed to go. Thanks to the imagination of the apocalypsists, however, it became a place of fire, first for evil angels,[3] and later for evil men.[4] A more fully developed doctrine of hell as a place of punishment appears in *Enoch*, 22:1–14. According to this passage, hell is divided into four sections: for the martyrs, the righteous, the sinners who lived prosperously on the earth, and sinners who had been to some degree punished on the earth. The souls of the

---

[1] *Ant.*, xviii, 1:3–5; *War*, ii, 8:2–14. [2] ii, 8:14. [3] *Enoch*, 21.

[4] *Enoch*, 27:2, 3; 48:9; 54:1, 2; 62:12, 13; 90:26, 27. It is worth noticing that in these passages there is no trace of the purgatorial fires of rabbinism.

third class were to be slain[1] in the day of judgment, but those of the fourth class were to be left in sheol, bereft of all hope of resurrection.

From these representations it is safe to infer that the chief reward to which the Pharisee looked forward was the resurrection of the body. Goodness was a matter of keeping the law, but not for its own sake. Rather was it a means by which one should escape the power of death, and, unlike the wicked, pass over into the glorious future set by the kingdom and conditioned by the obtaining of a new body. This identification of the heavenly reward of the righteous with the resurrection, coupled with the fact that such reward could only come to the righteous, *i. e.*, those who kept the law sufficiently to be acquitted at the day of judgment, furnishes an essential part of the Pauline scheme of justification and salvation.

With the introduction of the resurrection into the messianic concept, pharisaism reached the limits of its transcendental hope. Further it could not go and remain Jewish. The new world was a Jewish empire and the new Jerusalem, inhabited though it might be with risen saints, had still its temple and its worshiping Jews and proselytes. Logical difficulties might be numberless; they were as nothing in comparison with any teaching that de-ethnicized the new age. Lacking scientific habits of mind, the Pharisees had boundless confidence in their nation. To question its future supremacy was to question Jehovah's love and power.

SECTION V.   THE ESSENTIAL ELEMENTS OF ESCHATOLOGICAL MESSIANISM

Such considerations as these, reinforced as they are by the evident variety seen in the different survivals of Jewish literature, should warn us against believing that there ever

---

[1] This is not equivalent to annihilation, in the light of *Enoch*, 108:3 and 99:11. But what does it mean?

was an "orthodox" messianic hope among the Jews. Among the rabbis of the second century it may be that there are to be seen tendencies making toward an authoritative formulation of such a hope, but among the Pharisees of New Testament times messianism, both in its general and its specific character, was in process of development. Any systematic statement of its content is therefore liable to be misleading, and most of all any statement that depends upon a classified accumulation of the various elements of the various writings.[1] The only safe method of constructing any schematic statement is that which distinguishes those elements which are clearly universal and fundamental from those that are to a greater or less degree peculiar to any given document or teacher, and sets such variations in genetic relationship with the common elements.[2]

If now we formulate the common elements of eschatological messianism as found in the apocalyptic literature of pharisaism, we obtain the following results:

1. Two ages, the one present and the other future— "this age" and "the coming age."

2. The belief that the present age is evil, under the influence and even control of Satan,[3] and abounding in all sorts of misery, including disease and pain and death.[4]

3. The belief that the good age is to be introduced by

---

[1] As, for instance, is given by SCHÜRER, Vol. II, ii, and WEBER, Jüdische Theologie.

[2] SCHÜRER's elaborate presentation of the messianic hope, Gesch. jüd. Volkes [3], § 29, is misleading at this point. By his method of accumulation of materials, he gives the impression that all people held to all the elements he has tabulated. How far this is from the actual facts will be apparent to any person who reads his presentation of his data, or, better, reads the literature itself. SCHÜRER's text, Vol. II [3], pp. 550, 551, is apparently intended to correct any misapprehension caused by his method.

[3] It is worth noticing that this conception of Satan is of late origin. Very possibly it is the result of Parsic influence. Cf. STAVE, Einfluss des Parsismus auf das Judenthum, esp. pp. 272 f.; J. WEISS, Predigt Jesu [2], pp. 30–35,

[4] E. g. „Jubilees, 10:8; 17:16; Assum. Moses, 10:1 f.; Testament XII. Pat.; Dan. 5; Naph. 2, 3; Lev. 19; Issa. 6.

God or his representative through some sort of catastrophe.[1] In some cases this catastrophe is developed into a period of struggle between God's representative and his enemies.

4. The judgment, which is at times identified with the catastrophic punishment of the enemies of the Jews. The decisions of this judgment are final. The future of the gentiles, however, is not altogether distinct, varying between destruction in a gehenna of fire to a conversion and subjection to the new Jewish kingdom. The fact that reference is sometimes made to two judgments[2] emphasizes the central portion of the judicial element.

The judge is to be God, although occasionally the Messiah himself is so conceived.[3] Once also the righteous are regarded as judges.[4]

5. The introduction of the new kingdom of the Jews, which is also understood to be the kingdom of God or heaven. This kingdom is the great characteristic of the new age. It comes like it, not by way of evolution, but as God's gift. A variation at this point is the introduction of a messianic kingdom of limited duration—four hundred or a thousand years—which is followed by the final establishment of God's control over all men.

It is to be borne in mind that the Pharisee, as distinct

---

[1] A reference in *Assum. Moses*, 1:18, to repentance as in some way related to the coming of the kingdom, is unique in pre-rabbinic literature. How prominent it later became may be seen in *Sanh.*, 97b; *Pesitta*, 163b. See WEBER, *Jüdische Theologie*, pp. 348 f. In *Assum. Moses*, 1:18, the repentance does not condition the "consummation of the end of the days," but is the first result of such a consummation. *Cf.* also the relation of the conversion of the gentiles in *Assum. Moses*, chap. 12.

[2] *E. g.*, in *Apocalypse of Baruch*, *4 Esdras*, *Enoch* literature, and *Wisdom of Solomon*. In rabbinical literature there is even a threefold judgment. *Cf.* EISENMENGER, *Entdecktes Judenthum*, Vol. II, pp. 950 f.

[3] *Enoch*, 45:3; 55:4; 61:8; 62:2; 69:27; *Sib. Oracles*, iii, 286.

[4] *Wisdom of Solomon*, 3:8; *cf.* Ecclus. 4:15. See also the forecast of crowns and thrones prepared for the righteous and awaiting them at the resurrection, *Ascen. Is.*, 7:22; 8:26; 9:10-13, 18, 24, 25; 11:40. But these passages are of Christian origin. Later Jewish thought conceived of the messianic age as one of struggle and placed the judgment at its close. *Cf.* WEBER, *Jüdische Theologie*, § 88. It also demands the resurrection of the bodies of the righteous.

from the Zealot, did not desire to inaugurate this kingdom, but to wait God's pleasure. The later rabbis, it is true, were swept from this position, and under Akiba did attempt the establishment of a new Jewish and messianic state by force of arms, but the Pharisees simply waited for God's initiative.[1]

6. The resurrection of the righteous. Here variation is also to be seen in that sometimes the resurrection and the judgment are made contemporaneous, and occasionally there seem to be two resurrections, one preceding the messianic kingdom and the other introducing the final reign of God.[2]

7. The personal Messiah. This, however, is not an explicitly described element in all the messianic conceptions. He would of course be always implied. There is no contrast between a fighting and a judging Christ, and no reference to a dying or a suffering Christ. He might be a man especially "anointed" for his work, or a superhuman character.

The coming of Elijah, though not unexpected by pre-Christian Judaism, was not so prominent as in rabbinism proper.

[1] Josephus's refusal to give the one interpretation to Dan., chaps. 11 and 12, required by his context (*War*, iv, 6:3; *Ant.*, x, 11:7) shows that the Pharisees expected the future supremacy of the Jewish people.

[2] The status of the righteous dead between death and the resurrection is not set forth in Jewish literature with any consistency. Some rabbis evidently thought that this interval was spent in "paradise." *Cf. Enoch*, 39:3-12; 60:8-23; 61:12; 70:3, 4; 71:16, 17. *4 Esdras*, 7:30-34, speaks of the righteous dead as being in a "storehouse;" *cf.* 4:35. Such or similar views were especially held by the Jews of the Dispersion. See SCHÜRER, *Ges. jüd. Volkes*[3], Vol. II, p. 549, note. See also CASTELLI, "The Future Life in Rabbinical Literature," *Jewish Quarterly Review*, Vol. I (1889), pp. 314-52.

PART II

THE MESSIANISM OF JESUS

CHAPTER I

CRITICAL PRESUPPOSITIONS

In any discussion of the sayings of Jesus critical processes must always be presupposed. It is by no means to be assumed that the records contained in our four gospels are verbatim reports of the words of Jesus. With the evidence of textual criticism, the patristic gospels, and the Fourth Gospel at hand, it is to exercise but ordinary caution when we carefully scrutinize any reported saying. Above all, there must always be recognized the possibility that the universal eschatological messianism of the early church should have been read back into the sayings of Jesus.

At the same time, however, it is not difficult to reach certain critical positions without attempting at the outset a precise opinion as to just how great an allowance should be made for the subjectivism of the evangelists. While it is obviously impossible to enter fully into a discussion of the grounds for such positions, it will perhaps conduce to a better understanding of what may be said in the following pages, if such positions be briefly stated.

Sufficient evidence is already at hand to warrant us in believing that there exist in our synoptic gospels two classes of material.[1] One class is composed of narratives of the deeds of Jesus. Chief of such material is a collection to all intents and purposes the same as our present gospel of Mark.[2]

---

[1] Cf. especially WERNLE, *Die synoptische Frage;* BURTON, "Some Principles of Literary Criticism and their Application to the Synoptic Problem," *Decennial Publications of the University of Chicago;* and *A Short Introduction to the Gospels.*

[2] The question as to whether or not the original sources of the synoptic gospels were in Aramaic (as with Dalman) or in Hebrew (as with Resch) does not demand attention in the present study. Nor does it yet appear that we are likely to account for the variations in parallel sayings, and thus come nearer the actual words of

Another, and for our purpose much more important, class of sources is that comprising collections of the sayings of Jesus. Chief among these would be that known as the Logia of Matthew.

The combination of the different collections of these two classes of sources in varying proportions gave us our synoptic gospels. Just which collection in each group is the older, or whether any in the group of narratives antedates those in the group of sayings, it is not necessary for our purpose to decide. Far more important is it to decide which of the variant forms of a saying is the older and thus more probably represents the actual thought of Jesus. At this point we may safely use this canon: that saying is more probably genuine which treats of messianic matters in any other way than that which characterized apostolic belief. The trustworthiness of sayings which do not contradict, but agree with, apostolic belief must be decided on these more general critical grounds: (1) Such sayings as appear in Mark as well as in Matthew or Luke may be used with confidence. (2) Such sayings as are common to Matthew and Luke are also to be used with confidence as representing the thought of Jesus. (3) In the case of sayings which occur in both Luke and Matthew, but in different forms, the preference will, on the basis of internal evidence, be given sometimes to the Lukan and sometimes to the Matthean form. The reason for this uncertainty, as far as Matthew is concerned, lies in his tendency to give new literary form to his material, in the less specific character of his version of parallel sayings, and in the interpolatory use made by the first gospel of material

Jesus by retranslating our Greek gospels into either Aramaic or Hebrew. The results of such a method as yet are interesting rather than convincing.

That our present gospel of Mark shows the influence of Matthew or the Matthean Logia (BADHAM, *Influence of the Gospel of Matthew upon Mark*; J. WEISS, *Das älteste Evangelium*), and that it is itself composite, may very likely be true, but such highly refined critical processes as such a possibility demands, in order to become probability, have not brought very tangible results as yet. See J. WEISS, *Marcusevangelium*.

contained in proper contexts in the third. On the other hand, Luke seems at times to have made changes from subjective reasons.[1]

In certain cases Luke has apparently used narrative materials different from those employed by either Mark or Matthew. Here the Lukan account bears every evidence of late origin, and in no way proves an exception to the general principle, already enunciated, of the primary value of the Markan account. It is not impossible, also, that in the case of certain sayings dealing with questions of wealth the Lukan gospel includes material of Ebionitic origin. Such material, however, for our present purpose may be largely disregarded, as it is messianic only in the most general sense, and introduces no elements which are not found in sayings about which there can be no reasonable question.

A consideration of the utmost importance concerns the reworking of sayings in the different gospels. Practically without exception, these reworkings show an advance toward the schematic messianism of the apostolic age. It is not difficult to recognize these expansions and modifications, and their existence is a constant warning against a too ready attribution to Jesus of appeals to current messianic ideas.

The problem involved in any use of the Fourth Gospel is admittedly intricate. The general tendency of criticism seems to be, on the whole, toward insisting upon the impossibility of separating the sayings of Jesus from the editorial element of the gospel. Such agnosticism does not appear to be wholly justifiable. That the editorial element in the gospel is very large is apparent from even a superficial study, but much of the argument against the originality of Johannine sayings of Jesus is based upon the position that Jesus did not assume messianic importance until Cæsarea

---

[1] On the Sermon on the Mount see article by VOTAW in HASTINGS's *Dictionary of the Bible*, supplementary volume, and BACON, *The Sermon on the Mount.*

Philippi, and that therefore the early portion of the Fourth Gospel is without historical value. As will appear later in our discussion, this is a point which cannot be established on sufficiently independent grounds to warrant the rejection of the facts contained in the chapters of the gospel. For the purpose of discovering the sources to be used in tracing the messianic thought of Jesus, it would be a distinct begging of the question to declare that nothing can be genuine which portrays an early development of the messianic consciousness on the part of Jesus. Just when that consciousness dawned is the precise question under discussion. Before it can be answered it will be necessary to establish the worth of the Johannine material by the use of independent criteria. If it should appear that there is absolute contradiction between the messianic portrayal of Mark and that of John, the choice then necessary would favor Mark; but such contradiction has never yet been fairly established.

Nor is it by any means impossible at many points to distinguish sharply between the editorial comment and doctrine, and the sayings of Jesus which lie below them. Even when such line of cleavage is not immediately evident, it can be pretty thoroughly established that most of the sayings represented by the Fourth Gospel as those of Jesus are really echoes of similar sayings of Jesus contained in the synoptic tradition. It is true that the term "kingdom of God" is not commonly used in the Fourth Gospel, but the term "eternal life" is clearly an equivalent to the idea of membership in such kingdom. The eschatological point of view predominates in the Fourth Gospel quite as truly as in the synoptics. In so far, therefore, as the sayings of Jesus in their Johannine form are similar in content to those of the synoptic cycles, it is hard to see why they should not be used as sources for constructive statements. In cases where there is no such echo of the synoptic logia, the question of authenticity must be decided very largely through a decision as to whether or not a saying is in a section of editorial disquisition, and whether it is in general harmony with the thought in the synoptic cycle. Generally speaking, it will be found that, outside of the references to the early messianic career of Jesus, the Fourth Gospel contains nothing from Jesus that is new. More than the synoptics it emphasizes certain elements of Jesus' teaching, notably those of the Holy Spirit, and of the superhuman relationships existing between himself and God. Undoubtedly, too, it represents a more developed tendency toward apologetic interpretation than that discoverable even in Matthew. But, after all, it is a question of degree rather than of sort of treatment, and at least as far as messianic elements are concerned the problems involved are by no means beyond solution.

CHAPTER II

THE MESSIANISM OF JOHN THE BAPTIST

IT is by no means to be inferred from the discussion of the pharisaic literature that apocalyptic, eschatological messianism was universal among the Jewish people.[1] Popular messianism, as has already appeared, was rather of the political, revolutionary type. Yet both parties awaited the Day of Judgment, and either could use the vocabulary of the other. There was, further, always a possibility that the old message of prophetism might furnish a common ground upon which both might stand. That message, however, was never uttered. The call which stirred the common people, however it may have been interpreted by them, was eschatological, and not religio-political; apocalyptic, and not revolutionary. In the person who uttered it, John the Baptist, we have a man speaking, indeed, in the spirit of prophecy, but under the control of that messianism which had grown up in the pharisaic period.[2]

John the Baptist is always regarded by the New Testament writers[3] as the inaugurator of the great movement of

---

[1] BALDENSPERGER, *Selbstbewusstsein Jesu*[2], pp. 203-7, has probably underrated the diffusion of apocalyptic influences, especially since, as has already been noted, the book of Daniel was in universal use. There is, to my knowledge, no evidence, fit to be taken seriously, of the existence among the Jews of a sect of apocalyptic Pietists. It, like the similar body of religionists, " Die Stillen im Lande," may have existed, but the historical student must yet relegate that possibility to the region of conjecture.

[2] It is difficult to see why we should question the trustworthiness of the Lukan account of John's mission. There is certainly nothing in it that is in any way contradicted by the common synoptic source or by Matthew, or by later references of New Testament writers. The reference in JOSEPHUS (*Ant.*, xviii, 5:2), whose genuineness, indeed, is not above suspicion (SCHÜRER, *Geschichte des jüdischen Volkes*[3], Vol. I, p. 438, n. 24), compels us to believe that John's career and preaching were such as would suggest social revolution.

[3] Mark 1:1-3; John 1:1-6: Acts 1:22; 10:37; 13:24, 35.

which Christianity was the outcome. Although the New
Testament gives us few data, they are sufficient to enable us
to formulate an opinion concerning him and his work. The
appearance of the man and his methods were both adapted
to attract the attention of the people and to stir the nation.
Of agitators there had been many, and of revolutionists, but
there had been no one who so completely fulfilled the popular conception as to what a prophet should be.[1] His long
hair, his fasting, his rude clothing, his intensity, his own
estimate of himself, all argued the prophetic office. The
message which John delivered was exceedingly simple.[2]
The Christ was at hand, the judgment was soon to be established, and punishment was soon to be inflicted upon the
wicked. Such preaching is evidently a prophetic announce-
ment of an approaching messianic era. John does not
mention specifically the two ages, or Satan's kingdom, or
the messianic kingdom and the resurrection of the dead.
His attention seems to be entirely centered upon the coming
Judge. In this obviously he is in advance of messianism, as
we have seen it, in which the person of Christ is generally
subordinated to the idea of the kingdom. But he is in sympathy with the spirit of pharisaism in that he emphasizes
the idea of judgment and the necessity for righteousness on
the part of those who wish to be members of the kingdom.
It is to be noticed, further, that, as in pharisaism, this
repentance and achievement of righteousness do not condition the coming of the messiah. Repentance is the means
by which a man determines his fate. Righteousness neither
hastens nor delays the divinely fixed event.

The recognition of the redemptive work of Jesus contained in the phrase "the Lamb of God that taketh away
the sin of the world"[3] is certainly not so easily explained.

1 Mark 1:6 and parallels.   2 Mark 1:7; Matt. 3:7-12; Luke 3:7-9.
3 John 1:29.

In view of all the facts at our disposal, it is impossible to believe the Baptist conceived of Jesus as fundamentally a sacrifice for sin. Possibly the explanation is in part critical. John 1:29 may be an editorial expansion of John 1:36. The hypothesis is by no means improbable, in view of the general character of the Fourth Gospel, and would account for the appearance in a saying ascribed to the Baptist of a soteriological concept of later origin. If it be regarded as tenable, the characterization of Jesus as the Lamb of God would mean simply that the Baptist saw in him an utter absence of the revolutionary furor of the Zealots. Such a rôle he might well have believed to be temporary, and later have grown impatient for the establishment of the judgment he had predicted. When it is recalled that in the estimation of Jesus' own disciples his work as a teacher and healer delayed his assuming his proper functions of Messiah, it is not difficult to see how John could have been ready to believe that Jesus might begin his work in a quiet, undemonstrative way, and later take up a more obviously messianic rôle. His later attitude toward Jesus[1] would thus be one of disappointment rather than of curiosity or newly awakened interest.

It is, however, rather remarkable that John so expressly repudiates the idea that the acquittal in the judgment and membership in the kingdom are in any way conditioned by Jewish descent. Whether or not he could have stated the matter more positively and said that anyone, Jew or gentile who repented might became a member of the kingdom, it would hardly be safe to affirm. In view of his subsequent questionings concerning Jesus' conception of the rôle of Messiah,[2] it would probably be safer to conclude that his position was negative. That is, while holding to the general Israelitic character of the messianic kingdom, he made it

---

[1] Matt. 11:2, 3; Luke 7:18-21.   [2] Matt. 11:2-19; Luke 7:18-35.

clear that the Jew would not enter it simply as a Jew, but as a penitent Jew.   Repentance, not birth, was to be the ground of acquittal.

The act of baptism which John adopted to symbolize repentance as a preparation for entrance into the kingdom consequent upon the forgiveness of sins, can hardly be said to have been invented by him.   Ablutions were common throughout the Jewish cult, though administered by one's self rather than by another.   The real significance given the bath by John was however new.   Its symbolism was by him connected, as it proved inseparably, with the messianic hope.   And instead of the repeated ablutions of current Judaism, it was administered but once—a fit symbol of that one supreme act of penitence and abandonment of sin demanded of those who believed the good news of the coming salvation.[1]

That John was in no wise revolutionary or ascetic in his teaching, however he might himself live, is to be seen in directions given by him to the various classes of penitents, as recorded by Luke.[2]   These words enable us to see again how thoroughly he was in sympathy with the pharisaic rather than the Zealot messianism.   His converts were not to abandon their ordinary way of living, but were to maintain a righteous mode of life.   Such mode of life was, however, not conceived of by him as a part of the messianic kingdom proper, but rather as the sort of life which became penitents who were awaiting the messianic kingdom.   With John clearly the kingdom was still future, and it would be serious perversion of his thought to hold that these directions given the publicans, and the soldiers, and the people generally,

[1] WERNLE, *Beginnings of Christianity* (Eng. trans.), p. 36, very properly says that this baptism and the accompanying ascetic tendencies of John's teaching (*e. g.*, fasting) were toward pharisaism.   They might indeed conceivably, to judge from the tone of the Fourth Gospel, be even regarded as opposed to Christianity proper.

[2] Luke 3: 10–14.

concerned the kingdom itself. What life would be in the kingdom he never specified. He even refused to assume the rôle of Elijah. He was simply a voice calling for preparation for the coming King and Judge.[1]   As to what would happen after the judgment and the coming of the kingdom, John utters no word, except a general forecast of punishment. But he does most emphatically declare that whereas he baptized with water, the Coming One would baptize with the Holy Spirit. And that Coming One he believed was close at hand.

[1] Luke 3:15-17; John 1:19-27.

CHAPTER III

THE KINGDOM OF GOD IN THE TEACHING OF JESUS

LIKE his contemporaries, Jesus lived in the messianic atmosphere. It would, indeed, be interesting to speculate as to just the form in which he would have expressed his religious and ethical teachings, had he been a Greek rather than a Jew. Possibly like Plato he might have described an ideal city-state, or, like the Stoics, have spoken of Nature or Logoi. Our sources, however, make such speculation futile, and we are thrown back upon the fact that Jesus was a Jew, and, as one born under the Law, was inextricably and to no small degree genetically united with the thoughts and life and hopes for Judaism. That he gave new content to his people's language and thought-forms is true, but to understand him completely one must first of all understand his times. Yet, as one discovers in Jesus something quite other than a mere restatement of the better element of pharisaism in general, even more does one discover in his entire career the mingled rejection and acceptance of elements in current messianism.

I

1. From one point of view, Jesus seems utterly to reject both the popular and pharisaic messianic hopes, and to lay emphasis upon the essentially religious hope of deliverance through God's help, of which Jewish messianism was a historical and ethnic expression.[1] He apparently wished to be recognized as the founder of a society the members of which, whether Jews or gentiles, should resemble him, their Teacher

[1] WERNLE, *Die Anfänge unserer Religion*, English translation, *Beginnings of Christianity*, and *Reichgotteshoffnungen*, pp. 23–44, discusses this matter in detail.

and type, in their faith in a loving heavenly Father, in their
love of other men, and in such a willingness to count this
faith and love the highest good in life as to be ready to
sacrifice all else rather than them.   Where they went, as where
he was, the kingdom of God was.   The group of men thus
devoted to a religious and moral life—the kingdom of
God[1]—he seems to have believed would ultimately transform society into a great brotherhood of love and service
and trust in God.[2]

Evidently in such a conception Jesus made the kingdom

---

[1] The two terms ἡ βασιλεία τῶν οὐρανῶν and ἡ βασιλεία τοῦ θεοῦ are essentially
identical.   Each may very well be the translation of מַלְכוּתָא דִשְׁמַיָּא (Heb.
מַלְכוּת שָׁמַיִם).   So DALMAN, *Die Worte Jesu*, Vol. I, p. 75, who gives references to
Berachoth, ii, 2, and to similar expressions in *Ab.*, i, 3; *Sanhedrin*, vi, 4; ix, 6.   The
Aramaic form is made definite simply because the Aramaic has no other form.   It
should be noticed that the Hebrew is without the article.   See also SCHÜRER, *Jahr-
buch für protestantische Theologie*, 1876, pp. 171 f.; TAYLOR, *Sayings of the Jewish
Fathers*, p. 67.   Dalman rejects, the ideas of BALDENSPERGER, *Selbstbewusstsein
Jesu*[2], p. 197, and STANTON, *Jewish and Christian Messiah*, p. 209, that ἡ βασιλεία τοῦ
οὐρανοῦ emphasizes a transcendental element in the conception of the messianic kingdom.   So, too, BOUSSET, *Die Religion des Judenthums*, p. 208.   Dalman also holds that
Jesus chose the expression in order to avoid the use of God's name.   Luke and Mark,
in reporting his words, followed the usage of the LXX, which always uses ἡ βασιλεία
τοῦ θεοῦ.   The fundamental idea of מַלְכוּת he holds to be always "reign" (*Regiment,
Herrschaft*,) and not "domain" (*Reich*); so HOLTZMANN, *Leben Jesu*, pp. 125 f.; but
see KROP, *La pensée de Jésus sur le royaume de Dieu*, pp. 21 f.   Dalman's examples
certainly establish such a usage among the rabbis, but that it is the only usage is
contradicted by other literature.   And what easier and more inevitable metonymy
is there than that "dominion" should pass over to represent "those ruled"?

At all events, it is important to recognize clearly that in the present instance
we have an example of the fact that the study of a concept is more important than
the study of a term.   The expression ἡ βασιλεία τοῦ θεοῦ does not occur in the Jewish
literature contemporary with Jesus, unless it be Eth. *Enoch*, 41:1f.; 52:4; *Wis. Sol.*,
6:5; 10:10; *Ps. Sol.*, 5:21.   Yet, God's relation to the messianic kingdom is universally recognized as that of king (*e. g.*, Eth. *Enoch*, 25:3, 5, 7; 27:3).   And, more specifically, the kingdom is actually in heaven, according to *Test. XII. Pat.*, Lev. 2:3;
Ascension of Isaiah, 4:14.   In *Assumption of Moses* the victory of God's kingdom over
that of Satan is described at length (*cf.* especially 10:1f.; *cf. Test. XII. Pat.*, Dan 5).
Further, see *Ps. Sol.*, 17:4; *Tobit*, 13:1; Dan. (Song of Three Children) 3:54.

[2] Matt. 12:28; Luke 10:11; Matt. 13:24-30, 36-43, 47-50; Mark 4:26-29.   JÜLICHER,
Gleichnissreden Jesu, hardly does justice to these parables.   To these passages are
sometimes added Matt. 11:11, 12; (Luke 7:28; 16:16).   This social view of the kingdom of God has played a considerable, and doubtless helpful, rôle in recent literature.   I have myself adopted it in my *Social Teaching of Jesus*, chap. 3.   Such a
definition, however, is not the proper point of departure for a study of the social
teaching with which the gospels abound.

into a family, thereby utterly destroying its formal messianic content. It was to be a regenerate humanity, not a conquering Jewish nation. God was to be a father and not a king. Evidently, too, he has preserved the truth that lay in revolutionary messianism. If God is to deliver men from misery or sin, social results are inevitable. To postpone all effects of divine assistance to an indefinite future is to ostracize God and to threaten the very foundations of religion. That Jesus discountenanced revolution by no means argues against this position. He rejected violence as the mistaken idea of the Zealots, just as he agreed with them and the prophets in his forecast of social regeneration as inextricably united with that of the kingdom.

2. If this were the only form taken by Jesus' teaching as to the kingdom of God, apostolic teaching would be inexplicable. In the sayings that warrant this formulation of his doctrine the idea of an eschatological kingdom of God is lacking; with the apostles it is exclusively and invariably present. If the teaching of the apostles is the outgrowth of that of Jesus—a position few would question—the inference is unavoidable: Jesus' teaching must also have contained and emphasized the eschatological hope. That the apostles should have left unnoticed, or even have overlooked, certain elements of the teaching of Jesus, and in consequence should have made over-prominent other elements, is easy to believe. But it is quite inconceivable that they and the early church should have so utterly misunderstood his words as always to see eschatology where he intended a divinely directed social evolution. At least they must have dropped some hint which would suggest such a change of opinion.

We are not left, however, to merely *a priori* and negative considerations. The extant sayings of Jesus show beyond doubt his acceptance of elements of pharisaic eschatological messianism.

Even from the side of exegesis, the evidence that the kingdom is present is not free from objections. Chief among the supports for such a view are the parable of the seed growing secretly[1] and the saying of Luke 17:20. Any fair criticism will recognize the genuineness of these sayings, and any fair exegesis will admit their reference to the kingdom. The fact that the phrase with which a parable is introduced may be used (as, for example, Matt. 13:44–47; 20:1; cf. also Matt. 18:23; 22:2; 25:1) to denote a general analogy between certain things true of human experience and certain things true of the kingdom, does not necessarily argue that it has no more specific reference here. In this parable Jesus is evidently speaking of the kingdom itself. Yet it can be urged that these two sayings do not necessarily argue a present kingdom. In the case of the parable of Mark 4:26–29, the teaching as to a present evolving kingdom is wholly dependent upon a disregard of vs. 29. In the only other parable in which the figure of the harvest is used it is equivalent to the day of judgment.[2] This parable might very properly be interpreted eschatologically; that is, as intended to teach the necessity of waiting until the coming of the harvest with reaping long delayed by the growth of the grain. Thus the parable would to all intents and purposes have the same teaching as that of Matt. 13:24, 29. Similarly in the case of the saying of Luke 17:20. The context not improbably compels it to refer, not to the fact that the kingdom is present, but to the suddenness with which it will appear. One will not need to say that the kingdom is here or there; it will be instantaneously among people, as the lightning instantaneously crosses the entire heavens. Men will not

[1] Mark 4:26–29.

[2] Matt. 13:39. The figure is different in Matt. 9:37 and John 4:35.

need to look for it carefully, because it will suddenly be among them.[1]

Even the most superficial reading of the gospels reveals a terminology already made familiar by the study of the pharisaic apocalypses. Such terms as συντέλεια, παλιγγενεσία, αἰών and its cognates, ὁ υἱὸς τοῦ ἀνθρώπου, κόσμος, ὁ ἐκλελεγμένος, δαίμων, πτωχοί, ἅγιος, σωτηρία, ἀνάστασις, γεέννα, φῶς, βασιλεία, χριστός, indicate at once how great is the indebtedness of the gospels to current vocabularies.

Similarly in the case of specific concepts. A comparison of his words with apocalyptic literature will reveal a number of striking similarities. It is certainly no mere coincidence when we find Jesus referring to hell as prepared for the devil and his angels;[2] to wealth as the mammon of unrighteousness;[3] to the approaching redemption;[4] to the thrones prepared for his followers.[5]

When, however, one lays the general scheme of the teachings of Jesus over against the general scheme of pharisaic messianism already presented, the points of similarity are strikingly shown.

1. With him, as with the authors of the apocalypses, there are two ages, the present and the coming.[6]

---

[1] So also, JÜLICHER, *Gleichnissreden Jesu*, Vol. II, p. 136. WERNLE, *Reichgotteshoffnungen*, considers Matt. 11:11,12, with parallels, as arguing the presence of the kingdom, but his arguments are not convincing. In both sayings the reference may be quite as satisfactorily held to be to the eschatological kingdom.

[2] Matt. 25:41; Eth. *Enoch*, 54:5; if this verse is not actually from Jesus, it of course loses its weight.

[3] Luke 16:9; *Enoch*, 63:10.   [4] Luke 21:28; *Enoch*, 51:2.

[5] Matt. 19:28; *Enoch*, 108:12. These and similar references will be found given with some completeness in introductions to the various apocalypses. In particular see CHARLES, *Enoch*, *Jubilees*, *Assumption of Moses*, and *Ascension of Isaiah*. The matter is also treated in THOMSON, *Books which Influenced Our Lord and His Apostles*, and more generally by J. WEISS, *Predigt Jesu vom Reiche Gottes*[2]; BOUSSET, *Predigt Jesu in ihrem Gegensatz zu Judenthum*.

[6] There is only one saying unquestionably from Jesus (Mark 10:30), in which this distinction is explicitly drawn, and even in this instance the word καιρός is used in the first member of the antithesis. The one complete and precise saying attributed to him (Matt. 12:32), is an explanatory rewriting of Mark 3:28, in which no reference is made to the two ages. Similarly οὗτος ὁ αἰών of Luke 20:34, is an

2. The present age was evil and under the control of its prince, Satan.[1] Through his influence sickness[2] and temptations to evil,[3] suffering and "possession," had seized upon mankind.[4] Though Jesus had prophetically seen the fall of its prince,[5] one large part of his mission consisted in destroying this demoniacal kingdom,[6] and bringing its king and members to the fires of hell.[7] Demons were cast out by himself and his representatives,[8] the prince was to be overcome,[9] and the kingdom of God was to prevail.

3. With Jesus as with the Pharisees the kingdom of God was still future.[10] Repentance was urged, not as the means of bringing in the kingdom, but as a preparation for membership in it, when in the Father's good pleasure it should appear. The kingdom is thus a gift of God,[11] destined to come, not as the product of social evolution, but suddenly, as something already prepared before the foundation of the world.[12] It is to be inherited and found rather than constructed.[13]

explanatory expansion of Mark 12:25. In Luke 16:8, however, the contrast is drawn between the children of "this age" and "the children of light." This reticence of Jesus, which we cannot believe to be accidental, may well be contrasted with the usage of Paul. See, e. g., Rom. 12:2; 1 Cor. 1:20; 2:6, 8; 3:18; 2 Cor. 4 :4; Gal. 1 : 4.

[1] Mark 3:24; 4:15 (Luke 8:12); Luke 22:31; Matt. 4:8, 9; 12:26. In the Johannine logia this conception is very clearly expressed. See, for instance, John 12:31; 14:30; 16:11.

[2] Luke 13:11 f.   [3] Matt. 4:1-11 (Luke 4:1-13).

[4] On the kingdom of Satan as opposed to, and to be conquered by, Jesus see ISSEL, Reich Gottes, pp. 38–51; JACOBY, Neutestamentliche Ethik, pp. 55–62; WENDT, Teaching of Jesus, Vol. I, pp. 163–68; WEISS, Predigt Jesu vom Reiche Gottes[2], pp. 90–94.

[5] Luke 10:18.   [6] Mark 3:22; Matt. 12:22–37; Luke 11:14–23.

[7] Matt. 25:41; cf. Eth. Enoch 54:5 Ascen. Isa., 7:12; 10:12. In case this section be treated as a Christian homily, this reference should be omitted.

[8] Luke 9:11 f.; Mark 3:15; Luke 10:17.   [9] Luke 22:31; Mark 3:23.

[10] ἔρχεσθαι, Matt. 6:10; Mark 9:1; Luke 11:2; 17:20; ἐγγίζειν, Matt. 3:2; 4:17, etc.; φθανεῖν, Matt. 12:28; Luke 11:20.

[11] Luke 12:32; Matt. 25:1–45; Mark 13:3–42 (Matt. 24:3–42; Luke 21:5–58). It makes little difference whether or not this eschatological address is composite. The mass of evidence is too great to have the decision affected.

[12] Matt. 25:34. Even if this section of Matthew be no part of the original logia, but a little apocalypse incorporated into the gospel, it would be difficult not to believe that Jesus' words had given color to the belief in the pre-existence of the kingdom. Cf. the sentence in the model prayer, "Thy will be done in earth as it is in heaven," Matt. 6:10.

[13] Matt. 6:33 and parallels; cf. 13:44-46. See LÜTGERT, Reich Gottes, p. 26; HOLTZMANN, Neutestamentliche Theologie, p. 202; SANDAY, art. "Jesus Christ," in HASTINGS'S Dictionary of the Bible.

4. The judgment[1] also plays an important rôle in the teaching of Jesus. The Son of man was to appear in the clouds,[2] to accord rewards and punishments.[3] Once, also, Jesus is reported as speaking of his disciples sitting on thrones "judging the twelve tribes of Israel."[4]

5. Similarly the resurrection is distinctly taught by Jesus as one element of a complete transformation of the individual,[5] when the evil age should reach its "consummation" and the new messianic age should begin.[6] Indeed, the one extra-gospel saying of Jesus dealing with eschatological matters unmistakably deals with the resurrection.[7] The coming of Elijah as the precursor of the messianic age, which was to play so large a rôle in rabbinic messianism, is also distinctly recognized by Jesus.[8]

Thus of the seven fundamental elements of the pharisaic messianism, five and, since, as will be argued below, Jesus regarded himself as the Messiah, six are an integral and distinct part of his teaching. The seventh—the fifth of the summary—the restriction of membership in the coming kingdom to Jews, was distinctly repudiated by him. This divergence from current beliefs was inevitable because of his insistence upon the ethical nature of the new citizenship. The citizen was to have the character, not the nationality, of the king.[9]

[1] It is one of the merits of HOLTZMANN, *Leben Jesu* (*e. g.*, pp. 132 f.), that this is sufficiently recognized.

[2] Mark 14:61, 62.

[3] Matt. 13:41-43; 16:27, 28; 19:27-29; Luke 22:69. Here belong also the eschatological discourses of Mark, chap. 13, and parallels, and Matt., chap. 25, as well as the parables of Matt. 13:24-30, 36-43, 47-50; Mark 4:26-29.

[4] Matt. 19:28; Luke 22:30.

Regeneration, Matt. 19:28, which is added to Mark 10:28.

[6] Mark 12:18-27; Matt. 22:23-33; Luke 20:27-38; John 5:28, 29; 6:39, 40, 44, 54.

[7] 1 Thess. 4:15-17. The force of the statement in the text would not be changed if vss. 16, 17 should be shown to be Paul's.

[8] Thus, Elijah, Mark 9:11 (Matt. 17:10-12); Matt. 11:14.

[9] It cannot be denied that there are sayings of Jesus which may be used to show that he thought of the kingdom as to be composed of Jews; *e. g.*, Luke 19:9; Mark 14:25. *Cf.* Luke 22:16, 30.

The transference of the kingdom from the Messiah to the Father he does not discuss, but as the supremacy of God in general was one of his most fundamental teachings, there can be nothing in opposition to such a relegation of the Messiah to a secondary position, when once his mission had been accomplished.[1]

II

We find, then, in the messianic teaching of Jesus a twofold representation of the kingdom. On the one side he is reported to have spoken of it as present and evolving; on the other, he far more commonly spoke of it as future, given by God to a waiting people who had prepared themselves for its coming by repentance and faith in the loving heavenly Father. The first conception is unique in Jewish and early Christian thought. The other is to all intents and purposes the same as that of literary eschatological messianism. The fact that superficially, at least, the one conception appears inconsistent with the other has led opposing schools of critics to deny the authenticity of each.

1. On the one hand it is claimed that the apocalyptic element is due to reading back apostolic hopes into the gospel record of the sayings of Jesus.[2] The social and religious, rather than the eschatological, elements are therefore treated, not only as an exegetical point of departure, but also as a critical and exegetical norm.

In general, such criticism is under the direction of dogmatic presuppositions as regards the kingdom of God, due to the influence of Ritschl. For those who approach the subject from the theological-sociological point of view the term is essentially identical with the church—a present evolving institution. The kingdom from their point of view is not to

---

[1] *Cf.* Matt. 10:32; Luke 12:8.

[2] So, MUIRHEAD, *The Eschatology of Jesus;* and, cautiously, STEVENS, *Biblical Theology of the New Testament*, pp. 37–40; *Teaching of Jesus*, chap. xiv.

come suddenly, but gradually; it is in no sense apocalyptic, but genuinely social. It is not at all difficult, therefore, to understand that Jesus' references to eschatological matters should either be accounted for in terms of a developing organism or be judged unauthentic.

While there is the possibility, if not the probability, that a certain amount of apostolic thought has been read back into the words of Jesus, such a rough and ready treatment of a genuinely difficult problem can hardly be considered satisfactory. As a matter of fact, it clearly begs the question. If it were true that Jesus thought only of the kingdom of God as a present, growing institution, it would be necessary to reject as unauthentic all sayings attributed to him of a strictly eschatological import; but this is precisely the point at issue, and cannot be assumed.

Again, there are those who hold that the eschatological element was adopted by Jesus to bring himself in touch with the thought of his day. It cannot be denied that such a position embodies a very important truth, but it is far from being a complete answer to the problem. If Jesus employed a term which was in common use, and gave to it a definition which was different from that which it ordinarily possessed, we should certainly expect that in some way he would have attempted to disabuse the minds of his disciples of false impressions. At least we should expect some explicit references to the definition he held to be correct, as over against that which others held to be correct. As a matter of fact, however, we do not have any such correction in our records. If it is argued that it is to be expected that the apostles would overlook such teaching, the reply must again be made as before that, while there would be no improbability in holding that the disciples overlooked many of the sayings of Jesus, because of their failure to understand and so to remember them, it is altogether beyond the

range of probability that they should have completely overlooked any explicit correction of current ideas as regards the
kingdom of God.   They certainly remembered his criticism
of the current conception of the Messiah as a son of David.
With this argument from silence removed, our way is plain.
To think of Jesus as deliberately using a term with a
meaning different from what it would have for others is not
only to raise a question as to his morals, but as to his
capacity as a teacher.

There remains one other critical hypothesis for the
removal of at least a large element in the eschatological
teaching of Jesus.   It is in effect that Matt. 25:31–46 is an
apocalypse of early Christian origin which has been incorporated into the gospels, and that, similarly, the eschatological elements of Mark 13 and parallels[1] did not come
from Jesus, but are a "little apocalypse" that have been
inserted in his teaching.   But even if this, by no means
improbable, hypothesis be granted, it by no means follows[2]
that the eschatological element in the teaching of Jesus
vanishes.   There are still left on practically indisputable
critical grounds such eschatological sayings as those of
Matt. 16:27 f.; 26:29, 64; 10:23; 19:28 f.

2. Diametrically opposite to this attempt to eliminate the
eschatological elements from the teaching of Jesus is the
more or less pronounced tendency on the part of some
scholars to deny that Jesus himself spoke of the kingdom of
God in any other than an eschatological sense, and, consequently, to deny the authenticity of the passages which
involve any idea of a present kingdom.[3]   The basis of such

[1] See WENDT, *Die Lehre Jesu*, Vol. I, pp. 9 f.; SCHMIEDEL, art. "Gospels," *Encyclopædia Biblica*, § 124.   The "little apocalypse" here imbedded in the gospel
narrative is held to have been interwoven in authentic non-eschatological sayings
of Jesus concerning the fall of Jerusalem. This "little apocalypse" may be
recovered by uniting the following verses of Mark: 13:7–9a, 14–20, 24–27, 30.

[2] *Cf.* SCHMIEDEL, in article cited, §§ 145 f.

[3] See J. WEISS, *Predigt Jesu vom Reiche Gottes*[2]; SCHMOLLER, *Die Lehre vom
Reiche Gottes*; SCHNEDERMANN, *Reich Gottes*; ISSEL, *Reich Gottes*; WERNLE, *Die*

a denial is not exegetical, but critical.   Such sayings as in any clear way represent the kingdom as present are declared to be due to an introduction into the thought of Jesus of the apostolic conception of the church as a kingdom of Christ distinct from the kingdom of God.   The basis, however, of such an argument is by no means firm.   It cannot be denied that Paul conceived of a time when the Christ would transfer the kingdom to the Father,[1] but it is a mistake to conceive of this expectation as referring to the church.   The kingdom to which the apostle refers is evidently that to be inaugurated at the coming of Christ, and is truly as eschatological at its inception as it is at its completion.[2]   In the apostolic thought the church is not conceived of as the kingdom, but as the body[3] of Christ, and Christians are distinctly said to have their citizenship in heaven.[4]   To say, with J. Weiss,[5] that the idea of a present kingdom of Christ, as distinct from the coming kingdom of God, has here been read back into Jesus' teaching by primitive Christianity, is precisely to reverse the facts at our disposal.   Early Christianity, as represented both by the apostles and the Fathers, thought of the kingdom of Christ and of the kingdom of God as eschatological.   The use of 1 Cor. 15: 24 ff. to prove the contrary is unfortunate in the light of 1 Cor. 15: 22, 23. That the apostles believed that the Christ would some day deliver over the kingdom to the Father is undeniable, but this is very different from saying that his kingdom is present.   There is no one to be mentioned to whom the idea of a present kingdom can be attributed except Jesus himself.[6]

Anfänge unserer Religion; CONE, *Rich and Poor in the New Testament;* BALDEN-SPERGER, *Das Selbstbewusstsein Jesu;* BOUSSET, *Die Predigt Jesu in ihrem Gegensatz zu Judenthum.* See, however, LÜHR, "Das Bild Jesu bei den Eschatologen" in *Protestantische Monatshefte,* Vol. VII, pp. 64–78; HAUPT, *Die eschatologischen Aussagen Jesu.*

[1] 1 Cor. 15: 24, 25.   [2] 1 Cor. 15: 23.   [3] Eph. 1: 23; 5:30; 1 Cor. 12: 12–27.

[4] Phil. 3: 20.   [5] *Predigt Jesu vom Reiche Gottes*[2], p. 41.

[6] I wish to acknowledge assistance received at this point from a doctor's thesis by H. M. HERRICK, *The Kingdom of God in the Patristic Literature.*

Apart from this consideration, there is no critical argument which would lead one to doubt the authenticity of all the eschatological or all the religio-sociological passages, and the problem is left precisely where a fair exegesis leaves it: How may we reconcile the two contents given by Jesus to the term, "kingdom of God"?

III

Before attempting to solve this problem methodically, it may be well to consider a rather ingenious attempt at ruling it out of court by a sort of exegetical *tour de force*. This is the view that accepts the apocalyptical sayings attributed to Jesus as genuine, but holds them to be simply figurative expressions of judgment and of glory. The basis for such an argument lies in the admitted fact that the coming of the Son of man in *Enoch* has obviously to do with judgment. Apocalyptic being considered as a purely literary form without content, all references which Jesus makes to such a coming are therefore treated as figurative prophecies of the judgment which is to be inflicted upon the Jewish nation. Such a view would see, for example, in the destruction of Jerusalem a fulfilment of the words of Jesus to the high-priest: "Ye shall see the Son of man coming in the clouds of heaven."[1] Indeed, the view may even be carried further[2] and involve an indefinite number of comings of the Son of man, in the sense that every great crisis in which suffering results from national or individual wrongdoing may be said to be a judgment of God, and so a coming of the Son of man.

The difficulty with such an interpretation lies not so much in the assertion that the coming of the Son of man was synonymous with judgment, as in the fact that it is a philosophical generalization which by no means is to be

1 Mark 14:62.

2 Burton and Mathews, *Constructive Studies in the Life of Christ*, p. 240.

found in the thought of Jesus. With him, as with the apocalyptic writers, there was to be but one coming of the Judge. To reduce the apocalyptic terminology to a mere figure of speech is to destroy, not merely a literary form, but a certain definite content as well. That this view has elements of truth in it cannot be denied, but as a complete explanation of the situation it raises more difficulties than it explains.

Nor can it be satisfactorily argued that the eschatological kingdom represents a completed kingdom, the beginnings of which are to be seen in Jesus and the community of disciples about him. It cannot be denied that such a view has great attractiveness. Certain passages, to which references have already been made, like the parable of the seed growing secretly, and of the leaven, might be argued in favor of such a position. The difficulty is, however, that Jesus himself never distinctly makes the combination. Nothing would have been easier for him than to have embodied such a view in his teaching. It is, of course, possible to think of a series of comings of the Son of man in judgment; but even thus it is exceedingly difficult to think of the kingdom in its eschatological shape as in any way growing out of the kingdom in the social sense. Whether or not Jesus actually used the term, the establishment of the new age was really a παλιγγενεσία—a new birth.[1]

The first step toward a proper reconciliation of the two usages of the term, must be a determination as to which of the two is really fundamental. The difficulty in making the idea of a present kingdon fundamental has already been seen to be insuperable, because of the difficulty of synthesizing with it the distinctly eschatological elements which are so prominent in the teaching of Jesus. If these elements had been but incidental, or if Jesus had referred to them in

[1] In the Syriac version of Matt. 19:28, παλιγγενεσία is translated " in the age new."

the way of accommodation, or if they had been but literary figures, the synthesis would be comparatively easy. The eschatological pictures of the kingdom could then be treated as a poetic representation of the completion of the evolving present kingdom. Such a hypothesis is untenable, not alone on the grounds already stated above, but because it involves a reversal of true exegetical method. At the very best the passages which can be quoted in favor of the existing present kingdom are exceedingly few, while those which more naturally must be interpreted to refer to the future kingdom are all but constant. But the objection rests not alone on the comparison of numbers. If a true exegetical method demands anything, it is that the interpreter come to a given thought with the stream of historical development. The burden of proof lies heavily upon him who gives a meaning to historical concepts which is contrary to the course of such development. Such burden of proof can be sustained in the case of certain elements of the messianic hope as taught by Jesus, notably those which concerned the office and the work of Christ himself; but, as has already appeared, the entire scheme of his teaching is so thoroughly like that which it has been shown he must have inherited, as to render the substitution of new definitions for those inherited improbable in the highest degree. The historico-grammatical process, if it is worth anything, demands that of the two uses of the term "kingdom" the eschatological be chosen as fundamental.

The practical question is therefore reversed. It is no longer one of adjusting the eschatological teachings of Jesus to his religio-sociological, but that of adjusting his references to a present kingdom to his entire eschatological scheme. Such an accommodation is by no means difficult when once it is undertaken.

The words of Jesus which apparently describe the present kingdom refer (1) to those who were to be received into the kingdom when it appeared, and (2) to the triumphs he and his followers were winning over Satan and his kingdom.

1. The kingdom was among those to whom he spoke, in the sense that there were men present who were to enter it when it appeared. This simple explanation has very much in its favor. To begin with, it is precisely the conception of the relation of the individual believer to the kingdom held by the early church. Then, further, it necessitates no redefinition of the term "kingdom of God," but simply a metaphorical use of the term to refer to those who were to be its subjects. To attempt to give to the words of Jesus any double definition seems very hazardous; to think of him as at one time speaking of the kingdom as sociological, and at another as apocalyptic-eschatological, is to raise the suspicion that he himself had no clear idea of the term. To say that he uses the term with a constant sense of the new kingdom which was to be established by God in the new age, but also in a figurative way to refer to the people who are actually to belong to it, is to allow him no more than a conventional freedom in his references to and use of an inherited concept.

From this point of view it is easy to see how Jesus could speak of the immediate group of his disciples as growing in the world like leaven in the meal, or like the mustard seed. The small beginnings were, indeed, to have a great ending, numerically as well as in dignity.

2. Jesus could speak of the kingdom as present in the sense that there already was to be seen an expression of that divine power and authority which later would establish the complete overthrow of Satan's kingdom. In the person of himself and his disciples that struggle between the two kingdoms which has already been noted as a part of his general thought was in progress. The first intimations of the final triumph were already seen. The disciples were

given authority to, and are reported to have, cast out demons.[1] Jesus himself by the finger of God cast them out, and was himself the strong man who was to bind and spoil his opponent. When the kingdom had in a precise sense come, Satan would be completely vanquished. In the meantime Jesus, in the full assurance of that victory, could speak of having seen him fall from heaven.[2] How easy it was for the apostolic age to interpret the historical work of Jesus as that of one who introduced, not the kingdom, but the messianic last days, will appear in our subsequent discussion.

None of these considerations, however, affect the conclusions which one must draw concerning the primary and the derived messianic conception of Jesus. Any strict definition of the kingdom of God as used by Jesus must be eschatological.[3] With Jesus as with his contemporaries the kingdom was yet to come. Its appearance would be the result of no social evolution, but sudden, as the gift of God; men could not hasten its coming; they could only prepare for membership in it.

IV

The discussion thus far may now be summarized:

Formally considered, the kingdom of God in the estimation of Jesus was that community over whom God was to rule, whose members were like God in character and in that they were not possessed of physical bodies. When God saw fit, it was to be miraculously triumphant over the Satanic kingdom and established upon the earth by the Christ. Those who had prepared to enter it by living a life of love, might be conceived of proleptically as the kingdom, so certain were

[1] Mark 3:15; Luke 10:17.

[2] Luke 10:18. It is the merit of WERNLE (*Reichgotteshoffnungen*) that he has seen distinctly the significance of this latter point. He is less happy in his adoption of the distinction drawn by J. Weiss between the kingdom of Christ and the kingdom of God. See also his chapters iv and vi in *The Beginnings of Christianity*.

[3] See, for similar statement, TITIUS, *Neutestamentliche Lehre von Seligkeit*, Vol. I, p. 5.

they to enjoy its unmeasured happiness.   It was Jesus' duty, both by teaching and example, to prepare men to enter and to prepare others to enter it when he, the Christ, should come to establish it.

Yet this is by no means the end of the matter.   It would be a grievous mistake to think that Jesus appropriated without discrimination the beliefs current among his people.   He was far too original a thinker not to see limitations in the religious world whose life he shared.   While the kingdom of God as he conceived it resembled the kingdom of God as the Pharisee conceived it, there were radical differences in the two conceptions.   Just what these differences were can be best considered, however, in connection, not with abstract teaching, but with the formulation of his own self-consciousness.

CHAPTER IV

JESUS' CONCEPTION OF HIMSELF AS MESSIAH

THE question as to how Jesus regarded his own relations to the kingdom he foretold is one of first importance, both from the point of view of Christology and from that of constructive theology. Such a question has but two possible answers; either he regarded himself as the Christ, or he did not so regard himself.

Which of these two alternatives is to be chosen will appear only after a detailed examination of the material of the gospels.

I

The chief argument against messianic self-consciousness in Jesus is critical, and amounts to the complete denial of the historical value of the early chapters of the Fourth Gospel and the assertion that such passages in the synoptic gospels as imply messianic self-estimate on the part of Jesus are either misinterpretations or unauthentic. Sometimes, it is true, such criticism does not lead to a denial that Jesus considered himself to be the Messiah. As in the case of Wrede,[1] the gospel material may be held to show that Jesus did believe himself to be the Christ, but that he kept it a secret except from his most intimate friends. From such a point of view, all sayings as appear to give publicity to this belief are untrustworthy. The self-designations which have commonly been held to imply the messianic character on the part of Jesus are now held by an increasing number of scholars to be either mistranslations of

[1] *Das Messiasgeheimniss Jesu.*

84

some original Aramaic expression, or interpolating additions
of the evangelists or editor of the gospel.[1]

So complicated and discordant is this criticism, and so
subjective are the criteria which it employs, that detailed
discussion is here impracticable.   Yet it is not difficult to
see that, wholly apart from any philosophical bias against
the miraculous, such criticism makes three untenable presuppositions.

In the first place, it assumes that a confession of belief in
Jesus as the Christ involved also the belief that Jesus was
at the time of the confession engaged in recognizable messianic work.

In the second place it assumes that Jesus could not have
considered himself the Messiah unless the kingdom had
actually come.

In the third place it assumes that any similarity between
the messianic teaching of Jesus and the messianic belief of
the apostolic church is due to a reading back of such apostolic
faith into the sayings of Jesus.

To all three presuppositions it may be replied, in general, that they embody the precise matter under investigation and cannot be used as critical criteria.   That there are
independent criteria at our disposal is undeniable, and the
problem before the investigator must be answered by em-
ploying them.

But this general consideration is by no means the end of
the matter.   Each of the presuppositions is open to particular objections.

The assumption that Jesus must needs be doing recognizable messianic work in order to be accepted as the
Messiah is fundamentally incorrect.   The entire church of

[1] See CARY, *The Synoptic Gospels*, pp. 360 f.; MARTINEAU, *Seat of Authority in
Religion*, pp. 355 f.; MEINHOLD, *Jesus und das Alte Testament*, pp. 98 f.; HAVET,
Le Christianisme et ses origines, Vol. IV, pp. 15 f.; KÄHLER, *Der sogenannte historische
Jesus und der geschichtliche biblische Christus*; SCHMIDT, art. "Son of Man" in
Encyclopædia Biblica.

the New Testament times had no difficulty in believing the precise opposite. To its members Jesus was the Christ, but a Christ who in their own time had not established his kingdom. Nor was this position wholly precluded by eschatological messianism as it existed among the Pharisees. While, as has already appeared, it is true that the current expectation knew nothing of a suffering and dying Christ, it is quite as true that it included a period of messianic activity in which the Christ should not have completed his work. It will be recalled that his reign was held to include, if not to constitute, a period of struggle. It is obvious that at some point within this period the Christ would not have attained his real messianic supremacy. Such a consideration as this does not prove that one could be the Christ who was not actually engaged in messianic work, but it does suggest caution as to holding that, in order to be the Christ, one must be *recognized* as doing the full, or even recognizable, messianic work. That which constituted a personality messianic was not so much his deeds as the presence in his life of the spirit of God. Accordingly, if, instead of assuming that messianic quality and recognizable messianic activity are inseparable, one admits possible periods in a progressive messianic activity, there is no difficulty in holding that, in case the evidence of the synoptic gospels warrant the view, Jesus might both be and be considered the Christ. His activity, before he was seen to be a messianic king, may be conceived of as falling into two periods—the preparatory or prophetic and the eschatologically messianic. Finally, to hold that all similarities between the teaching of Jesus and that of the apostles originate in the latter is the most arrant subjectivism. Why might they not have originated with Jesus and have been reproduced in the apostolic teaching? Or, as is indeed the case, why might they not have originated in Judaism and have been reproduced by both Jesus and his disciples? There may very well be certain cases in which the evangelical tradition has been somewhat reworked by the evangelists or by those who subsequently edited their writings, but such reworkings and interpretations and substitutions of verbal equivalents can generally be detected and controlled by critical methods that are independent of the result they seek to establish. The simple fact is that the method by which it is sought to prove that Jesus did not hold himself to be the Christ proves too much. It destroys the entire historicity of the gospel narrative. How, for instance, is one to deny the genuineness of Jesus' reply to the high-priest[1] and hold to any part of Mark as historical data? But if such a saying as this is admitted, it is sheer waste of time to argue that Jesus did not, at least in the latter part of his career, think of himself as the Christ.

As might be expected, these presuppositions find their chief critical result in the rejection of the early sections of the Fourth Gospel. Jesus is there represented as having been pointed out by John the Baptist and accepted by certain disciples as Christ at the very beginning of his ministry. The precise content of the testimony of the Baptist to Jesus will be considered later; at present it is enough to consider the broader aspects of the matter. It cannot be denied that there is, superficially at least, some discrepancy between the early acceptance of Jesus as the Messiah recorded by the Fourth Gospel, and the silence of the synoptists as to the faith on the part of the disciples before the scene at Cæsarea Philippi. This discrepancy, however, loses much, if not all, of its force when one recalls that neither in the Fourth Gospel nor in the synoptics is messianic faith in Jesus anything more than an expectation that he would do messianic work in the future. In neither is there any clear acceptance of him as Christ on the basis of qualifying messianic acts.

[1] Mark 14:61, 62.

From the point of view of the early church, there is no
a priori reason why such a conviction might not have come
early as well as late in Jesus' ministry, provided only some-
one had the insight to perceive the real character of Jesus.
The question, therefore, becomes simply a matter of evidence to be decided by the use of the synoptic gospels as
controlling data. If they do not make it impossible to hold
that the disciples could have accepted Jesus as the future
Christ during the lifetime of John the Baptist, we may
safely estimate and use the Johannine material. The one
assumption in which this position may involve the investi
gator concerns the prophetic insight of John the Baptist.
If Jesus were pointed out by him as Christ before he had
presented, so to speak, his messianic credentials, John certainly had powers of insight beyond the ordinary. But as
to the possibility of John's believing that Jesus was the
Christ and so describing him, it is hard to find *a priori*
objections. No serious scholar would deny some plus element in the prophetic self-consciousness.

It is the investigator's first duty to discover in the synoptic
sources how distinct was the messianic consciousness in Jesus
himself throughout his public ministry; in short, to determine whether Jesus actually did consider himself the Messiah.

II

In any constructive statement as to the self-consciousness
of Jesus the point of departure must be his baptism rather
than his birth. It is true, as will appear in this discussion
sooner or later, that any estimate of his personality arrives
at ontological conclusions. It is also doubtless true that for
minds of a Greek tendency statements concerning origins are
more intelligible than those which deal with the "coming
of the Spirit" upon a person. At the same time outside
of the infancy sections, the New Testament writers never

approach Jesus through his miraculous conception.[1] Mark
expressly states[2] that the beginning of the gospel was the
work of John, and implies that a new consciousness came
to Jesus at the baptism.[3]

But was this new consciousness genuinely messianic ?
Might it not have been simply prophetic ? It is impossible
so to interpret the data. A messianic content is intended by
the synoptic writers, and is reaffirmed by the Fourth Gospel[4]
and the early church.[5] The recognition on their part of the
inseparable connection between the baptism of the believer
and his reception of the Holy Spirit is always taken as
proof of a messianic relation. If it be replied that such
experience of the Christian was wholly subjective, it can
be said that the subjective character of Jesus' experience
after baptism is now seldom doubted even by scholars not
subject to suspicion of extreme rationalism.[6] The opened

---

[1] The first dogmatic use made of the infancy sections in Matthew and Luke is
that of IGNATIUS, *Eph.*, 7:21; 18:2; 19:1; 20:2; *Smyr.*, 1; *Magn.*, 11. *Cf.* HOBEN,
The Virgin Birth in "Historical and Literature Studies," etc.; also *American Journal
of Theology*, Vol. VI (1902), pp. 481-83.

[2] Mark 1:1.

[3] The phrase "messianic self-consciousness " is at best an unhappy one, and is
without strictly scientific definition. In the interest of precision, it would be well
if it could be abandoned. At the same time, it has acquired a general usage and is
convenient for expressing that which otherwise would require considerable circum-
locution. In using the term, I do not wish to be understood as implying that Jesus
had two origins of consciousness, the one that of the ordinary Jew, and the other
that of the Christ. Any such duality is foreign to the entire New Testament conception. By "messianic self-consciousness " is meant simply that recognition of his own
personality as possessed of certain powers and characteristics to which he gave
a messianic value. On the messianic self-consciousness see BALDENSPERGER, *Das
Selbstbewusstsein Jesu* [3]; SCHMIDT, "Bildung und Gehalt des messianischen Be-
wusstseins Jesu," *Studien und Kritiken*, 1889, pp. 423-507; HOLSTEN, "Zur Ent-
stehung und Entwicklung des Messiasbewusstseins in Jesus," *Zeitschrift für
wissenschaftliche Theologie*, 1891, pp. 385-449; BOVON, *Théologie du Nouveau Testament* [2], Vol. I, pp. 262-90; HOLTZMANN, *Das Leben Jesu*, chaps. 6, 7; SCHMIDT, "Son of
Man," in *Encyclopædia Biblica;* WREDE, *Das Messiasgeheimniss Jesu;* SCHWARTZ-
KOPFF, *The Prophecies of Jesus Christ concerning His Death and Resurrection;*
BARTH, *Die Hauptprobleme des Lebens Jesu*, pp. 229-84.

[4] John 1:30-34.   [5] Acts 10:38.

[6] See, for instance, BRUCE, *Expositor's Greek Testament*, on Matt. 3:16, 17; Luke
3:22; SANDAY, art. "Jesus Christ," in HASTINGS's *Dictionary of the Bible;* J.
WEISS, *Life of Jesus Christ*, Vol. I, p. 324. See also KEIM, *Jesus of Nazara*, Vol. II
p. 286; BEYSCHLAG, *Leben Jesu*, Vol. II, p. 112.

heavens must certainly be figurative. The dove is a rabbinic analogy of the Holy Spirit.[1] The *Bath Qol*, "the daughter of the voice" (of Jehovah), is frequently met with in rabbinic literature to denote a divine revelation to some teacher in the form of an oracular sentence.[2]

Described thus in terms almost conventional among the rabbis to express the idea of divine revelation, the tendency seen in Luke to describe the baptism in more concrete terms cannot for a moment affect the general conclusions. It is a picture of the inner experience of Jesus. Jesus himself must have been the source of the story, at least in its fundamental elements. That is to say, he must either have used the figures which we find in the synoptic gospels, or have simply stated that at his baptism he became aware of his messianic office. His subsequent references to himself at Nazareth and in his reply to the question of John the Baptist are fully in accord with this view. The Spirit of the Lord was upon him.[3] The sin of misinterpreting his beneficent work of conquering Satan lay, not in the attack upon himself, but in that upon the Holy Spirit who was working through him.[4]

[1] *Chag.*, 15a; but see Edersheim, *Life and Times of Jesus the Messiah*, Vol. I, p. 287.

[2] See Weber, *Jüdische Theologie*[2], pp. 190–95, especially pp. 194, 195 The origin of this belief is held by Bousset, *Die Religion des Judenthums*, p. 319, n. 3, to have lain in *Jubilees*, 17:15; Eth. *Enoch*, 65:4; *Baruch*, 13:1; 22:1; *4 Esdras*, 6:13 f. That the term was in use in the time of Jesus is implied by its appearance in the Mishnah, *Yeb.*, xvi, 6; *Abhoth*, vi, 2. Dalman, *Words of Jesus*, pp. 204, 205, and art. "Bath Kol" in *PRE.*, Vol. II[3], p. 443, distinguishes between two species of such "voices" the one directly from God (as in the case of Jesus), and the other some chance expression of a man which seemed, to express oracular quality. See, further, Wünsche, *Neue Beiträge*, pp. 22, 23; Hamburger, *Realencyclopädie*, and *Jewish Cyclopædia*, art. "Bath Qol." In our synoptic sources the later accounts of Matthew, and especially of Luke, show a decided tendency to materialize the account of Mark.

[3] Luke 4:18; *cf.* Luke 7:22, 23; see also Mark 1:12; Matt. 4:1; Luke 4:1, 14.

[4] Mark 3:29, 30; Matt. 12:28–32; Luke 12:10. The statement of the text is not affected by a rejection of the non-Markan form of the saying of Jesus as a reworking of the Markan material. It is interesting to note, in this connection, such an expression as Luke 10:21.

It is possible, however, that it may still be insisted that Jesus' experience of the Spirit does not differ fundamentally from the experience of the prophet, and that it would consequently be incorrect to speak of it as necessarily implying a messianic consciousness. Such a hypothesis is not absolutely impossible, but, in the light of the data at our disposal, it must be pronounced highly improbable. As has already been pointed out, the early church evidently conceived of this experience as one of messianic rather than merely prophetic importance.[1] Further than this, as appears especially clear in the original account in Mark,[2] the spiritual experience of Jesus at the baptism was the basis of what is commonly known as the temptation. In this latter experience, as described by Matthew,[3] and Luke,[4] Jesus is not confronted with any doubt as to a possible deception in the baptismal experience, or as to the reality of his new self-consciousness, but rather with the possibility of misusing miraculous powers known to be his through that experience. It is exceedingly difficult to believe that such a struggle resulted from anything else than a consciousness of messianic importance. The critic who denies the historicity of the account may of course avoid such a conclusion, but the burden of proof lies upon him in making such a denial.

Throughout Jesus' life his attitude is always that of one superior to the prophet. The force of this statement can be broken only by a denial of the historicity of the passages to which appeal is made. Thus he clearly regards himself as greater than Jonah, Solomon,[5] his own dis-

[1] This statement would perhaps gain still further strength if DALMAN, *Words of Jesus*, pp. 276–80, be right in insisting that "the evangelists give an account of the voice, not on account of any importance which the reception of such a divine voice might possibly have for Jesus, but in the sense of impressive testimonies that Jesus really was what his disciples before the world proclaimed him to be."

[2] 1 : 9–13.   [3] 4 : 1–11.   [4] 4 : 1–13.

[5] Matt. 12 : 41, 42; Luke 11 : 31, 32.

ciples,[1] and Satan himself.[2]   If we add to this the further consideration of his frequent recurrence to his intimacy with God, the conclusion as to his sense of superiority to the prophetic office is much strengthened.[3]   But the strongest argument for the messianic self-estimate of Jesus is cumulative, and to be stated best by a careful consideration and combination of all the other facts at our disposal.   To this we now pass.

The beginning of the public career of Jesus is said by all the synoptists to have followed the temptation.   He came into Galilee announcing that the kingdom of heaven was close at hand, and calling upon his fellow countrymen to believe the good news.[4]   Further than this we know nothing of his teaching.   His own relation to his message must be determined by an appeal to the experiences of the baptism and temptation, as well as to his conception of the kingdom he announced.   In no case, however, are there good grounds for holding that he regarded himself as "founding" the kingdom in the ordinary sense of the word.   So far as his mere summons is concerned, it implies messianic character in his case no more than in the case of John.   Its real messianic significance can be established only by establishing the messianic character of Jesus himself.

Yet this argument from silence must not be pushed too far.   At the time he called the four fishermen, he must have

[1] Matt. 10 : 24, 25 ; Luke 6 : 40 ; Matt. 23: 10. These passages are very liable to critical objections, but that Jesus did consider himself the superior to his disciples will not be questioned. In the Fourth Gospel this superiority is developed at some length. See, for instance, John 13:12-16.

[2] Mark 3:23-27, and parallels; Matt. 12 : 28. As to the kingdom of Satan *cf.* *Assump. Moses*, 10: 1.

[3] The reference here is not to the Johannine addresses, although it would be rash to deny absolutely their historical worth, but to the sayings of Matt. 11:27, and Luke 10:22. Whatever critical position one may take as to the parallel saying of the last half of the verse, that of the first half is clearly more than the expression of a simple prophetic ecstasy akin to it though it may be; *cf.* Matt. 10:40. It is probable that when the structure of the Fourth Gospel is better understood, such sayings as those of John 6:46, and 13:20 will be seen to be echoes of these synoptic logia.

[4] Mark 1 : 14-20.

been already known in some exceptional capacity.   It is certainly not to be supposed that men would have abandoned their occupations if an utterly unknown and irresponsible person had promised to make them fishers of men.   The only satisfactory explanation of the action of the two sets of Galilean brothers lies in the assumption that they had known Jesus prior to their summons, and that they had accepted him in some way as related to the messianic future. It is, of course, true that the synoptic material in itself does not warrant the inference that they accepted Jesus as one who was superior to John the Baptist.   Without the Johannine material we should never have suspected that they had been associated with the Baptist,[1] and their acceptance of Jesus as master at the beginning of his Galilean ministry would in itself compel us to hold only that they considered him the successor of John the Baptist, who, according to the synoptic source, had just been arrested and imprisoned.[2]

Yet, after all such due allowance is made, there is nothing here contradictory of the Johannine story.   Nor is there anything intrinsically improbable in the statement of the Fourth Gospel that some disciples of John should have abandoned him and followed Jesus.   And if so, why should they have chosen Jesus, had it not been that John had in some way recognized him as more than an ordinary disciple ? If one be ready to admit that the Fourth Gospel correctly represents this change of discipleship as involving a faith in the messianic future of Jesus on the part of both John and

[1] *Cf.* the comparison between the Twelve and the disciples of John ; Luke 11 : 1 ; Mark 2 : 18.

[2] See also the highly subjective criticism of BRIGGS, *New Light on the Life of Jesus*, chaps. 1, 2. If it were possible to adopt the general thesis of this latest *tour de force* of harmonization, and bring in the Samaritan visit with its express messianic claims (John 4 : 4-43), after John 11 : 54 ; Mark 10 : 1, and Luke 13 : 22, many difficulties would certainly be avoided. But it is hard to see the justification for such a readjustment. The order in Luke when compared with that in Mark shows a rearrangement for the sake of explaining the basis for the obedience of the force to the call of Jesus.

some of his disciples, the explanation of the readiness with which the four subsequently left their employment is readily seen. They believed that Jesus was now about to take up the work that such a future involved, but which he had postponed when there was danger that the preparatory steps might interfere with the similar work of John.[1] That such a view involves difficulties cannot be denied, but it is hardly to be rejected as improbable simply because it treats the Johannine account with respect. The chief business of a historian is to utilize material that is not absolutely irreconcilable. And most unprejudiced students will admit that, in the light of the baptism and temptation of Jesus, the account of the Fourth Gospel gives a very satisfactory explanation for the sudden abandonment of their business interests by James and John, Peter and Andrew.

From any difficulty herein involved it would, however, be altogether unjustifiable to argue that Jesus did not consider himself as anything more than a second John. His sense of his superiority, with its awful responsibilities was already keen. He kept it a secret from the masses, perhaps from many of his disciples,[2] but—if such a hypothesis be not judged too speculative—not from those who were peculiarly sensitive to mental suggestion, the so-called demoniacs.[3] For some reason these unfortunate persons were accustomed to address Jesus in messianic terms. Is it too much to suppose that in some mysterious way they caught a suggestion from his own conviction as to himself?

[1] John 4 : 1–3.

[2] For an elaborate treatment of this position see WREDE, *Das Messiasgeheimniss Jesu.*

[3] Mark 1:24; *cf.* Mark 3:11; 5:7, and parallels. The tendency among interpreters to regard these instances of "casting out demons" as the cure of persons afflicted with peculiar forms of nervous diseases is the warrant for the conjecture in the text. The critical basis for their cures is as good as for any part of the gospel narrative. The hypothesis I suggest amounts to this: these persons responded to the thought and will of Jesus as the clairvoyant to his enquirer. There is no larger difficulty here than is recognized in hypnotism and allied phenomena.

However we may estimate the worth of this speculation, it is clear that it is only from the point of view of a conception of himself as Christ that one grasps the full significance of the words of Jesus concerning his conquest of Satan to which reference has already been made.[1] Perplexing as such sayings are to the modern man, they are at once intelligible from the point of view of messianism. Such a conquest argued the beginning of the victory of the kingdom of God. But the Christ and the Christ alone would be strong enough to overcome the kingdom of evil that overshadowed and embittered the pre-messianic age.

The interpreter stands, however, on surer grounds when dealing with the answer given by Jesus to the query of John the Baptist as to whether he was the Coming One. It has been held that this answer does not involve any messianic claim. Such a position is certainly not that of the evangelists or of anyone who is not determined to give every saying of Jesus a non-messianic force. Just as certainly it is not of Jesus. Unless the reply be an affirmation of his messiahship, the entire anecdote is meaningless. John asked him point blank whether he were the "Coming One" —the Christ. Jesus must have known that he either was or was not such a Personage. If he thought he was not the Christ, it would have been only elementary honesty to have said so. But he does not make any such declaration. On the contrary, he declared that he was fulfilling a text of scripture which John must have recognized as messianic.[2] And, what is more, if he had not intended John to understand his reply as an affirmation of his messiahship, he would scarcely have referred to the blessing awaiting the one who did not "stumble" over him. Once take Jesus' own point of view, that he was the Christ who was engaged in a work

[1] See especially Mark 3:23-26, and parallels: Luke 11:18; 13:16; cf. Acts 10:38.

[2] Isa. 35:5, 6, is repeatedly applied to messianic times by the rabbis. EDERSHEIM, *Life and Times of Jesus the Messiah*, Vol. II, p. 725.

of preparation while he awaited the Father's call to establish
the kingdom, and all difficulty vanishes. The fact that
Jesus did not explicitly say "Yes" to John's question was
simply due to caution. He had his idea of the true messianic work; the people had theirs. He could not and he
would not endanger his own ideal by even apparently yielding to theirs. He that had ears to hear could hear, and he
that had eyes to see could see.[1]

While there is not quite the same distinctness in the
words of Jesus at Nazareth,[2] their general import is obviously
the same. The reference to the fact that the Spirit of the
Lord was upon him might possibly imply only his prophetic
call to announce the acceptable year of the Lord. Yet the
reference is clearly to himself, and, taken in connection with
his reply to John and his experience at the baptism, it may
certainly be interpreted as expressing the same distinct
consciousness of his messiahship.

It is generally admitted that Jesus accepted the messianic title at Cæsarea Philippi.[3] For the purpose of the
present discussion there is no need to consider again the
question as to whether this was the first time that his disciples considered him as Christ. This matter is not so vital
as the fact that they did so accept him. What their confession involved it is easy to see. They believed that he
was the Christ, in the sense that his personality was so
august and mighty as to convince them that he must in the
near future take up the messianic work. In other words,
they ascribed to him future messianic power. That they
expected this future to be in general similar to that expected

---

[1] HOLTZMANN, *Leben Jesu*, pp. 169–71, makes the words of Jesus apply to the
kingdom and the messianic age rather than to himself. But what point has such an
answer? John knew the messianic age was close at hand. What he wished to
know was whether Jesus was the Christ. Even on Holtzmann's own ground it follows that the words of Jesus form an affirmative reply to the Baptist's question.
For if the messianic age was really shown to be present by his works, then certainly
he must have been understood to be the one who introduced it.

[2] Luke 4:16–30.   [3] Mark 8:27–30 and parallels.

by the Pharisees appears not only from the hope of the New
Testament church, which will be considered presently, but
from their own words and Peter's rebuke of Jesus.[1] It was in
this sense that Jesus must have accepted their confession of
faith in himself. For it can hardly be doubted that he did
accept the title. The oldest source, it is true, does not state
this explicitly, but, on the other hand, there is recorded no
refusal of the title on his part, and the story evidently
implies acceptance. If the additional material in Matthew[2]
be accepted, any question as to the attitude of Jesus is super-
fluous. He is there represented as giving Peter the keys of
the kingdom of heaven, and as making him the foundation
of his church. His subsequent conversation with Peter
concerning the suffering which awaited him at Jerusalem is
most naturally understood as implying that Jesus was by
both himself and Peter assumed to be Christ. Here again
the account in Matthew[3] adds an explanatory saying which
makes the reference more distinct, but the Markan source[4]
can be understood in only one way. What this interpretation is will at once appear from the fact that in the latter
part of the words spoken at this time[5] the reference is both
to the speedy coming of the kingdom and to his own return
"in the glory of his father with the holy angels."

From the time of the confession of Peter at Cæsarea Philippi until his death, Jesus is represented as more openly
disclosing his messianic position, though often with emphasis upon matters like suffering and death which the Twelve
could not recognize as compatible with messianic felicity
and glory. At the same time, he more completely appropri-
ates an eschatological significance. He treats with increasing emphasis the future kingdom and its world-judgment.
It is true that in some cases his teaching concerning the

[1] Mark 8:31:33; 9:11; 10:35-37; 11:1-10 (parallels in each case); cf. also Acts 1:6.
[2] 16:17-19.   [3] 16:20 f.   [4] Mark 8:31-33.   [5] Mark 8:34-39.

kingdom does not expressly involve his own messianic position, and might have been spoken by one who held himself
a prophet rather than the Messiah; but, on the other hand,
there are events and sayings which must be eliminated
before the general content and connotation of his words can
acquire a non-messianic character. It is not merely that
Jesus permits himself to be called "son of David."[1] He
promised those of his disciples who have made great earthly
sacrifices the reward of eternal life in the world to come.[2]
In the case of the request of James and John,[3] he does not
deny their assumption that he is to sit as king in glory, but
replies to them from their own point of view, denying only
that he himself has the right to distribute those honors
which should be given by God himself. Such a denial as
this can by no means be interpreted to imply that Jesus
conceived of himself as something less than the Messiah.
Had this been the case, it would have been simple honesty
for him to have disabused his disciples' minds, and to have
declared that not he, but another, was to come in royal
glory. As it stands, his reference is to the fact commonly
recognized by all Messianists, that the Messiah himself was
subordinate to God.

The triumphal entry[4] is not interpreted in the oldest
source as in any way intended by Jesus to be a dramatic
presentation of messianic claim, although this interpretation
is given it by both the first and the fourth evangelists.[5]
None the less, he allowed the crowds to attribute to him
messianic importance, if not the messianic title.[6] A comparison of the four gospels shows that the cry of the people
is essentially the same in all accounts except that of Mark.

---

[1] Mark 10:46–48 and parallels.　　[2] Mark 10:28–30.　　[3] Mark 10:35–45.

[4] Mark 11:1–11 and parallels.　　[5] Matt. 21:4, 5; John 12:14–16.

[6] The oldest source simply speaks of the kingdom of David. According to Matt.
21:9, the people saluted him as the Son of David. Similarly Luke 19:38 and John
12:13 speak of him expressly as the King.

In that, although Jesus is said to be coming in the name of the Lord, he is not spoken of expressly as King. The difference does not seem to be important. He who came in the name of the Lord, introducing the kingdom of David, could hardly be other than the Christ.[1]

The cleansing of the temple can hardly be counted as other than an expression of the same sense of messianic importance. This would be true whether it be held that there were two cleansings or one, although, if there were but one cleansing, and if that occurred at the end of the ministry, such an interpretation would appear the more certain.[2] The ready yielding of the Sadducean officials of the temple to commands of Jesus is easily explicable in

[1] The additional verses of Luke 19:39, 40, in which he refuses to rebuke his disciples for saluting him thus messianically, add nothing of importance beyond what is fairly implied by the other accounts.

[2] The questions at issue in harmonizing the two stories of the cleansing are certainly perplexing. The similarity between the accounts of John 2:13–22, and Mark 11:15–19 and parallels is too striking to argue that the two are independent accounts of separate events. The only serious objection to our immediately identifying them lies in the position accorded the event in the two sets of sources. (Yet see HUTTON, *Theological Essays*.) From the point of view of a reasonable criticism, however, this difficulty vanishes, and it is permissible to follow obvious probabilities and identify the two accounts. The question, however, as to whether the cleansing belongs at the beginning or at the end of the public ministry of Jesus is one on which there will always be difference of opinion until we have reached a more definite conclusion concerning the composition of the Fourth Gospel. Briefly stated, the situation amounts to this: Everything in the nature of the event favors the position accorded it by the synoptists. So far as the general character of the sources is concerned, it must be argued also that it is easier to transfer the section John 2:13 f. than it is that of Mark 11:15–19. Tatian follows the synoptists' order. On the other hand, the chronological expression τεσσεράκοντα καὶ ἓξ ἔτεσιν οἰκοδομήθη in John 2:20 can most easily be interpreted in the sense that the forty and six years had already elapsed and the building was still in the process of erection. *Cf. 4 Esdras*, 5:16. Yet the fact that the aorist was used with the dative may possibly indicate that the temple was not still in process of erection, but that it had taken forty-six years to build it. In that case the expression has no chronological bearing whatever. When one balances all these data, it seems on the whole more reasonable to argue that the datum of the forty and six years was due to a careful calculation on the part of the editor of the Fourth Gospel, made in the interest of his peculiar chronology. Certainly such a view is no more extreme than that compelled by the discrepancy which exists between his statements concerning the date of the Last Supper and those of the synoptists. If no other way of adjusting the chronology is discovered, and one is shut down to a choice between such a view as to the forty and six years, and the results which follow from transferring the cleansing, recorded in the Markan source, to the early Judean ministry, the former is certainly preferable.

view of the reception accorded him at his entry to Jerusalem, and the act, though by no means unlike those of a prophet, is entirely in keeping with the general antagonism of Jesus toward the Pharisees, consequent upon his messianic consciousness.

Most clearly do the gospel records show that during his last days Jesus spoke of himself in messianic terms.[1] Among the sayings of these days attention must first be called to the eschatological address of Mark, chap. 13.[2] Before, however, we can safely use material contained in it, a conclusion must be reached as to whether or not it truly represents the teaching of Jesus. Recent critics[3] have regarded the section as composite, vss. 7, 8, 14–20, 24–27, 30, 31 being held to be no part of the original discourse of Jesus.[4] Whatever position one may take as regards this proposed critical division, it is clear that in vss. 5 and 6 there is a reference of Jesus to his messianic position. Many were to come in his name, saying: "I am He," that is, the Christ. If vss. 24–27 be not an apostolic addition, such a reference becomes

[1] At a first glance it might appear that reference cannot be made fairly to Matt. 23:34, because Luke 11:49 substitutes "the wisdom of God" for "I;" but the real content of both passages is applicable only to the time of speaking, and although it is possible that the saying is in its more original form in Luke, the passage in Matt. 23:37-39 certainly contains a logion which refers to Jesus himself (*cf.* Luke 13:34, 35). It will be impossible therefore, without destroying the text, to deny that the passage in some way gives expression to Jesus' conception of his own mission.

[2] In general, see HAUPT, *Die eschatologischen Aussagen Jesu.*

[3] Notably, WENDT, *Lehre Jesu*, Vol. I, pp. 10 f.; H. J. HOLTZMANN, *Einleitung, N. T. Theol.;* O. HOLTZMANN, *Leben Jesu*, pp. 359 f.; CHARLES, *Eschatology*, pp. 323-29; BOUSSET, *Lehre Jesu.*

[4] The grounds for such an opinion are, first, a comparison of Mark 13:10 with Matt. 10:23; second, vss. 14-20, in the light of the call ὁ ἀναγιγνώσκων νοείτω, could hardly have come from Jesus; third, there seems to be contradiction between vss. 13 and 18-20; fourth, the two sections of the discourse deal with different subjects, vss. 7, 8, 14-20, 24-27, 30, 31, dealing with terrible sufferings which are the result of wars, famines, the destruction of Jerusalem, rising at last into apocalyptic prediction, while the other half, vss. 5, 6, 21-23, 9-13, 28, 29, 32-37, deal with the persecutions to which the disciples are to be subjected and with the reward which is certainly to be theirs. It is held that the first-named verses constitute a section of the discourse which is a Jewish Christian apocalypse, written in 67-68 A. D., which has been added to genuine sayings of Jesus.

genuinely apocalyptic.[1]   Certainly the specific reference to the destruction of Jerusalem, in the light of our discussion,[2] seems more foreign to the method of Jesus than the apocalyptic presentation of the future.

The vision of judgment in Matt. 25:31–46 is possibly a homily of the early church, for it seems out of keeping with the general method of Jesus.   In view of what we know as to the literary habits of the early Christians,[3] it would have been by no means strange if there should have developed an apocalyptic teaching which attempted to do for the ethical life what this section so forcibly does.   Further, the general tone of the address is impersonal.   In no case is Jesus represented as uttering the various sentences, but they are put into the mouth of "the King."[4]   The general teaching is in harmony with that of Jesus, but it will probably be safer not to use the section as coming from him.

No such doubt can, however, fairly rest upon the words of Jesus uttered at the Last Supper.[5]   Although their precise meaning is very difficult to grasp, the only explanation which is possible lies in the fact that, anticipating death, Jesus yet expected that he would share in a resurrection and so enter the kingdom of God.[6]   Such a belief in his own resurrection had already appeared in his own words to his disciples[7] just subsequent to the confession of Peter at Cæsarea Philippi.[8]

[1] It is this fact that leads Charles, *Eschatology*, p. 328, to reject them as non-authentic. The reason for this decision is that he finds so many parallels to the sayings in the apocalyptic half of the chapter in Jewish literature. Such an argument does not appear conclusive. It is a fair question whether the test proposed by Wendt and adopted by Charles and others be not too subjective. *A priori* is it any more probable that Jesus would have predicted the sufferings of his disciples than that he would have dealt in a general apocalyptic fashion with the end of the age?

[2] *Cf.* especially the influence of Dan. 7:13.   [3] *Cf. The Shepherd of Hermas.*
[4] Matt. 25:34, 40, 41, 45.   [5] Luke 22:15, 16.

[6] The possibility that Jesus expected that before he ate another passover the kingdom would be established on the earth is not to be denied, but hardly to be treated very seriously.

[7] Mark 8:31; 9:31; 10:34.

[8] The reference in Matt. 12:40 to the similarity between the circumstances of the mission of Jonah and that of the Son of man must be disregarded as an interpola-

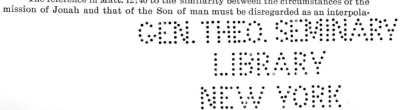

By all means the most important of the messianic affirmations of Jesus are those which are to be found in the account of his trial. Both before the Jewish authorities and the Roman Jesus was charged with being the Christ. At the first trial, it is true, the Jewish authorities seemed to have endeavored at the start to condemn him on other grounds, but, these attempts failing, the high-priest adjured, him in the name of the living God[1] to tell them whether or not he was the Christ. The reply of Jesus in Mark is unmistakable. "I am," he said—and immediately made reference to an eschatological coming of the Son of man. Because of these words he was condemned. It was the same charge of being the Messiah, although cast in words fit to appeal to the Roman authorities, that was made against Jesus in his trial before Pilate. The Jews, however, at that time gave the term "Christ" the Zealot significance. Again he admitted the charge and as the king of the Jews Jesus was finally crucified.[2]

III

It is at this point we can best consider the terms which Jesus uses as self-designations.

1. First and most important of these is the term "Son of man," ὁ υἱὸς τοῦ ἀνθρώπου.

Within recent years there has been much discussion as to whether or not this term is the outcome of a mistranslation due to the misinterpretation of the Aramaic phrase (א)בר אנש. It is urged by Wellhausen,[3] Lietzmann,[4] Schmidt,[5] that the

tion. The original account made the repentance of the Ninevites the real sign of Jonah. The reference is lacking in Mark and Luke 11:32. In the entire matter of the reference of Jesus to his resurrection see SCHWARTZKOPFF, *Prophecies of Jesus Christ.*

[1] Mark 14:53-64; Matt. 26:57-66. [2] Mark 15:1-15.

Skizzen und Vorarbeiten, Vol. VI, pp. 187-215. [4] *Der Menschensohn.*

[5] *Encyclopœdia Biblica,* art. "Son of Man;" *The Son of Man and The Son of God.* See for summary of recent discussion DRUMMOND, "Son of Man." *Journal of Biblical Studies,* 1902.

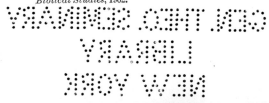

Aramaic term בַּר אֲנָשָׁא means simply "man," and that its translation ὁ υἱὸς τοῦ ἀνθρώπου is due to the failure of the Christian writers to grasp its real force.   On the other hand, Dalman[1] criticises very vigorously this position and insists that the Greek translation is by no means untrue to the Aramaic original.   But it is hard to see that the matter is one to be settled on purely philological grounds.   Even though Dalman's position be mistaken and Wellhausen's be correct, there is no reason why "the Man" or "Man" should not have been given a peculiar force and reference by Jesus. In no case is the idea of *sonship* of man vital to the term as he used it.   Whatever force one finds in it must be one of connotation, not of strict translation.[2]   Most scholars would admit that certain sayings in which the term appears were uttered by Jesus, and it is from this fact that we must proceed.   The point at issue in these instances becomes one of exegesis, not of criticism.   To argue that all the expressions in which the phrase is used have reference to humanity in general is to do violence to any true exegetical method.[3] But this is not all.   The phrase is represented as being used by Jesus to refer to himself as Judge.[4]   To argue that these passages are Christian comments added to the words of Jesus is certainly to base conclusions on no clear evidence. Let it be repeated: we are dealing, not with a question of translation or mistranslation, but with a question as to what the term, whether properly "Man" or "Son of man," connoted.   We may grant that in such a passage as Matt. 8:20 and Luke 9:58 it may have simply the force of "a man," but it is certainly unnecessary to argue that Jesus could not

[1] *Words of Jesus*, pp. 234–67.   See also SCHMIEDEL, *Protestantische Monatshefte*, 1848, pp. 252–67, 291–308; 1901, pp. 333–51; BOUSSET, *Religion des Judenthums*, pp. 248–55.

[2] A view very similar to this is that of BOUSSET, *Religion des Judenthums*, p. 252.

[3] *Cf.* Matt. 11:18, 19; Luke 7:33, 34, where any contrast between John the Baptist and humanity at large is altogether meaningless. So, too, Mark 10:44, 45; Luke 19:10.

[4] Mark 8:38; 14:62.

at other times have used the term with special reference to himself as the type of the kingdom.[1]

There are three considerations here of primary importance: the use of the term in the Enoch literature;[2] the wide influence of the book of Daniel; and the practical absence of any use of the term by the early church as descriptive of Jesus.

a) As regards the use of the term in the Enoch literature, there has been no small attempt to show that the sections in which the term occurs are either Christian interpolations or due to the influence of Christian thought. Recent criticism,[3] however, has shown conclusively the impossibility of attributing these sections to Christian influences. There is in them absolutely nothing that can reasonably argue Christian origin; but, on the contrary, they are thoroughly pharisaic in spirit.

b) The probability that the term did have some messianic connotation gains strength from the fact that the apocalyptic sections of Daniel were in general use in the time of Jesus. We have here at our disposal not only the existence of the apocalyptic literature, so full of echoes of the Daniel apocalypse, but also clear evidence of the appeal to and interpretation of the book by Josephus as one commonly read and accepted.[4] In fact, every argument for the existence of Daniel in the time of Jesus is an argument for the currency

---

[1] FIEBIG, *Der Menschensohn*, holds that the Aramaic בַּר אֱנָשָׁא and בַּר אֱנָשׁ may be translated "man" in a collective sense (*der Mensch*), "a man," or "anyone," according to its context. The only difference he sees between ὁ ἄνθρωπος and ὁ υἱὸς τοῦ ἀνθρώπου as used by the gospels is that the latter refers to Dan. 7:13, which he takes in a personal sense. According to this view, Jesus used the word with a messianic connotation (*Der Menschensohn*, p. 120). The definite Greek form with the article as distinct from υἱὸς ἀνθρώπου of the LXX rendering of Dan. 7:13 is a new translation of the Aramaic of that passage.

[2] Eth. *Enoch*, 46:2–4; 48:2; 62:5–9; 63:11; 69:26, 29; 70:1.

[3] BOUSSET, *Religion des Judenthums*, pp. 13, 248; SCHÜRER, *Geschichte*, etc.[3], Vol. III, pp. 200–202; KAUTZSCH, *Apoc. und Pseud.*, Vol. II, p. 252.

[4] See for details GERLACH, *Die Weissagungen d. A. T. in den Schriften d. Fl. Josephus.*

of the book among the people. It may therefore be assumed that the term בַּר אֱנָשׁ, used in Dan. 7:13 to symbolize the coming kingdom of the saints, was in current use and given a more or less distinct messianic content. This is not of necessity to argue that the Jews commonly conceived of the term as referring to a personal Messiah. In this sense its use by the Enoch literature is unique in pre-Christian writings, being approached, indeed, only once in post-Christian Jewish literature.[1] It does, however, argue that Jesus could use it in the symbolical force of Daniel and be understood by his hearers to portray the character of the kingdom.[2]

c) In the literature of the early church other than the gospels it is to be noticed that the term is never used of Jesus except in Acts 7: 56.[3] Various conjectures have been made to account for this fact, but its most plausible explanation seems to be that after his death the followers of Jesus used the term "Christ" as a precise description of their belief in him. There was, indeed, no good reason for early Christians to use a more obscure term. Most of the New Testament literature, it is true, was written before the gospels, and this fact might conceivably argue that the term was the invention of the second generation of Christians. But it is impossible to discover a motive for such invention, or in any way to account for its appearance, unless the evangelists may have mistranslated the Aramaic words of Jesus—a hypothesis already considered. That when the

---

[1] *4 Esdras*, 13:3, 5, 12, 25, 51.

[2] FIEBIG, *Der Menschensohn*, pp. 75 f., discusses fully Dan. 7:13 as point of departure from the force of the term as used by Jesus. He finds the similarities in the two usages to be largely in their eschatology. The differences he discovers to be numerous. Fiebig's opinion that the term in Dan. 7:13 is personal and refers to the Messiah can hardly be accepted. That kingdom was to be like the "Son of Man" or "The Man." To set himself forward as that "Son of Man" or "Man" would be by no means to be understood as indicating that Jesus considered himself the Christ. It would, however, undoubtedly lead to his being understood as presenting himself as the type of such a kingdom, whether it were to be founded by himself or another.

[3] In Rev. 1:13; 14:14, the phrase ὅμοιον υἱὸν ἀνθρώπου is used, but evidently in a general sense of "a man."

term was used by the evangelists it was regarded as a self-appellation of Jesus seems clear from a comparison of Mark 8:27 with the parallel question of Matt. 16:13.

In view of these facts, therefore, the most satisfactory conclusion seems to be this: Totally apart from its etymological force, Jesus used the Aramaic term translated ὁ υἱὸς τοῦ ἀνθρώπου (a) as a self-appellation; (b) derived from the messianic passage of Dan. 7:13; (c) with a meaning which while not necessarily seen by all his hearers to be a claim to personal messianic character, would be seen by all those familiar with Dan. 7:13 to imply that he regarded his life as in some way typifying that life which should characterize those who were preparing for the coming kingdom. In other words, in the mind of Jesus himself it would express his messianic character in its moral and exemplary aspects.

2. The term "Christ" is never found in the gospels as a self-appellation of Jesus. In the synoptic account the word is not used except by the evangelists as a descriptive term,[1] and in the Johannine account Jesus does not call himself the Christ except by implication to the woman at Samaria.[2] Even after the confession of Peter at Cæsarea Philippi, he never used the word with explicit reference to himself. It is lacking even in Mark 14:61, when Jesus answers the high-priest's question in the affirmative.[3]

3. So also in the case of the term "Son of God." Jesus himself does not use the expression, although others use it with reference to him.[4] It is, of course, true that Jesus frequently speaks of God as "Father" and of himself as

---

[1] Matt. 1:1, 18; 11:2; Mark 1:1, 34; Luke 4:41.   [2] John 4:25, 26.

[3] DALMAN, *Words of Jesus*, pp. 289 f., gives full treatment of the meaning of the term "Christ."

[4] Mark 3:11; 5:7; 15:39; John 1:49. A possible exception should be made to this general statement in the text of John 10:36; 11:4; but in the light of the general character of the Fourth Gospel, it would be hardly safe to say that the evangelist had not substituted a term expressive of his own estimate of Jesus for the word which Jesus himself used.

"the Son," but this is quite another matter from speaking of himself as ὁ υἱὸς τοῦ θεοῦ.[1] This title is, indeed, applied by Peter to Jesus, according to Matt. 16:16, but this is clearly an addition of the evangelist. It is not found in the original account in Mark 8:29. That Jesus spoke of God as his Father in some unique sense cannot be denied, but such sayings as imply this do not employ either ὁ υἱὸς τοῦ θεοῦ or υἱὸς θεοῦ, and can be considered more properly where the content of the messianic consciousness of Jesus is under consideration.

After thus examining the sayings of Jesus concerning his relation to the kingdom, it is impossible to reach any other conclusion than that he was convinced that he was the Christ and that he was to inaugurate the kingdom he foretold, and the influence of which he was already bringing to bear upon men. Yet such a conclusion as yet is largely formal. The content of this estimate of himself, both personally and as conditioned by his relation to the kingdom, must now be considered.

---

[1] For elaborate discussion see DALMAN, *Words of Jesus*, pp. 268–89. His conclusion is that the term is sometimes a synonym of Messiah, and at other times (*e. g.*, Matt. 16:16; Luke 1:35; 3:38) is used in a Hellenistic sense involving paternity.

CHAPTER V

THE CONTENT OF THE MESSIANIC SELF-CONSCIOUSNESS

If it be true that Jesus conceived of himself as the Christ, the next question to be answered concerns the content which he gave the term. It has always been the opinion of students of his life, and of the church generally, that he gave to the term a somewhat different force from that given by his contemporaries. How justifiable is such an opinion will at once appear.

I

1. The first modification is fundamental: he broke utterly with pharisaism as a system. Eschatological messianism was peculiarly the property of the Pharisee and the Essene. New Testament scholars have long since abandoned any hope of showing that Jesus was an Essene or intimately connected with the fraternity. His relations to pharisaism cannot be determined so promptly. On the one side, he certainly had much in common with their fundamental religious opinions. Even in the process of his denunciation of their mistakes he distinctly says that the scribes and lawyers sit in Moses's seat, and bids his disciples follow their instructions,[1] though avoiding their practice. In such a saying he bears deserved testimony to the position which ideally the representatives of the law of Jehovah occupied.

Further, it would seem probable that in the early part of his ministry the Pharisees saw in Jesus one who was at vital points apparently in sympathy with them. It was not until he began the more positive instruction of his disciples, and showed indifference to the oral law, that their suspicions

[1] Matt. 23:2.

were aroused.   Little by little these suspicions grew into distrust and enmity.   In each step, however, the develop-ment of hostility was the outcome of some positive act or word of Jesus himself.   It is a serious mistake to think of Jesus as being a passive martyr; on the contrary, it was he who was the aggressor, and it is in his positive rejection of certain elements of pharisaism that we have an expression of those general principles which led him to modify the messianic conception he had inherited.

Apart from their expectation of the coming kingdom of Israel, four things were the special mark of the Pharisee movement: the elaboration of sabbath observance, scrupu-lousness as to the requirement to pay tithes, an equally scrupulous regard for the laws of ceremonial purity, and a close adherence to the rapidly developing oral law.   All four could be classified under the fundamental conception of the society-holiness through separation.

Every student of the life and teaching of Jesus will at once recognize that these four traits, with their consequent idea of the separation of the good man from the evil, are the very points at which Jesus made his attack.   Not only was he a friend of the despised masses,[1] but he distinctly repu-diated the pharisaic teaching concerning the sabbath;[2] de-clared that nothing a man ate could defile him, even though he was not ceremonially clean;[3] declared the Pharisee was making the word of God of no avail through his tradition;[4] and censured the tendency to substitute the principles of tithing for fundamental morality and religion.[5]   Indeed, he went farther, and excused his disciples for not following the disciples of John the Baptist in adopting the incipient asceticism of the Pharisees shown in their new regard for

[1] Mark 2:15, 16; Matt. 11:19; Luke 15:1.
[2] Mark 2:23-27; 3:2 f.; Matt. 12:10, 11; John 5:1 f.; 7:22 f.; 9:1 f.
[3] Mark 7:1 f.   [4] Mark 7:8-13; cf. Matt. 23:5 f.   [5] Matt. 23:23-25.

fasting.[1] In the light of this attitude toward pharisaism as a system, it is not surprising to find him constantly censuring the Pharisees as a class for insincerity and casuistry in the maintenance of their religious reputation.[2] But so to break with pharisaism was to abandon many of the very principles that controlled pharisaic messianism, and to substitute for formal requirements the recognition of actual ethical conditions.

2. More distinctly revolutionary was the new teaching of Jesus concerning God. It is absolutely essential for the entire messianic scheme of pharisaism that God be thought of in precisely the same way as the Pharisee thought of him, namely, as a Judge and King. In Judaism such a conception is not a matter of analogy; it is description. As it has already appeared from our survey of Jewish literature, the kingdom of God was really to be a kingdom of Jews, and God was to reign over them just as truly as Herod reigned over Judea. The Judge no more than the judgment was a figure of speech. God was actually to undertake judicial functions.

Jesus does not attempt a precise definition of the Deity. His language is always one of analogy descriptive of the moral character of God and his attitude toward mankind. But even by way of analogy he seldom speaks of God as a King or Judge. To him God was to be thought of as a Father. Such an analogy, of course, did not exclude the other and sterner conception, but it goes far toward modifying any religious or theological teaching derived from the forensic concept. The great effort of Jesus was to induce men and women to see fatherliness in the divine ruler; not severity, or even bald justice. How far this modified his conception of messiahship is immediately evident. The Christ who was to reveal God's will and prepare men for the

[1] Mark 2:18-22. [2] For instance, Matt. 22:14-33.

coming kingdom could not insist upon judgment so much as upon the love that welcomed the penitent; not so much upon the destruction of one's enemies as upon that self-sacrifice revealed by the heavenly Father in his treatment of bad men.[1]

3. More specific was Jesus' rejection of the current conception of the Christ as the Son of David.[2] The point at issue in his well-known question as to the messianic teaching of the scribes was not merely of descent. The term "Son of David" had become expressive of the entire messianic idea as held by all Jews, whether scribes or common people. It indicated that the new kingdom was to be essentially Jewish, just as its king was to be the representative of the most typical royal family of Hebrew history. More than that, it declared the new kingdom to be essentially military, for to the Jew David was essentially a man of war, a conqueror of the enemies of Israel.[3] To describe the messianic king as his son was to ascribe to him the same military prowess.[4] All this Jesus rejected. The Messiah was to be greater than David; his glory was to be his own and not derived from descent.

4. Similarly, at least in the latter part of his ministry, he clearly repudiated the idea that the Jews had any monopoly upon the coming kingdom. Those who were brought to the wedding feast from the highways and hedges were the outcast of Jews and gentiles.[5] Many were to come from the east and the west, the north and the south, and sit down with Abraham, while the children of the kingdom, the Jews, were to be cast out.[6] And the risen Lord commanded his apostles to disciple all nations.[7] It is to be noticed also that in thus extending the kingdom to the gentiles Jesus does not make proselytism a condition of entering it. In his

[1] Matt. 5:44–48. [2] Mark 12:35. [3] 1 Sam. 16:18; 2 Sam. 17:8; 1 Chron. 28:3.
[4] Cf. Ps. 72:8. [5] Matt. 22:1–14. [6] Matt. 8:11, 12. [7] Matt. 28:19.

entire teaching there is not the slightest reference to the claim, subsequently urged by his followers in Jerusalem[1] that it was necessary for a man to keep the law of Moses in order to be saved. The condition of entrance was clearly ethical. The pure in heart were to see God; the peacemakers were to be called the children of God; the meek were to inherit the earth.[2] This teaching of Jesus concerning the subjects of the kingdom supplements his teaching as to the supreme dignity of the Christ. A Jewish king could expect only Jewish subjects or proselytes. The kingdom of one greater than David would be hampered by no such limitation. Such a universalizing of the messianic concept does not modify the idea of the kingdom as an eschatological institution, but introduces a fundamental change in the conditions of membership in it. It goes far also to show that in the teaching of Jesus the most fundamental thing was not the kingdom itself, but that quality of life which assured a participation in its blessings.

5. More revolutionary, if possible, than this universalizing of the messianic ideas is Jesus' belief in the necessity of the Christ's suffering. In all Jewish literature such a belief had been wanting. Later, it is true, doubtless under the force of Christian argument, the rabbis developed a theory of a Messiah who was to suffer, but it was never a universal belief.[3] The source of so original and radical a modification of the messianic concept as this of Jesus is really twofold. On the one side was his own experience, which led him to see how inevitable and fatal would be the hostility of the religious authorities of his people; and on the other were those scriptural statements, like Isa., chap. 53, overlooked or repudiated[4] by the Jews, which foretold the suffering of the

1 Acts 15:1.   2 Matt. 5:3-12.

3 DALMAN, *Der leidende und der sterbende Messias;* WÜNSCHE, *Die Leiden des Messias.*

4 *Cf. Targum of Jonathan, in loco.*

Servant of Jehovah. The full meaning of this element of his messianic concept can be appreciated only as one grasps Jesus' conviction that suffering and death were not merely accidental to his career, but were an essential part of his messianic work. It was the Father's will that he drink the cup; it was the Father's will that he suffer and die. He saw clearly that his was not a mere individual's fate. He died and knew he must die, not as Jesus the carpenter or teacher, but as Jesus the Christ. His blood was to be shed for many.[1]

It was doubtless in part because of this growing conviction of the necessity of his death as a part of his revelation that God was fatherly, and that all things in life could be accepted as an expression of divine love, that Jesus maintained the silence already noticed concerning his messiahship. As modified by him, the term "Messiah" could not have been apprehended by the people; to use it without the change of content would be to confirm his followers and the people in those very opinions as to the kingdom and its Christ which he was seeking to change. How impossible it would have been to induce the people at large to believe that the Christ was to suffer is to be seen in the impossibility of inducing even the Twelve to accept his forecast of his death. They could not understand what he meant by his sad words, and believed that he must certainly be mistaken. Their preconception as to the career of the Christ completely excluded all expectation of anything but glorious victory. And they feared to question him concerning the new teaching.[2]

6. It is not difficult from this point of view to appreciate the reference by Jesus to his resurrection. It is true that certain of the sayings attributed to him may not be authentic,[3] but there is no good *a priori* ground for refusing to

[1] 1 Cor. 11:25 f.; Mark 14:24. The words in Matt. 26:28, εἰς ἄφεσιν ἁμαρτίων, while probably expressing a legitimate implication of the thought of Jesus, clearly are an explanatory addition of the evangelist. Yet see DENNEY, *The Death of Christ*, pp. 56 f.

[2] Mark 8:31—9:1; 9:30-32.   [3] Matt. 12:40.

believe that a Christ who believed that he must suffer and die would also believe that, simply because he was the Christ he would have power enough to accomplish his results after death. It is to be borne in mind that the resurrection of the righteous dead was an essential part of the pharisaic belief as to the kingdom. If, then, the Christ were to die before he had completed his messianic work, the inference would be inevitable that he himself must partake of this same resurrection. Here, too, the disciples seemed to have been utterly at a loss to understand what he meant, and the conception of a Christ who attained supreme power by resurrection was as original with Jesus as that of a Christ who shared humanity's common lot of suffering and death.[1]

II

To a considerable extent, any decision as to the general messianic position of Jesus, and especially concerning his idea of the kingdom, carry with them a determination as to the term "Christ." If Jesus thought of the kingdom of God as fundamentally eschatological, then he must have thought of himself as the eschatological Christ. Such a conclusion will be reached also by a process of elimination. Evidently he did not think of himself as the political revolutionist, and in the same proportion as the kingdom was to be the gift of God rather than a result of the growth of the disciples in number and influence, his messianic work would be future. Such considerations mark the point of departure for any study of the content of his messianic consciousness. The problem of his messiahship, like the problem of his kingdom, is one that concerns the adjustment of the eschatological expectation with an actual historical career.

Jesus' teaching concerning the kingdom gives us also data for determining his conception of messiahship. For-

[1] See Schwartzkopff, *Prophecies of Jesus Christ concerning His Death and Resurrection.*

mally speaking, the kingdom was eschatological, but, while
its coming was delayed, the struggle with the kingdom of
Satan had already begun, and its future members, while
preparing to enter it, were in a prophetic sense the kingdom
itself. Co-ordinate with these two periods in the history of
the kingdom would be naturally two periods of messiahship.
In the first the Messiah would be engaged in prophetic work;
in the second, which would open with the coming of the
kingdom, he would be the messianic "Judge" and "King."
That Jesus himself believed that he was not only the Messiah,
but was actually doing messianic work during the ministry,
has already appeared. Herein he differed from his disciples.
They could believe that he was the Christ, but could not see
that his work of teaching and of self-sacrificing service was
a part of the messianic career. Still less during their association with him could they believe that death formed any part
of messianic work.

What was the adjustment which Jesus made in his own
mind concerning his work of preparing men for the coming
kingdom, and his work as the King and Judge of the kingdom when it came? Any difficulty involved in an answer
to this question lies rather in the preconceptions of the
interpreter rather than with Jesus himself. If we may
judge from the simplest interpretation of his words, in his
own mind the problem was one simply of two stages in his
messianic activity—the one prophetic and the other judicial
and royal. Between the two lay death. That the harmonization of the two careers gave rise to no moral struggles
on the part of Jesus we cannot assert. The whole significance of the temptation argues the contrary. Convinced as
he was that he must undertake the new duties and exercise
the new powers which were his because of the experience at
the baptism, he was brought face to face with the fate of
the prophets. If they suffered as the servants of God, cer-

tainly he must. Nor is it too much to believe that he had
already formulated that conception of the meaning of suffering which it was to be his great mission to exemplify. If
God were the Father of righteous men, then certainly the
sufferings which they underwent must be a part of the divine
plan; and if he, the Christ, were to bring to the world the
revelation of God's fatherliness, then he must himself be
ready to do this through sharing the fate of the noble army
of martyrs. From the very beginning of his ministry it
appears that he foresaw with more or less distinctness the
tragedy through which he was to pass,[1] and it is his own
experience that he seeks to make that of his disciples when
he insists that they must take up their cross and follow him.
Yet such a period of humiliation and agony was but temporary. He was to return again. Death was to be but the
supreme sacrifice which he was to make in preparing men
for the coming kingdom. He was to return as King and
Judge. Of this assurance the evangelists do not permit us
for a moment to doubt. It was this that nerved him for
the final agony, as he foresaw it at the Last Supper. It
was this future that he distinctly laid before the high-priest
at his trial, and it was because of this, as much as anything
else, that he was condemned to death as a blasphemer.[2] In
the mind of the early church there was no necessary chasm
between the present and the coming glorious life, nor was
there in the mind of Jesus. That personality which suffered
in order to show men how to prepare for the coming kingdom
was the same personality that was to return to introduce
that kingdom.[3] The resurrection would be the connecting
link between the two messianic periods.

[1] *Cf.* Mark 2:19 f.   [2] Mark 14:60 f.

[3] There is no alternative for this view, except that which sees in Jesus' death a
complete demolition of all his plans and in the words ascribed to him relative to
the new kingdom, the beliefs of the early church. The question here is, however,
precisely that which we have already discussed, and if Jesus believed that the
kingdom was future, and at the same time believed that he was the Christ, the
position taken in the text seems beyond question.

As to the precise time when he should take up the full messianic work, Jesus is said[1] expressly to have confessed ignorance. It must be admitted, however, that this verse sounds much like a gloss or editorial comment. At all events, however, it is clear that Jesus foretold his appearance as sudden and unexpected.[2] It was to be preceded by persecution and preaching on the part of his disciples.[3] If we follow the line of criticism already indicated and remove Mark 13:7–9b, 14–20, 24–27, 30, 31 from their context, the program of events preceding and accompanying the coming of the Messiah is very indefinite.[4] If, however, they are retained it would appear that Jesus in some way correlated his return with the fall of Jerusalem. However that may be, the limit within which the messianic kingdom was to be established, and the Son of man was to return, is expressly stated to be the life of the generation to whom he preached.[5]   And it is in accordance with such conviction that the apostolic churches ordered their lives and hopes.

Just what relation Jesus saw existed between his death and the entrance of his followers into the blessings of the heavenly kingdom is not clearly exhibited in the gospels. It is, indeed, possible to construct an argument[6] which would show that even at his baptism he consciously took up the work of the Suffering Servant. From such a point of departure it is easy, by the aid of the "ransom" saying,[7] to discover in the words of Jesus a complete Pauline doctrine of the atonement. Yet such a dogmatic exegesis does

---

[1] Mark 13:32.

[2] Mark 13:35; Luke 12:35, 46; Matt. 25:1, 13; possibly also Luke 17:20 f.

[3] Matt. 10:24, 25; Mark 4:17; Matt. 10:23.

[4] These verses contain striking parallelisms with the thought of the apocalyptic literature, such as *Apoc. Bar.*, 27:2, 7; 48:32, 34, 37; 70:2, 3, 6, 7, 8; 6:24; 9:3; 4 Esdras, 5:9. As to the shortening of the days, see *Apoc. Bar.*, 83:1, 4.

[5] Mark 9:1 and parallels; Matt. 10:23; 14:62. The current belief of the early church is to be seen also in John 21:20-23.

[6] Thus DENNEY, *The Death of Christ*.   [7] Mark 10:43.

not quite bring conviction. Jesus believed that his death
was an integral part of his redemptive work as Messiah; of
this we may be sure. In this sense it was vicarious and
atoning. But this is far from saying that he regarded his
death as in any true sense a "buying off" of God or Satan.[1]
It was in behalf of others; it was not necessarily in the
place of others. Through it many would be freed from the
punishment which otherwise might be inflicted upon them.
For the messianic work without it would be incomplete; and
without that messianic work the way of salvation would have
been incomplete.

So far we can go with assurance. But can we go farther?
Did Jesus consider his death as having, wholly apart from
his career as Messiah, an efficiency in itself? On this we
cannot speak from unquestionable data, and if we are to
confine ourselves to the evangelists' records at our disposal,
we must plead ignorance of any more precise thought than
that he saved them as a Messiah who died. But the deliverance was no less real. The fear of death, the power of
death, the distrust of God's love because of suffering—all
these vanished when the Christ died. In very truth he
submitted to that penalty which all lives must endure, but
he suffered to conquer, and he died to rise. And all for the
sake of others.[2]

Yet it must be constantly borne in mind that the content
of the term in Jesus' teaching is not historically discon-
nected with the messianism of his day. Such differences as
may appear between the two systems are not radical, but
modifications on the part of Jesus. The ground-work of

---

[1] The force of λύτρον ἀντὶ πολλῶν is not to be pushed into a literalizing of the
figure. It is "deliverance at a cost" that is here set forth, not primarily a ransom
in its literal sense.

[2] See WENDT, *Teaching of Jesus*, Vol. II, pp. 218 f.; STEVENS, *Teaching of Jesus*,
chap. xii; *Theology of the New Testament*, Part I, chap. x; STALKER, *Christology of
Jesus*, chap. x; BEYSCHLAG, *New Testament Theology*, Book I, chap. vi; FEINE,
Jesus Christus und Paulus, pp. 113-35.

his entire conception of the Messiah's work is conditioned by the eschatological kingdom. On this point Jesus was in accord with John the Baptist and with the entire apostolic church. He was to come in his kingdom;[1] as the Son of man he was to be the judge sent by God.[2] In the Johannine reworking of his sayings he is represented as promising to raise up those who believe upon him at the last day[3] and as going to prepare places for his followers, whom he is to return to take to himself.[4] Yet neither the kingdom nor the Messiah of the gospels is precisely that of Judaism. For Jesus was not utterly dependent upon his inherited concepts. A review of the modifications noted above will show that they appear *wherever the inherited concept would be affected by his self-consciousness.*

[1] Matt. 16:27, 28.   [2] Mark 14:62.   [3] John 6:40-45.   [4] John 14:1f.

CHAPTER VI

THE ESSENTIAL ELEMENTS IN THE MESSIANISM OF JESUS

THE results reached in the preceding chapter lead us out from the region of an historical, to that of a normative investigation. We should do Jesus an injustice were we to leave the discussion of his messianic self-estimate at this point. The significance of the modifications made by him in Jewish messianism are too important to be overlooked. It is inconceivable that Christianity should have been the result of the mere belief either on the part of himself or of his disciples that he was in future to be the Christ of apocalyptic hopes. It is necessary above all things to discover just what rôle messianism, as it has been seen to exist in his teaching both as a general scheme and as a mold of his own self-consciousness, played in the entire body of teaching which he has bequeathed to us. The problem should be stated sharply. Were these modified messianic concepts so regulative and so absolutely essential to his function and his doctrine that to remove them would destroy his religious significance, or do they stand in such a relationship that they may be allowed for? Might they be removed and still leave in the teaching and personality of Jesus truth of eternal significance? In other words, in order to have faith in Jesus is it necessary, on the basis of the gospels, to accept him as Christ in the strictly historical Jewish sense of the word?

I

The answer to such a question is not to be found in an appeal merely to the distinction between that which was

120

original with Jesus and that which was inherited by him from his Jewish environment. The question as to what is true and what is false in his teaching is not to be confused with the question as to what is inherited and what is original in his thought. The study of the messianism of his times gives us clearly the interpretative medium through which we must study him, and it further shows elements that were inherited rather than, strictly speaking, originated by himself. It would be a mistake, however, to hold that all such heritage is to be rejected out of hand as utterly false. The two questions run, so to speak, at right angles to each other. Much of what he inherited was, as has already appeared, rejected by him. Some of that which he did not reject will be rejected by men in different intellectual conditions; but he would be an exceedingly rash man who should say that the entire messianic concept, as it reached Jesus, was without elements of truth. The practical problem for today lies just here. After a study of messianism enables us to understand Jesus better, there is still left the question as to what in his teaching is eternally true.

It will, of course, be easier to discover what this permanent element is after one has discovered what actually was original and what was inherited by him, but such a distinction is not the final criterion. The entire eschatological scheme in which his teachings are apparently cast is not mere speculation. As it appears in the teaching of Jesus, the eschatological element was undoubtedly inherited, but none the less it included in itself at least two elements which are not at all dependent upon any particular coloring of the future, but summarize the deepest experiences which the Jew shared in common with all peoples. These two elements are the belief that the good man must survive death, and the belief that God is bound to come to the assistance of those who trust him. Such fundamental beliefs may be expressed in a great variety of ways—by the stoic, the cynic, and the mystic, as well as by the messianist. The fact that Jesus expressed these truths in the forms of messianism can be easily accounted for, but such an explanation does not destroy the truths themselves. Jesus, it will be recalled, made this plain when he made the enjoyment of the kingdom dependent upon one's possession of a life like God's. His rejection of many of the conceptions upon which messianism was really founded forces us to abandon any belief in the permanence of the particular form of his teaching given by these two elements of Jewish hope, but not in the truths they embody.

For the Jewish eschatology does, indeed, embody truths. It may be and undoubtedly is true that the Jew did not analyze his hope; but none the less messianism may properly be conceived of as a way of thinking of matters which are in no sense dependent upon the peculiar form in which they are portrayed. The portrayal of the Day of Judgment may be quite too naïve for an age dominated by the concepts of physical science to accept, but its fundamental conception that goodness must lead to blessing, and badness to suffering, is certainly undeniable. The idea that the souls of the righteous dead should enter new physical bodies—if, indeed, that were commonly held by the Jews—is quite excluded by today's psychology, but the persistence of a self-sufficient personality after death is assuredly one element of this conception which is not to be denied. The glorious and eternal kingdom of the Jew was a dream which was never fulfilled, but the hope of a society in which righteousness is supreme is certainly one of the greatest treasures of humanity. The kingdom of Satan may be the outcome of Persian dualism, and the pit filled with fire prepared for demons and evil men may lie quite outside any scientific cosmogony, but the great religious and moral principles which the Jew embodied in these concrete forms will never be denied.

One would hardly be justified in assuming *a priori* that
Jesus treated the messianic expectation in such a generalized
way as this, but just as truly is it unsafe to declare *a priori*
that he used messianic terms as finalities in his thought, or
as concepts which must be accepted before one can assent to
his explicit moral and religious teaching.   He was possessed
of the idea of an impending eternity.[1]   To him life had
meaning and the need of moral decisions was pressing
because of the possibilities of eternal woe or weal.   Eschatology in his teaching is essentially a recognition of immortality.   The center of his teaching is not the kingdom of
God, with its mingled ethnic and political connotation; it is
eternal life—the life which, because it is like God's, persists
across death into the joy of the divine life.   He could
teach it because he possessed it.   To tell one of its certainty
and the way to possess it was in truth to preach a gospel.
It is to this life, born of the Spirit of God, that any study of
the messianic elements of the New Testament will continually lead.   The conception was not given by Judaism, it
was given by the conscious experience of Jesus.   Because
he lived, his disciples were to live also.   Life in the conviction of an impending eternity!—that is exhortation of
Jesus.   Life in the enjoyment of eternity!—that is the
supreme good.

II

But, more specifically, it can never be forgotten that
much of the teaching of Jesus has value wholly apart from
its connection with the messianic concept.   In fact, so true
is this statement that, as has already appeared, scholars have

---

[1] WERNLE, *Beginnings of Christianity*, Vol. I, chaps. 4, 5, discusses this matter
admirably, and with substantially the same results as those presented in the present
volume.   In many points a comparison of his positions with mine shows differences,
especially in matters of criticism, but that two studies so independent as these
should reach results so similar gives me, at least, added confidence both in them and
in the method employed.

sometimes been able to convince themselves that the whole significance of Jesus is unmessianic. Throughout his teaching there runs the note of universality rather than of Judaism. That for which the religious soul turns to his teaching is his reference, not to the kingdom of God, but to God himself; not for his reference to the judgment, but for his exposition of the moral values and outcomes of life possessed of eternal capacities.

If we ask ourselves as to the origin of these teachings, so independent in their content from his inherited messianism, our answer is not hard to find. In the first place, Jesus re-emphasized the noble ethics of the prophets. All through the history of the Jews there persisted the struggle between the prophet, on the one hand, and the priest and the legalist, on the other. Tragic as this contest sometimes became, it gathers an element of pathos when we recall that the prophet himself sometimes found it necessary to further the policy of those to whom he was really opposed. But of one thing the prophet was never ignorant: Whether he expressed his words in terms of prophecy, or in great principles embodied in the Codes of his people's lawgivers, he never forgot that life was something more than ceremony, and that duty to God was something more than the keeping of rules. Back of every specific act he saw a dominating motive, and back of every law he saw his God. It was this perception of the moral significance of religious faith that gave the great prophets their ethical passion, and it was this that Jesus himself appropriated. He, too, would say, with the writer of Deuteronomy, that the two greatest commands of the law were to love God and to love one's neighbor.

Jesus saw also the supreme truth which lay in the prophet's interpretation of suffering. It was this, quite as much as his perception of the inevitable outcome of his struggle with the Pharisees, that taught him the necessity of his death. In the description of the Suffering Servant he saw the fate that would be his as the Christ. In a profound sense he fulfilled this prophecy. It was not merely that he expounded the principles of the prophets even better than they themselves; beyond this he saw that he who would be the truly messianic representative of God must fulfil those forecasts with which the second Isaiah so wonderfully interpreted the sufferings of Jehovah's Servant, but which the pride of the Jew had refused to see must picture his Christ. But, at the same time, it is noteworthy that in his teaching Jesus does not magnify the messianic aspect of his suffering or of the world suffering. The note which he strikes most insistently is the note of the fatherliness of God. But when Jesus reached this conception he had passed quite beyond the sphere of the messianic expectation and had entered that of universal religious faith.

It is here in this conception of God as love that we see the basis of the ethical teaching of Jesus. It too, although occasionally couched in terms of messianism, is not dependent upon the concepts of messianism. The supreme duty of man is to believe that God is love, and to live with others as God himself would live. That is to say, he is to live a life of love. How far removed this is from the traditional messianism of his day will appear at once. The kingdom of God may or may not be considered as necessary in our modern religious vocabularies, but it is no mere archæological concept. Deep within it is the thought that men must embody the love of God in their social relations. It is not only heaven, it is a community of "children of God" who are like the Master Jesus, who are brothers because they are like their heavenly Father. They are to be immortally blessed because they are possessed of that character, gained by the life of divine quality, which will make immortality blessed. Any others, consciously refusing to be godlike, must find immortality a curse. In a word, love is the social correlate of the sacrificial individualism of Jesus—the great dynamic element of eternal life.

But such elements as these in the teaching of Jesus emphasize distinctions not merely between messianism and ethics, or between messianism and religion, but between truth and the form of truth; between the substance of teaching and the form which that teaching took in a given age. From this point of view the student of the life of Jesus becomes increasingly convinced that none of the essential teachings of Jesus are dependent upon the messianic scheme as such. Jesus does not use the idea of the kingdom as inclusive of all his teaching. If it be abandoned, his general ethical and religious teaching would not be injured. The idea of the kingdom is a point of contact between himself and his hearers. Could he, conceivably, have been a Greek, it must have been something different. His own experience of God, his own personality, led him to enlarge upon eternal life rather than upon the kingdom. But that is a term of his own personality, not of an inherited hope. Its content is moral, not ethnic.

III

Yet even here we have not reached the most significant help that lies in the messianic interpretation which Jesus gave himself and his life. That lies in the very word "Christ," the Anointed One, in which Jesus conceived himself.

When Jesus made his own inner life the object of attention, and disclosed his self-conscious life, his words are susceptible of being ranged in two general classes. On the one side are those in which he speaks of his personality as thoroughly under the influence of the Spirit, and on the other are those in which he used the filial analogy to express

his relations with God.   But it would be a mistake to think
of these two self-descriptions either as involving a double
personality, or in fact as expressive of any radical difference.
To think of God as Father was at bottom no more different
from thinking of himself as having the Spirit of God than
to think of himself as Son of man was different from thinking of himself as Christ.   The distinction between the two
terms is rather one of point of view.   The very account
which describes the coming of the Spirit upon him also
describes the new experience as one of sonship.

The nearest analogy which we have to the experience of
Jesus is that of the prophet, but the psychological formula to
describe his and the prophetic experience is not the same.
Jesus was conscious, not of a momentary indwelling of the
Spirit,[1] but of a personality constantly and exceptionally and
supremely filled with the divine personality—of a divine
incarnation.   Otherwise he would not have conceived of
himself as the Christ.

Again, however, a careful distinction is necessary.   Such
a consciousness of himself as Messiah and of the significance
of his own personality would be impossible without experiences which antedated the baptism.   Whatever new experience
of God and new perception of duty may have come to him
by the Jordan must have been conditioned by his previous
life.   It is, of course, possible, with some of the Docetic
teachers, to hold that there was such an incarnation of the
Spirit of God at that time as would have been unconditioned
by any previous character or capacity of his personality; but
such a position is unlikely on *a priori* grounds, as well as
opposed to such information as we have as to the early life
of Jesus.   The words uttered by him as a boy in the temple
certainly do not refer to his parentage.   Otherwise his
father and mother could not have failed to understand him.

---

[1] *Cf.* John 1: 32, 34.   So, too, J. WEISS, *Reich Gottes*[2], p. 155.

Wholly apart, therefore, from the question as to the historicity of the infancy sections of Matthew and Luke, we are forced to believe that by these words Jesus intended to express his developing consciousness of God in his own life. It would in very truth be contrary to all the data and probabilities of psychology to find such a supreme experience as that of the baptism unconditioned by previous states of personality. Just what the difference was between the state of soul of which Jesus was conscious before his baptism, and that of which he was conscious after his baptism, it would be impossible to state with accuracy, but one thing is clear: the personality of Jesus made the new self-consciousness possible. Thereafter he believed himself to be so great and so possessed of God as to be absolutely and unquestionably convinced that all the glories of the eschatological kingdom were to be secondary to his own position as its king. A greater thought than this probably never entered a man's mind and left it sane. That Jesus should have believed such a future should be his, is a most important datum for assisting us to judge his own self-estimate. From the day of his baptism onward this conviction set Jesus in a different class from that to which other men belonged. Never for a moment does he consider himself as a mere climax of humanity. In his experiences, in his duties, and, most of all, in his consciousness of his own superhuman self he puts himself over against humanity as its divine Master. Otherwise he would not have been the Christ.

To come to a consideration of his self-consciousness from this point of view is to find one's self convinced anew that the real meaning of Jesus in history is not in the ascription to him of a messianic future on the part of his followers, but rather in a personality which, when fully read by himself, compelled him to regard himself as the one destined to undertake and enjoy a messianic future. Even though it should be shown that such an expectation was historically to be disappointed, the greatness of the personality which compelled itself to forecast its future in such ultimate conceptions is indisputable.

Almost unexpectedly eschatology is thus seen to be of the utmost interpretative importance. It would not have been such an extraordinary thing to have regarded one's self as Christ, if that had meant simply to teach men about God, to do good, and to organize a great movement of social regeneration which sooner or later should transform humanity. But consider only what it must have meant for one so eminently sane as Jesus to attach to himself the eschatological concept. He was doing nothing that the eschatological Christ was expected to perform. The judgment throne was not set; the dead were not raised; the wicked were not being thrust down to hell; the sun and moon and stars were not being shaken from their places; the earth was not being renewed. Why did he forecast his future as involving such expectations? The answer is close at hand. It was because he saw himself so supreme that he was forced to use the extremest valuations of his day and people to express his own self-consciousness. He could not interpret himself as a reformer, as a prophet, as Elijah. He was the Christ. Had such an interpretation been forced upon him, had others believed that he was doing messianic work, the situation would be radically different. As it was, it is a tribute to something in his personality that compelled him to regard himself as Christ. And that element was God. The coming of God into a man's life was implied in the very word, "Christ." It is that which the apostles saw and that which Jesus himself saw. He regarded himself as the Christ— the Anointed of God—because he was conscious of God in his personality. What "unction" was in Semitic thought, incarnation was in Greek thought. Jesus believed that he was Christ because he knew that when he read his own personality he read God. As this deep consciousness had led him to abandon certain elements of pharisaic messianism, and to modify others, so, too, did it become a contribution to religion wholly independent of the self-appellation with which Jesus was constrained to express it. It is the personality of the historical Jesus, not a descriptive title, that is God's best revelation to men. In very truth, in him was life that was to be the light of men.

Similarly in the case of the resurrection. While it is true that men believed Jesus to be the Christ before they believed that he had been raised from the dead, it is true that they believed he was raised from the dead because he was the Christ. Clearly, the fact that he was raised from the dead did not make Jesus the Christ; but it showed him to be such. It is on the basis of this fact that men attached to him the messianic conception. As has already appeared, there was absolutely nothing in the conception of messiahship which would have involved the belief that the Messiah should die and be raised from the dead. On the contrary, there was everything in the concept to argue the opposite conclusion. It was this which Peter evidently had in mind at Cæsarea Philippi: the Christ could not die. Account for the belief of the disciples in Jesus' resurrection as one will, it is the reverse of any genuine historical method to hold that the belief was derived from a belief in his messiahship.

It is well to state this fact distinctly. The belief that Jesus had been raised from the dead was the basis of a messianic interpretation, not the result of that interpretation. If one, therefore, is convinced that this belief of the apostles was well grounded, and that Jesus actually did manifest himself in some objective sense to the disciples, it is impossible to deny that in this fact the Christian church has a supreme historical datum wholly distinct from the messianic concept. The death of Christ might be used by the Jews to argue that Jesus was the Christ; for the man who does not care to reach that particular conclusion it stands equally significant as a fact in the history of the race, a testimony to the superhuman personality of the historical Jesus. It matters not in what schematic relation it is placed; whether it be systematized as an element in the messianic expectation, or in some scientific hypothesis like that of evolution. The fact of the resurrection itself is independent of any interpretation and stands out ready for correlation with whatever other facts one may care to join it. Whether or not one accept Jesus as the Christ of Jewish hopes, he is the Risen One.

IV

Thus we come in sight of the permanent, as distinct from the interpretative, elements in the story of Jesus. There are those fundamental human needs and hopes which messianism in itself expressed, and far beyond them is that personality of Jesus which was the test of truth in his own experience and lies back of his teaching, making him more than human teachers. When we combine these two elements, we have the permanent element of the gospels. Once given such facts, and it is easy to systematize them. They have but to be brought into correlation with any other group of facts to have their value appear. As we shall see, that is the use made of them by the apostles. By their aid the early church solved the theological and philosophical difficulties of its own age. So to use them is to put them to their true purpose. The life and resurrection and teaching of Jesus were not intended to be sources of mystery to the world. In such a case the gospel would be far enough from good news. They were rather intended to serve as a means by which the man who makes them supreme in his own conduct may better understand the world in which he is, better trust the forgiving grace of God, better perceive the life he ought to live, and be more fully assured of the life that may hereafter be his.

It is here, far above traditional messianism, that we reach our final word concerning Jesus and see most clearly his significance. Jesus, as all will admit, was something more than a teacher; he was a life, and the life was the light of man. His teachings are the expositions of this life; the ideal which he set forth as the divine way of living he himself first lived. To think of him as in any way disingenuous is impossible. If ever a man was transparently honest, it was he. In this assurance lies the great authority which we attribute to his teaching. He was not a theorist. He set forth his own inner life in the words which he bade other men to believe. This life he does not obtrusively set forth as messianic, but rather as that of the Son of God, the one in most perfect harmony with the divine soul, the one in whom the divine Spirit himself was incarnate. It was his inner life that forced upon him the messianic interpretation. It was his inner life that he formulated in his teachings. It is his personality, his vocalization of his self-conscious life with God, his triumph over death, that survive when all archæological concepts are removed. Jesus taught how one should live to insure the kingdom which the Jew expected and he himself so lived. But this way of living—this life of faith and love and sacrifice—remains imperative as a moral ideal, whether or not one correlates it with the Jewish pictures with which it was correlated by him as he spoke to Jews. He taught and demonstrated the certainty of the immortality of the man who possessed his sort of life. The truth of such teaching lies, not in the fact that he described it in terms of messianic hope, but in the historical fact of his own resurrection. Cast these facts and these teachings born of experience in any vocabulary and they are true.

The criterion by which to judge between the interpretative and the permanent elements in the words of Jesus is, in a word, Jesus himself. Such inherited thought employed by him as cannot be demonstrated true by his personality may be assumed as pedagogic and economic—the means by which he expressed to his own age the truth born of his own conscious experience.

In conclusion: On the basis of Jesus' own self-estimate and the results of a reverent criticism, a man may believe in him as the incarnation of God, as the revealer of a forgiving God, as the type and teacher of the perfect human life, as the Risen One who brought life and incorruption to light, without necessarily committing himself to a formal acceptance of his strictly messianic interpretation. The interpretation was born of Judaism and will be dynamic only as one assents to Judaistic preconceptions. The life will ever be the light of men.

PART III

THE MESSIANISM OF THE APOSTLES

CHAPTER I

THE MESSIANISM OF PRIMITIVE CHRISTIANITY

THE disciples who composed the original church at Jerusalem were those who had been associated with Jesus. Most of them were Galileans, and farthest possible removed from the academic discussions of the Sanhedrin. To them Jesus was not a doctrine, but a real person. Their faith in him was the product of their association with him—in no way was systematized into a theology. He was the Christ —of this they were certain from their daily contact with his supreme personality and from his resurrection. Their hopes were conditioned by the awfulness of the future which his return promised, and their daily life was full of the joy resulting from a conviction that they were to share in the glories of an eternity he in his kingdom would inaugurate. He was to them more than a teacher of religion, or the founder of a new religion. He had stirred their deepest souls by his constant insistence upon preparation for the impending eternity, and they were living in daily expectation that this eternity would break in upon them. Already they were living the same eternal life he had lived in humiliation and was living in glory. Property might well be sacrificed to alleviate the poverty of brethren during the brief period of waiting for his return to usher in that eternity, while the highest honor that could come to them was to be considered worthy of suffering for acknowledging belief in his messianic dignity.[1]

Four literary sources furnish us material for portraying the faith and hope of this group of Christians—the book

[1] Acts 3:44, 45; *cf.* 4:32-35; 5:41.

of Acts, the epistles of James and Peter, and the Revelation of John. With the exception of certain of the material of Acts, none of these literary survivals dates from the church at Jerusalem, but all alike furnish data for reconstructing the thought of those Christians who were not directly under the influence of Paul, and who preserved that general messianic point of view and habit of mind which the Apostle to the Gentiles was so characteristically to preserve, modify, and surpass.

I

The question as to the sources and authorship of the earlier chapters of the book of Acts is admittedly one of the most perplexing of all the critical questions concerning New Testament criticism. On the one hand are those who hold that these chapters are hardly more than a collection of late legends, which have been roughly grouped together and edited in the interest of a compromise between the Jewish and the Pauline wings of the early church.[1] In whatever form this view takes, whether or not it recognizes the possibility that original trustworthy records and recollections of the Jerusalem church have been preserved along with less trustworthy material, in general it discredits the historical value of the early portions of the book. To those who, on the contrary, hold that the book is the unedited, or but slightly edited, work of Luke, the first twelve chapters are of unquestioned value. On *a priori* ground it might seem that a mediate position which recognizes the authenticity of certain sources and certain elements

---

[1] Baur and the Tübingen school (especially Zeller) and the tangential Dutch school headed by Van Manen, represent this in its most elaborate form. The Tübingen scholars' theory of early church history compelled them to regard the book as a fictitious "tendency" writing seeking to further the interests of a nascent Catholicism. Harnack and Weizsäcker represent something of a mediating view between this and that of tradition. *Cf.* HARNACK, *History of Dogma*, Vol. I, p. 56, and WEIZSÄCKER, *Apostolic Age, passim*. The traditional view is argued vigorously by SALMON, *Introduction to the New Testament*, and KNOWLING, in *Expositor's Greek Testament*.

in the account, but allows also for a considerable redaction, would be thoroughly tenable. Such a position is, in my opinion, justified by a study of the literary character and the contents of the volume. That this early material has been edited at a time considerably later than the events narrated can be shown with all but certainty by internal evidence, but such a position is far removed from that which would insist that these early chapters are without historical value. The actual inconsistencies which they present with Pauline letters can either be resolved, or without serious difficulty be laid at the door of some of the late redactors. The general line of preaching, at all events, bespeaks a condition which, on the one hand, would be impossible after the destruction of Jerusalem, and, on the other, cannot be held to have been suggested by the conditions in the churches of the gentile world with which the editor was evidently associated.[1] The duplication of accounts in these early chapters also argues the originality of the substance of their accounts. There is certainly no more difficulty in recognizing a double group of sources in Acts than there is in recognizing the same phenomenon in Luke—a work admittedly from the same hand. And it is steadily growing apparent that philological argument and literary analysis have been pushed too far. A broad historical treatment certainly gives more tenable, as well as more conservative, results.

If it were not that such an argument would be obviously begging the question, appeal might here be made especially to the general messianic concept ascribed to the apostles and the primitive church of Jerusalem. Yet, if such views as are ascribed to the primitive Jerusalem community exhibit features which we should expect from Jews under the influence of apocalyptic messianism, the conclusion is hard to avoid that they must have been very early. Such a con-

---

[1] This is, after all, the great objection to the position of Van Manen.

clusion would only be strengthened if it should be shown that such a messianic concept had been modified by an editor or editors in the interest of ecclesiastical peace. Critical processes must always, to a considerable extent, approach the *petitio principii*, and can escape the danger only when, as in the case of Acts, a thorough comparison of the contents of a document with those of clearly established later and earlier writings enables us to trace tendencies, and so to establish the document under consideration in a probable historical perspective. In the case of Acts, such a comparison supplies sufficient evidence to warrant us in taking its early chapters and the general contents of its speeches at their face value, in so far as they purport to record the opinions of the Jerusalem church before the period of expansion. Thus a study of the messianic concept therein contained can be made independently of any question as to the details of authorship.

By far the largest part of the material in Acts representing the beliefs of the primitive church of Jerusalem is to be found in speeches attributed to Peter. While recent criticism has urged the composite character of these speeches, its results, if substantiated, would not materially affect the results which a non-analytical study of them produces. No one would claim that they are verbatim reports of the addresses of the apostle; but, on the other hand, the historical student, rather than the devotee to analytical criticism, cannot fail to see in their substance precisely the sort of teaching to be expected of a group of Jewish messianists who believed their hopes were about to be realized, and who had not been forced to consider the problems arising from the conversion of non-Jewish peoples. However clearly we may discover in them Judean and Pauline documents, the distinction between the two sets of material does not lie in the region of the messianic hope so much as in the general attitude of the various authors to gentile converts and a universal Christianity.[1] The same messianic hopes are in both sets of documents.

All the evidence at our disposal makes it clear that the sympathies of the primitive church were not with Zealotism. There is nowhere in the entire literature of primitive or Pauline Christianity any appeal for political action.[2] Jesus, it is true, had been executed as a political agitator, but his followers knew better than to see in his career anything to justify such a charge. In their own lives they were as far as possible removed from anything like revolution, either social or political. In their common life they held their meetings in private houses[3] and daily went to the temple to pray.[4] There is every indication that they regarded themselves as under obligation to maintain the Jewish law as conscientiously as before their association with Jesus.[5] In a word, they were Jews who believed that the Christ had appeared in the person of Jesus, and would again appear to undertake his messianic work. There is not the slightest suggestion that this faith in any way affected their devotion to their traditional religion, or led them to feel that the gentile world could share in the blessings of the messianic kingdom except by its members becoming proselytes.

How thoroughly these early Christians were Jewish messianists appears when we place the scheme of the pharisaic messianism already formulated over against the too scant records of the faith of the primitive church.

1. Peter, it is true, does not mention distinctly the two ages, but the distinction is clearly implied by his references

---

[1] For various analyses see SPITTA, *Die Apostelgeschichte, ihre Quellen, etc.;* CLEMEN, *Die Chronologie der Paulinischen Briefe;* JÜNGST, *Die Quellen der Apostelgeschichte;* HILGENFELD, in *Zeitschrift für wissenschaftliche Theologie,* 1895-96; J. WEISS, *Die Apostelgeschichte.*

[2] On the contrary, *cf.* Rom. 13:1-7; 1 Pet. 2:13, 17.

[3] Acts 1:13; 12:12.   [4] Acts 2:46; 3:1.

[5] This appears clearly in the great controversy from which Galatians sprang.

to the fact that his generation lived in "the last days,"[1] that is to say, those just preceding the coming of Christ. It argues the end of one epoch, while the approaching judgment argued just as strongly the approach of another—the truly messianic.

2. There is no express reference to the evil age being under the control of Satan in sayings attributed to the Jerusalem church in Acts.[2] That the primitive Christians believed it to be true, however, is beyond question.[3]

3. It goes without saying that the first Christians believed that the messianic age was to be introduced by the return of Jesus. There is no evidence that they conceived that they themselves had anything to do with its coming, except to prepare themselves and others for it.[4] They believed that it would come soon, since Jesus was already in possession of messianic authority in heaven—a conclusion drawn from the gift of the Spirit.[5] A similar argument is to be seen in the "name," belief in which led to cures.[6]

4. The judgment was central in the entire thought of the primitive Christian church. It was the expectation of that dreadful day to which Peter appealed at Pentecost.[7] Jesus whom the Jews had killed was the Christ whose enemies were to be put under his feet. Naturally his auditors were terrified and, reverting to the passage from Joel (3:22-25) just quoted by Peter, asked what they might do to be saved.[8] This is the first appearance of the concept of "salvation,"[9] and

---

[1] Acts 2:14-21. The passage here used is from Joel 3:1-5. The term of vs. 17, ἐν ταῖς ἡμέραις ἐσχάταις, is the apostolic substitute for μετὰ ταῦτα of the LXX. The origin of the term is doubtless Mic. 4:1, which is clearly messianic. *Cf.* Mic. 2:10; 3:1; Jas. 5:3; Heb. 1:1.

[2] This statement needs modification if Acts 5:3 be considered as strictly historical.

[3] *Cf.* the general scheme of Revelation of John and the entire thought of Paul.

[4] Acts 3:19-21.   [5] Acts 2:33; 5:30-33.

[6] Acts 2:38; 3:6, 16; 4:10, and often.   [7] Acts 2:19-21, 35. See also 4:8-12; 10:42.

[8] Acts 3:37; *cf.* vs. 40.   [9] Acts 2:21; 4:12; 13:26.

it is worth noticing that it is correlated with the forgiveness of sins, and that in turn is correlated with escaping the punishment of the judgment. The believer in Jesus as Christ was to be saved from an evil generation's punishment.[1] The essential identity of this belief with the alleged exclusively Pauline doctrine of justification by faith is evident.[2] This was only the negative side of the matter, to be complemented by that which was the current belief of the early church, viz., salvation was release from death and entrance into the messianic kingdom. But of this the records of Acts do not precisely speak.[3] As a precondition of obtaining such salvation there were necessary repentance, and faith (indicated by baptism) in Jesus as the Christ. Evidence of such acquittal would be seen in the gift of the Spirit.[4]

5. A party in the primitive church at Jerusalem clearly believed[5] that entrance into the coming kingdom—that is salvation—was to be for Jews only.[6] That this party represented the entire body of Jerusalem Christians is probable, although doubtless[7] they were more zealous in propagating their belief than other members of the church. The fact that "those from James" should have made Peter and Barnabas unwilling to continue eating with the gentiles at Antioch,[8] as well as Paul's reference to other matters in connection with Judaistic controversy, argue strongly that the prevailing sentiment of the Jerusalem church was pharisaic. This conclusion is guaranteed by the history of the church. By the

[1] Acts 2:40.

[2] That the primitive church held to this doctrine is expressly stated by Paul, Gal. 2:14–16.

[3] Acts 2:21; 4:12; 13:26. See *Pss. Sol.*, 10:9; 12:7; Lk. 1:69, 71, 77; Acts 4:22; 13:26.

[4] See page 142, note 9.

[5] Acts 15:1. Doubtless this is the same party as οἱ ἐκ περιτομῆς of Gal. 2:12.

[6] *Cf.* Acts 1:3; 2:39.

[7] *Cf.* οἱ ἀπὸ Ἰακώβου; Gal. 2:12. Yet the account of Acts, chap. 15, especially vs. 5, supports the view that the Jerusalem church was divided between the extreme and the moderate Jewish party.

[8] Gal. 2:12.

time of Paul's visit to Jerusalem[1] the Christian community there numbered thousands of Jews, "all zealous for the law." What we know from Hegesippus concerning the punctilious righteousness of James is of the same tenor.[2] There is no reason for doubting that this ethnic conviction included most of the old expectations of the subjugation of the gentile world to the regenerate and glorified Jewish state.[3]

6. The resurrection of Jesus is the central argument in the apostolic preaching. Because of it Jesus was seen to be the Messiah. However, in the speeches of Peter there is no clear reference to the resurrection of the believer. At the same time it would be impossible to doubt that the primitive church held the resurrection to be one of its fundamental hopes. It was involved in the idea of salvation.

7. As regards the personal Messiah there is, of course, no question that the early church believed that Jesus was the Christ who had returned to heaven, whence he would come to introduce the new age and the new kingdom. This was the very core of the entire Christian movement.[4]

Jesus was assuredly the Christ, for he fufilled newly discovered messianic prophecies by his death and resurrection; but he is never spoken of as having performed a truly messianic act. His kingdom was to appear only when he himself reappeared. And that was to be soon.[5]

It is commonly said that Jesus was not the sort of Christ that the Jews of his day expected, and if one thinks only of

---

[1] Acts 21:20; cf. 15:5. [2] EUSEBIUS, *His. Ecc.*, 2:23.

[3] See further in the discussion of Revelation. An interesting commentary on this attitude of the mind is to be seen in the words of Peter, both in his vision on the housetop and in his address to Cornelius, Acts 10:9-16, 28.

[4] *E. g.*, Acts 5:42.

[5] The ground for this statement lies not in specific texts, but in the general expectation as seen both in the synoptic gospels, the Revelation of John, and in Pauline thought. Indeed all apocalyptic looked to a speedily approaching relief. What force would the appeals of primitive Christianity have had if they had been understood to refer to an event to come in the indefinite future—say within ten thousand years? *Cf.* 2 Pet. 3:1-10. See also *Apoc. Baruch*, 20:6.

his brief career as teacher and philanthropist, such a view is of course true. No orthodox Jew of his day or of any day could for a moment admit that his historical career in any degree squared with the messianic ideal. That Jesus himself recognized this fact is equally clear from all of his few references to his conception of a truly messianic work. If, however, one looks to the apostolic conception of messiahship, another aspect of the matter at once appears. In the estimation of the Twelve, Jesus was the Messiah, but his career was prospective. His messianic life of humility was not a part of his messianic work. That lay still in the future. And when they and Paul undertook to picture what this work and what he himself was to be, they appropriated the apocalyptic hopes of the day. They did not believe he was to be a Zealot Christ, but, with certain modifications, they did believe he was to be the Pharisee Christ.

This consideration will go far to convince one of the error of those who hold that the kingdom of God plays no important rôle in apostolic Christianity; that all matters eschatological were no more to the primitive church and Paul and the first Fathers than they are to a modern treatise upon systematic theology. Such a view both lacks historical perspective and is at variance with the entire thought of the literature of apostolic Christianity. The very name of the new movement, *Christ*ianity, would suggest the contrary opinion. So far from the eschatological kingdom of God being a secondary element in the early church, it is its great conditioning belief.[1]

The preaching of the first evangelists was not a call to ethical ideals or an argument as to certain truths. Rather it was the proclamation of a message. They told of the nearness of the kingdom of God and of a preliminary earthly

[1] So HARNACK, *History of Dogma*, Vol. I, p. 58 : "The Gospel entered the world as an apocalyptical eschatological message, apocalyptical and eschatological not only in its form, but also in its content."

appearance of the coming Christ.[1] To them this preliminary career had been that of "the prophet"[2] who had
attained his superiority by the coming of God's spirit upon
him. This is the earliest Christology. There is in it no
reference to a miraculous birth or to a messianic pre-existence. Jesus was the Anointed.[3] And the decisive proof of
this messiahship was the resurrection.[4] The coming of the
Spirit upon his followers was evidence that messianic
authority was already his.

It is at this point that we reach the first of new and
modifying elements in the new messianism. The Jews had
not expected that the Spirit of God would come upon all
flesh in the messianic days.[5] The Messiah would, of course,
be anointed of God,[6] but the members of the kingdom were
promised no such experience. The entire movement of
John and Jesus, however, evidently included the belief that
the followers of the Anointed were also to be anointed.
The origin of this hope cannot be discovered in Jewish
literature. John the Baptist is the first reported to have
given it utterance,[7] but he refers to it as a matter of current

---

[1] See the admirable discussion by WEISS, *Biblical Theology*, Vol. I, p. 173.

[2] Acts 3:22; 7:36; 10:36-38. *Cf.* Isa. 42:1; 61:1; 52:7.   [3] Acts 10:36-38.

[4] Acts 2:25-31. It is interesting to see how readily the early Christian apologetic used new interpretations of the Old Testament gained by a knowledge of the historical Jesus.

[5] See GLOEL, *Der heilige Geist*, pp. 91-136.

[6] *Pss. Sol.*, 17:42; *cf.* 18:8; *Eth. Enoch*, 49:3: *cf.* 61:7, 11. Angels also are under the influence of the Spirit according to 68:2. According to *Wis.*, 1:5, 6, the holy spirit of instruction will come and impart wisdom to those who are pure in thought and deed. Philo treats the matter somewhat more elaborately. Moses (*Decalog.*, 33), the prophets (*Quis. Rer. Div. Her.*, 53), Abraham (*Nobil.*, 5), all had the spirit of God in exceptional degree. See SCHOEMAKER, "The Use of רוח and of πνεῦμα," *Jour. Bib. Lit.*, 1904, 13-67. WOOD, *The Spirit of God in Bib. Lit.*, pp. 64, 65, gives *Test. XII, Pat.* Levi 18, Judah 24, but these show Christian influence.

[7] Mark 1:8; John 1:33. Reference ought perhaps here to be made to *Eth. Enoch*, 90:38, when the sheep (the Pious) are to become white oxen like the white bull (the Messiah). From this it might be possible to argue that the author believed that all men were to be anointed.

expectation.[1] Nor would it be in the least surprising if such should have been the case. But in such an event current expectation would have been nothing else than the speech of Peter explains—an explanation of an experience.

That this new experience was an actual speaking in foreign tongues most critical scholars have come to question,[2] the interpretation to that effect being ascribed to the editor of Acts, who wrote after the phenomena of "tongues" had ceased to be common in the Christian churches. Yet such a position does not invalidate the report that the early disciples experienced a religious ecstasy which took some strange form, and was to be often repeated in the Christian communities both in Judea and throughout the Roman empire. Later a sharp distinction came to be drawn between such spectacular manifestations of religious enthusiasm and the normal influence of the divine life. It is enough now to note carefully that the acceptance of Jesus as Christ did lead to new experience. And it was the Spirit that was really supreme in the church. The apostles' authority was from him, and they it was who brought to others the same gift. It was the Spirit who forced the Jerusalem-centered church out into the world. Account for it as one may, the historic fact is indubitable that with the death of Jesus there sprang up innumerable men of the old prophetic spirit. God was again in vital union with his creatures. The neutralizing influence of Pharisaism was outflanked. Apostles were reinforced by the Seven Hellenists with Stephen and Philip at their head. Prophets like Agabus

[1] EDERSHEIM, *Life and Times of Jesus the Messiah*, Vol. II, p. 734, says that Joel 2:28 is explained by the Midrashim as "referring to the latter days when all Israel will be prophets." But such references as he gives are all post-Christian and very likely reflect the effect of the Christian polemics. In general see WOOD, *The Spirit of God in Bib. Lit.*, pp. 151-97.

[2] An exception should be noted in the case of WRIGHT, *Some New Testament Problems*. See also CHASE, *Hulsean Lectures*, and BARTLETT, *Acts* (Century Bible).

again began to utter their message. The humblest believer
had his particular "charism." The early church was full
of ebullient life. For men were coming straight to God.
Eternal life was being lived. Grant that the Christ never
came as the primitive Christians expected he would come—
God came.

A second modification that stands out clearly in the
messianic faith of the Jerusalem church is the emphasis laid
upon the death of Jesus the Christ. Throughout the
association of the Twelve with Jesus they had been quite
incapable of grasping the possibility of any such catastrophe
coming to one whom they believed to be the Christ of their
hopes.[1] It certainly was the opposite of their Jewish hope.
In the speeches of Peter, however, this death is argued to
be a necessary part of the divine plan of the messianic
revelation,[2] foretold by the prophets and the occasion of the
exposition of divine power in the resurrection. At last
they saw the truth in the teaching of Jesus they had rejected
during his life.

There is, however, in the Petrine section of the Acts no
distinct correlation of this death of Christ with the forgiveness
of sins—a fact to be borne in mind when formulating the
New Testament doctrine of the atonement. Men were to be
saved by repenting and believing on Jesus[3] as Christ. They
were not urged to accept any basis for the forgiveness of
their sins which such faith and salvation involved. At the
same time, caution should be exercised in arguing that this
silence of the Petrine section of the Acts constitutes a positive denial that the early church regarded the death of Christ
as having any relation to the forgiveness of sins. Paul[4]
expressly states that he "received" the teaching that "Christ

---

[1] Mark 9:9, 10, 30–32; 10:32–34; Matt. 16:21–23; Luke 24:13–27.

[2] Acts 2:22, 23; 3:18; 4:27, 28.

[3] Acts 3:19; 10:43.   [4] 1 Cor. 15:3.

died for our sins, according to the Scriptures." Unless we hold this to be a Pauline interpretative statement of facts, this certainly implies that the early apostles held to something closely akin to the late belief of a vicarious death. The same conclusion is in some degree involved in Philip's indentification of Jesus as the suffering Servant of Isaiah.[1] Yet, had it not been for Pauline thought, it is hardly possible that Christianity would ever have included any distinct doctrine of the substitutionary death of Jesus.[2] Justification by faith was indeed distinctly a tenet of the Jerusalem community (although not carried to its logical conclusions) but the Atonement as a doctrine is the gift of Paul.

One point further demands attention. Did Peter expect that the death of Christ, or some other aspect of his messianic work, would guarantee the ultimate participation of all men in the messianic salvation? This has been argued strenuously from the fact that he said that it was necessary for heaven to receive the Christ Jesus until the times of the restoration of all things of which God spoke through the prophets.[3] But obviously the reference here is to the messianic glories which are to be established in the future, and it would be natural to interpret it, from that point of view, as involving only such an extension of the messianic joys as would be conditioned by the whole scheme of messianism. This is substantiated by the fact that Peter urged his hearers to repent. If he were thinking about universal salvation, it is difficult to see the force of this appeal. Further, the reference is very probably to the prophetic picture of the restored Israel found in Mic. 4:5, 6; and finally there is nothing in the word ἀποκατάστασις to

---

[1] Acts 8: 35. In so far as the Gospel of Matthew reflects the belief of the Jerusalem community it evidences the same probability.

[2] DENNEY, *Death of Christ*, pp. 76-91, makes the best possible statement of the case, but fails to establish clearly any position in advance of that stated above. For complete treatment see KÄHLER, *Zur Lehre der Versöhnung*.

[3] Acts 3: 19. 21.

argue that the reference is to the fate of individuals. It is rather an echo of the general belief that God's reign, which was once supreme, and has been to some extent threatened by the power of Satan, was to be re-established, and in the glorious messianic kingdom. The Fall was to be overcome by the Restoration.

II

Only one of the two epistles bearing the name of Peter need concern us here. 2 Peter is all but unanimously held to belong to the second century and to be pseudonymous.[1] Concerning 1 Peter there are also many doubts, but there is no compelling reason for rejecting it as, in the main at least, the genuine work of the apostle. Apart from the admitted difficulties of date suggested by chap. 4, the chief ground upon which late authorship is built is its affinity with Paulinism. Jülicher[2] and Harnack[3] put the argument against its authenticity strongly and about to this effect: While the epistle contains nothing that is un-Pauline, it is thoroughly filled with the Pauline spirit and uses Pauline formulas. And to this may be added the general habit of the second century to produce a Petrine literature.[4] Yet external evidence in its favor is by no means weak.[5] So far as Paulinism is concerned, it is limited almost entirely to parallelisms between it and Romans and Ephesians. Some

---

[1] For summary of arguments in this case see JÜLICHER, *Einleitung;* BACON, *Introduction;* and the articles in *Encyclopædia Biblica,* and HASTINGS, *Dictionary of the Bible.*

[2] *Einleitung,* p. 133.   [3] *Chronologie,* pp. 451 ff.

[4] Thus we know of a Gospel of Peter, the Acts of Peter, the Teaching of Peter, the Preaching of Peter, the Apocalypse of Peter, and at least three epistles of Peter.

[5] Especially note the parallelisms between it and 1 Clement. The most important are given in BACON, *Introduction,* p. 151, note. The epistle was probably used by Polycarp and Papias. If it be felt that the fisherman apostle could not have written such good Greek as the letter contains, recourse may be had, with Bacon, to the hypothesis of some amanuensis, possibly Silvanus. But a study of the very numerous participial constructions of the epistle will certainly suggest caution in too liberal praise of its literary form.

degree of dependence must certainly be admitted.[1] It is hard
to see, however, why this should necessarily argue against
Petrine authorship. Intercourse between Paul and Peter is
certainly recognized in the New Testament,[2] and it is hardly
open to question that Paul must have influenced his compan-
ion. Nor is there anything improbable in the supposition that
the letter of Paul to the Romans, or, for that matter, to the
Asiatic churches, was known to Peter.

If it be further urged that there is nothing un-Pauline
in the letter, it can be replied that our discussion has shown
that the distinction between Paulinism and primitive Christianity is by no means as sharp as has been sometimes
urged. Both alike include, with varying distinctness, the
fundamental doctrines which result from the attachment of
the messianic dignity to Jesus. The peculiarity of Paulinism was not its insistence upon justification by faith, but its
insistence that such justification was not limited to those
who observed Mosaism. Peter, as is indicated not only by
Acts, but by church traditions, had himself removed this
limitation and so far stood on Pauline ground.

These considerations make it clear that, although we cannot
safely ascribe to primitive Christianity all the doctrines
which lie in 1 Peter,[3] a summary of the positions taken in
the epistle will show that it, like primitive Christianity,
reproduces pharisaic messianism.

1. With Peter as with pharisaic messianism there were two
ages. The end of the times was already come,[4] and a new
age—the last time[5]—was yet to come. The end of all
things was at hand.[6]

2. While there is no mention of the existence of the

[1] So SANDAY AND HEADLAM, *Romans*, lxxiv f.

[2] Gal. 1:18; 2:9-14. Acts, chap. 15, unless it be rejected completely, certainly contains evidence of an interplay of apostolic thought in line with the Galatian passage.

[3] See the somewhat extreme statement of this view in STEVENS, *Theology of the
New Testament*, where the question of the date of the epistle is not fully considered.

[4] 1 Pet. 1:19, 20; Mic. 4:1; Isa. 2:2.   [5] 1 Pet. 1:5-7.   [6] 1 Pet. 4:7.

kingdom of Satan, the essential idea involved in that belief is recognized in ascribing to Satan the causes of persecution.[1]

3. The kingdom was to be established by the Christ.[2] It was to include certain of the dead,[3] and was to be established at the revelation of the Christ in glory.[4] All of these forecasts imply a period of struggle which was involved in all expectations of the establishment of the messianic kingdom. The idea of an evolving kingdom is foreign to the entire outlook of the epistle. Its coming was to be catastrophic.

4. The judgment is both referred to specifically and implied.[5] The idea of salvation, the correlate of the belief in the judgment, is frequently expressed. The Christian's hope in salvation is perhaps the key-word to the epistle.[6] The judgment is conducted both by God and Christ.[7]

5. The letter is directed to the "sojourners of the dispersion," i. e., Jewish Christians. While there is no antagonism to gentile Christians, and the church has become an "elect race," it seems clear that Peter regards the Jews as composing its main body. In this connection it is interesting to note the steady parallelism which the epistle draws between the ancient prophecies of the glories of the Hebrew nation and those of this "elect" nation.[8] No distinct statement in the epistle describes the relation of the church to the messianic kingdom, but it was hardly needed. The members of the "elect nation" are obviously the subjects of the coming kingdom.

6. The resurrection lies in the background of the epistle as a part of the salvation which awaits the believer. The Christian's hope was one begotten by the resurrection of

[1] 1 Pet. 5:8, 9.   [2] 1 Pet. 1:7; 2:12; 4:5.
[3] 1 Pet. 4:5, 6.   [4] 1 Pet. 1:7, 8; 4:13; 5:1, 4.

[5] 1 Pet. 4:5, 6, where the reference includes the dead; 2:23; 4:17. This latter reference is somewhat enigmatical. The reference is probably to the persecutions under which the church was laboring, and which were to be shortly ended at the appearance of the Christ; 1 Pet. 1:6, 7; 5:10.

[6] 1 Pet. 1:5–10; 2:22.   [7] 1 Pet. 2:23 and 4:5; cf. Acts 10:42.

[8] For instance, the hope for the κληρονομία, as in Lev. 20:24; Deut. 19:10; 20:16, reappears in 1 Pet. 1:4. Cf. also 1 Pet. 3:9.

Jesus the Christ from the dead, and so could be called a living hope—that is to say, a hope which looked forward to life,[1] and that life was to be like that of God.[2]

7. Jesus throughout the epistle is always conceived of as the Christ. He is at the right hand of God, and supreme over all angels and other heavenly beings.[3] Yet his glory is to be seen only when he is revealed in the last time.[4]

How far Peter had moved away from Pharisaism is to be seen, however, in his Christology. This is precisely what is to be expected. The insistence that Jesus was to fulfil the messianic hope would of necessity tend to center attention upon him. Such facts, therefore, as actually lay in his life would of necessity be given large value. How far this could be carried into systematic thought will appear in the discussion of Paulinism. It is enough now to recognize the fact that in 1 Peter the death of Jesus is regarded as a means of redemption,[5] and that all his sufferings are held to have been in accordance with messianic prophecy.[6] The Petrine Christology is strictly messianic. It is centered, not in any metaphysical conception of deity, but in the divine spirit which was in Christ, spoke by the prophets, and was accordingly pre-existent. It was this spirit that raised Jesus from the grave,[7] and it was in the spirit—that is, with his human spirit anointed with the divine spirit—that between his death and his resurrection, Jesus, without his physical body, preached to the spirits "in prison" in order that his mission might include the dead as well as the living.[8]

[1] 1 Pet. 1:3; cf. 1:23; 5:4.   [2] 1 Pet. 4:6, 13; 5:1.

[3] 1 Pet. 3:22; cf. 4:11.   [4] 1 Pet. 1:7, 8; 4:13; 5:1.

[5] 1 Pet. 3:18, 19–24; 3:18.   [6] 1 Pet. 1:11.

[7] 1 Pet. 3:18.

[8] 1 Pet. 3:19 f. Cf. Acts 2:27, according to which the spirit of the Messiah could not be left in Sheol. For the force of "in prison" cf. Apoc. Baruch, 23:4; 4 Esdras, 7:85, 95. This passage in 1 Peter has given rise to a large literature. Chief among others, reference can be made to STEVENS, Theology of the New Testament, pp. 304–11; SPITTA, Christi Predigt an die Geister; SALMOND, Christian Doctrine of Immortality[2], pp. 450–86.

The Peter of the epistle is at one with the Peter of Acts in holding that this same spirit came to the believer. From this divine source came the Christian's power and impulse to service and to endure persecution. Thence, too, came the certainty of the blessings of life in the messianic kingdom.[1] From the spirit came also sanctification,[2] with its attendant forgiveness and salvation. That the epistle does not elaborate this aspect of the Christian life should not obscure the fact that matters of religious experience are recognized. Here, as throughout the thought of the New Testament, we can clearly distinguish between the phenomena of spiritual life and their interpretation.

III

It is only in the sense that it is not Pauline that the epistle of James can fairly be correlated with primitive Christianity. Even more than in the case of 1 Peter is it probable that it represents chronologically a period much later than the apostolic times. External evidence all but forces us to such a conclusion.[3] That the book was written by the brother of Jesus is an honor which it never claims, nor indeed could claim, for itself. It is an early homily, with more or less polemic purpose against Paulinism. It is more concerned with conduct than with hope, and the messianic element in it is all but missing.[4] None the less, back of the exhortations of the epistle lies the expectation of the new age which is to come when the believer is to have a crown of life;[5] and, furthermore, the judgment and the judge were always to be expected.[6] The kingdom was to come to

---

[1] 1 Pet. 4:6, 10, 11, 14. [2] 1 Pet. 1:2.

[3] See O. CONE, "Epistle of James," in *Encyclopædia Biblica*. An independent judgment can be readily formed by examining the evidence in CHARTERIS, *Canonicity*. To the contrary see MAYOR, *Introduction to the Epistle of St. James*. BACON's discussion in his *Introduction*, pp. 159 ff., is a lucid presentation of the essential elements of the problem.

[4] This wholly apart from the question of the genuineness of Ἰησοῦ Χριστοῦ in 2:1.

[5] James 1:12. [6] James 4:12.

those who loved Jesus as Christ,[1] and condemnation was to come to those who broke the law.[2] Jesus the Lord was to come soon.[3] These elemental matters of Christian hope had become by the time the letter was written the source of inspiration and a basis for warning in the matter of conduct. Christian life was paramount to Christian profession,[4] but the work of the spirit is all but unmentioned.[5]

IV

At the opposite extreme from the scantiness of data in the epistle of James is the wealth of material in the Apocalypse of John. The time of its composition is now pretty generally held to be in the reign of Domitian, and at first sight it may seem, therefore, a mistake to use it as a source for primitive Christianity. At the same time, it is certainly not controlled by Paulinism, and its Jewish element is very pronounced. In fact, it is now commonly held to be composed of a number of Jewish apocalypses which have been rewritten and united by a Christian author into a strikingly unified Christian production.[6]

[1] James 2:5.

[2] James 2:11. It is worth noticing, however, that this "royal law" (vs. 8) or law of liberty (vs. 12) is subjective—something far more authoritative than Mosaism. Cf. GOULD, Biblical Theology of the New Testament, pp. 110–18.

[3] James 5:7, 8.   [4] James 2:14 f.

[5] James 4:5. This passage is capable of two renderings, but in either case it refers to the residence of a πνεῦμα in the Christian which is the gift of God.

[6] See BOUSSET, art. "Apocalypse of John," in Ency. Bib., and PORTER, art. "Revelation," in HASTINGS, Dictionary of the Bible. For various partition theories see BOUSSET, Der Antichrist (Eng. trans., Legend of the Antichrist); and works by SPITTA, Die Offenbarung Johannis; VISCHER, Die Offenbarung Johannis; SCHMIDT, Anmerkungen über die Komposition der Offenbarung Johannis; VÖLTER, Das Problem der Apocalypse; GUNKEL, Schöpfung und Chaos; BRIGGS, Messiah of the Apostles. A good general account of these views is given by BARTON, "The Apocalypse and Recent Criticism," in the American Journal of Theology, October, 1898. For our present purpose we may well waive the decision of the vexed problem of authorship, involving as it does the determination as to whether there were two Johns—the apostle and the presbyter—the latter of whom may have written or edited the Apocalypse. The data at our disposal are too vague and the criteria are too subjective to warrant complete certainty, and in any case the contents are intelligible enough to be dated with considerable precision. The habits of the apocalypse writers would lead one to favor the view that the work is pseudonymous, were it not for the persistent external evidence in favor of the Johannine authorship.

The general character of the book is clearly enough that of the other apocalypses. There are the same pictures of distress, the same promises of deliverance, the same use of symbols, and the same forecast of punishment for oppressors. Coupled with these strictly apocalyptic materials are the letters to the seven churches which are intended to show the ideal which should obtain among those bodies of Christians who are awaiting their Lord's return to establish a messianic era. It is to be expected, therefore, that, more than in any other book of the New Testament, the Revelation of John should conform to the general messianic scheme of the apocalypses. Nor are we disappointed. In it are the chief elements which belong to all Jewish messianism, with the exception that the kingdom is not expressly limited to Jews. Yet even its pictures of the New Jerusalem followed the general Jewish scheme. It was to have twelve gates, one for each tribe of Israel.[1]

The main purpose of the book is to describe the misery of the church, its assured deliverance by its Christ who is to return from heaven, the punishment which he will inflict after a desperate struggle upon his enemies, and the blessings of the redeemed, especially of the Christian martyrs.

More particularly, the main elements of messianism are always in evidence:

1. The two ages are clearly recognized.[2]

2. The present age is under the control of Satan, who besides being active is represented by anti-Christ, false prophets, and the Beast.[3]

3. The kingdom is to be established in the near future by Christ, not by social evolution. The attitude of the

---

[1] Rev. 21:10-12.

[2] There is no use of the two contrasted terms οὗτος ὁ αἰών and ὁ μέλλων αἰών, but the entire scheme of the book involves the end of one era and the beginning of another. Most of the book is devoted to portraying the events accompanying and preceding the transition.

[3] Rev. 12:9, 12; 20:2. *Cf.* the references under paragraph 4 below.

believer is one of prayer that it should come quickly.[1]
Already prepared in heaven, it is shown to the seer by an
angel, and its glories are described in detail.[2]

4. The period of judgment is very elaborately defined.
Here, even more than in the other portions of the New
Testament, the struggle between the two kingdoms is
elaborated. Satan is to be bound for a thousand years, and
Christ is to reign with those who, because of martyrdom,
are first to share in the resurrection.[3] This is the only
passage in the New Testament in which there is any reference to the reign of Christ for a thousand years upon the
present earth.[4] Subsequent to this period of joy there is to
be a fearful struggle, when Satan is to be loosed and the
nations, under Gog and Magog,[5] are to make a terrific onset
upon the messianic kingdom. They are to be utterly destroyed
by God, and the devil with the Beast and false prophets are
to be cast into the lake of fire.[6] This period of struggle
leads immediately to the establishment of the great judgment by God of the living and the dead. In accordance
with the Jewish expectation,[7] the records of every man
are in the heavenly books, and the judgment is pronounced
by God in accordance with these records.[8] As a result
of this judgment the wicked are sent to the lake of fire,[9]

[1] Eth. *Enoch*, 90:27-29; Slav. *Enoch*, 55:2; *4 Esdr.*, 19:26; 10:27 f.; 13:36; *Apoc.
Baruch*, 4:2-6; 32:2.

[2] Rev., chap. 21. This view of course assumes that the New Jerusalem is to be
identified with the messianic kingdom. See *Pss. Sol.*, 17:33, 34. For rabbinic references see VOLZ, *Jüdische Eschatologie*, 334 f. The figure of Jerusalem as the bride of
the Messiah is not found in Jewish apocalypses, *4 Esdr.*, 7:26, being probably a
Christian interpolation.

[3] Rev. 20:1-6.

[4] The nearest approach to it is 1 Cor. 15:24-27. The origin of a " thousand
years," as has already appeared, is to be seen in Slav. *Enoch*, chaps. 32, 33.

[5] *Cf.* Ezek. 38:2; 39:16.   [6] Rev. 20:7-10.

[7] See the important discussions of VOLZ, *Jüdische Eschatologie*, pp. 93 f. ; BOUSSET,
Religion des Judentums, p. 47.

[8] Rev. 20:11 f. *Cf.* Eth. *Enoch*, 47:3; 90:20; 97:6; *4 Esdr.*, 6:20.

[9] Rev. 21:8.

while the righteous are raised and sent to paradise. The wicked thus pass into the second death or endless period of torment.[1]

5. The kingdom is not to be Jewish, but Jews are represented as forming an integral part of the redeemed.[2]

6. The resurrection of the righteous is clearly taught and is one of the chief things which distinguish their future from that of the wicked, who apparently are only to be brought from Sheol to the judgment. There are in Revelation two resurrections; the first preceding the millennium, and the second following. At the first resurrection the martyrs alone are raised, while in the second all the righteous are raised to live in the new heavenly Jerusalem.[3] This new Jerusalem is established in the new earth, the old earth and the old heavens having passed away.[4] Throughout this glorious period the distinction between the Jews and the gentiles is not to be removed, but they are both alike to enjoy the privileges of the new universe in which joy is supreme.[5]

The chronological relation of these resurrections with the judgment is not elaborated, but a probable order seems to be: the parousia and the triumph over earthly foes and binding of Satan; the first resurrection (of martyrs); the millennium, the messianic conquest of evil spirits, the second resurrection; the general judgment; the punishment of the

---

[1] It is to be borne in mind that this concept of the second death is not one of annihilation, but is in accordance with the general expectations of Jewish thought to which reference has already been made. *Cf.* VOLZ, *Jüdische Eschatologie*, pp. 270-92. It means the final determination that death is to be unrelieved. It is a hopeless condition in which punishment is to be put upon those who are wicked. It is further to be borne in mind that there is no consistent eschatology in this book, and that passages might be quoted which would give a different future to the wicked; *e. g.*, Rev. 22:14, 15.

[2] Rev. 7:1 f. The new Jerusalem was to have twelve gates (Rev. 21:12). There is no evidence that the seer expected that all Israel would be saved.

[3] Rev. 20:4, 5, chap. 21.   [4] Rev. 21:1, 5.

[5] This distinction does not injure the universalism to which the older Jewish material has been adapted. *Cf.* Rev. 7:4-17.

wicked and reward of the righteous; the new world with the new Jerusalem.[1]

So far the interpreter can go with the conviction that he has grasped the main elements of this wonderful piece of literature. But minute interpretation—as, for instance, of the seals, bowls, trumpets, plagues, the woman, and even Babylon itself, the new name, the white stone, and the hidden manna—is confessedly fraught with serious difficulties. For our present purpose minute identifications are not required. It is enough to see that behind this apocalyptic vocabulary and schema were undoubtedly realities that contemporary readers would grasp. For, in the light of other apocalypses, as well as in that of such identifications as seem probable, it is apparent that the Apocalypse of John, like all the literature of its class, was intended to encourage pious souls—in its case Christians—during moments of persecution. Whether the persecutors were Romans (as seems most likely[2]) or Jews (a view hard to substantiate), the followers of Jesus were to look forward to their defeat. The forbidding pictures of the Beast and of the False Prophet, the strange armies that afflict the earth —these are clearly drawn from life, and their defeat meant as truly political changes as do the pictures of Daniel. Only the end was not to be a new world-state such as the older apocalypses had expected. Human life in its ordinary forms was to end in a great cataclysm, or, rather, series of cataclysms, and the eschatological kingdom of God, without the need of temple or sun, with its subjects no longer clothed in flesh and blood, was to close human history.

[1] For the order in apocalyptic literature see VOLZ, *Jüdische Eschatologie*, p. 256. It is a fair question, however, whether some of the references given there (*e. g.*, *4 Esdras*, 7:32; *Sib. Or.*, iv, 180; *Apoc. Baruch* 42:7 f.; 36:10), do not show Christian influences. For references to rabbinic belief as to a temporal reign of the Messiah and a first (and limited) resurrection, see WEBER, *Jüdische Theologie*, pp. 364 f. As to the rewards, see BACHER, *Die Agada der Tannaiten*, Vol. I, pp. 15, 16.

[2] See especially chap. 17.

Nor is the probability of historical identifications destroyed by the recognition in the book of elements drawn from Babylonian mythology. Indeed, it is all but certain that back of the seven spirits of God,[1] the twenty-four elders,[2] the struggle with Satan and the dragon, lie the figures impressed upon Jewish thought by Babylonian literature.[3] This, however, is not to say that these figures were consciously used by the writer of the Apocalypse without historical allusion. The book is not an academic product concerned with abstract questions of future centuries. On the contrary, like all other apocalypses, it impresses the reader with its intense interest in the historical circumstances and persons that were causing misery to the Christian church. The origin of a concept and of a vocabulary is not to be confused with the usage accorded them by a writer living in later centuries. No historical interpreter would think of the book except as one intended to bring the hope of coming glory to bear upon conscious misery. Whether or not the pictures it uses were first found in Babylonian literature, the book is not archæological, but practical. From its letters to the seven churches to the last apocalyptic vision it is full of instructions and exhortations to actual Christian life.

Such considerations as these lead one into the real heart of the Apocalypse. No more than any other of the writings of the New Testament does it make mere dreams and words supreme. That to which it finally looks is not the introduction of the messianic kingdom; it is the Christian's achievement of eternal life. The great reward to him that overcomes is to eat of the tree of life, and to wear the crown of life.[4]

[1] Rev. 1:4; 3:1; 4:5; 5:6; *cf.* Eth. *Enoch*, 90:21.

[2] Rev. 4:4, 10.

[3] See especially GUNKEL, *Schöpfung und Chaos;* STAVE, *Parsismus;* BOUSSET, *The Anti-Christ Legend;* and various articles in the *Encyclopædia Biblica*, HASTINGS'S *Dictionary of the Bible*, and the *Jewish Encyclopædia.*

[4] Rev. 2:7, 10.

To have one's name taken from the book of life is equivalent to supreme misfortune,[1] and this life is clearly the
opposite of that second death, so terrible in its limitations
and in its misery, which is to come to those who have not
accepted Jesus as Christ.[2] As presented in the Johannine
Apocalypse, this life is conceived of eschatologically, and the
Christian apparently does not enjoy it while living in the
body. This fact, however, is not to be interpreted as indicating any radical difference from other New Testament
thought regarding the present life of the believer. In it, as
in the Petrine teaching, it is the Holy Spirit that watches
over the churches,[3] and the real witness of Jesus is the
spirit of prophecy.[4] Faith in Jesus as Christ involves something more than the mere intellectual conviction, viz., actual
morality. Entrance into the New Jerusalem is refused those
who live evil lives.[5] Those who are to inherit the glorious
future are the saints,[6] whose good works follow with them to
the judgment and into eternity.[7] In fact, in the Apocalypse
we get a very satisfactory combination of the idea of the
relation of faith and of works.[8] Men are not saved by their
good works, but, having faith, they are to live righteously
despite all temptation and persecution. And, finally, the
writer of the apocalypse, like Peter and all the other New
Testament writers, is so possessed with the sense of human
imperfection that the Christian's salvation is wholly one of
grace. He becomes clean only by the blood of the Lamb.[9]

Thus even in this apocalypse, with its insistence upon the
messianic eschatology, we find also a recognition of the
vicarious death of the Christ, and the belief that eternal

[1] Rev. 3:5; 13:8; 17:8; 20:12, 15; 21:27.   [2] Rev. 2:11; 20:6, 14; 21:8.
[3] Rev. 2:7, 11, 17, 29; 3:6, 13, 22.   [4] Rev. 19:10.
[5] Rev. 21:8; 22:15.   [6] Rev. 5:8; 8:3, 4.
[7] Rev. 14:13.
[8] For example, Rev. 2:5, 16, 21, 22, 26; 3:8, 11, 19; 12:17; 14:12.
[9] Rev. 7:10, 14; 12:10; 19:1; cf. extreme statement in 21:27.

life is possible through the union of the believer in the messiahship of Jesus with God. Glorious as is the future to be, the seer uses it as a basis of appeal for purity and holiness of life and obedience to the guidance of the Spirit. All the elaborate details of the book center about this. The idea of the historical Jesus has been submerged in that of the glorious Christ now in heaven but reigning over his followers upon earth. The Christian life is not a mere following of rules, but one in accord with the spirit of the heavenly kingdom rather than that of "Babylon." The conflict among the superhuman beings has its counterpart in the believer's soul. And, what is more, just as there is the certainty of victory when the two kingdoms come into conflict, so is there certainty of victory on the part of even the humblest of those who live the life of faith. The ethical appeal is based upon rewards and punishments, but, none the less, it is the ethical appeal that is the real heart of the book.

CHAPTER II

THE ESCHATOLOGICAL MESSIANISM OF PAUL

I

THE similarity existing between the messianic hope of Paul and that of contemporary eschatological messianism becomes at once manifest when we make our accustomed comparison.

1. The entire Pauline scheme is conditioned upon the belief in the two ages. The apostle's terminology is somewhat varied, and he does not seem to have any single term to denote the new age. Generally, the ordinary terminology is to speak of the pre-messianic epoch in which he himself lived as "this age" or "this present age."[1] This age (κόσμος) is passing away.[2] Occasionally the thought of the future is extended in the later epistles, and we have the idea of accumulated ages.[3]

2. The present age is evil.[4] It is not expressly said to be under the control of Satan,[5] but the entire thought of Paul is that the Christian — the citizen of the coming kingdom — is opposed by superhuman powers which God is to overcome.[6]

3. The age which is to come, the messianic age, is to be introduced by the appearance of Christ. The new kingdom

[1] Rom. 12:2; 1 Cor. 1:20; 2:6, 8; 3:18; 2 Cor. 4:4; Gal. 1:4; Eph. 1:21; cf. 2:2; 1 Tim. 6:17; 2 Tim. 4:10; Tit. 2:12.

[2] 1 Cor. 7:31. Paul never uses the correlate of "this age," i. e., "the coming age," ὁ μέλλων αἰών, but the distinction between the two æons is distinctly implied by the one term he does employ. See also Eph. 1:21; 1 Cor. 10:11. In addition to the passages given above, cf. Rom. 8:18; 1 Cor. 3:19; 5:10.

[3] Eph. 2:7.   [4] Gal. 1:4.

[5] Unless it be in Rom. 16:20; 2 Cor. 4:4; cf. 1 Cor. 2:8.

[6] Rom. 16:20; 1 Cor. 7:5; 2 Cor. 2:11; 11:14; 12:7; 1 Thess. 2:18; 2 Thess. 2:9. See also Eph. 2:2.

to be established is eschatological, not dependent upon social evolution.[1] It is to be inherited,[2] and men were "called" into it.[3] In a certain sense Paul believed that the pre-messianic age had already begun. It was a time of "present distress."[4] In this particular he is at one with the belief of primitive Christianity that Christians were living in the "last days."

The term ἡ βασιλεία τοῦ θεοῦ is sometimes used by Paul with an eschatological connotation,[5] but it obviously exposed the Christian movement to misinterpretation outside of Palestine, and it is not often in evidence. A belief in the appearance of the kingdom, however, is one of the assumptions which the entire Pauline literature makes, and the hope of sharing in it becomes the basis of ethical appeal.[6]

It is clearly a mistake to hold that in Paul the ἐκκλησία and βασιλεία are essentially identical. The members of the church, it is true, are to enter and inherit the kingdom, but the two concepts are complementary rather than identical. The church was the body of Christ in the sense that he exercised authority over it from his heavenly throne.

The hypothesis that Paul distinguishes βασιλεία τοῦ

---

[1] The truth of this statement is apparent in the light of the entire attitude of Paul, as indicated in his social teachings, which will be considered in detail later. Especial attention, however, should be called to passages given below dealing with the coming (παρουσία) of Jesus as Christ.

[2] Gal. 5:21; 1 Cor. 6:9 f.   [3] 1 Thess. 2:12.

[4] 1 Cor. 7:26; *cf. 4 Esdras*, 5:8; 6:21; Eth. *Enoch*, 99:5. This passage, however, is not in the text as given by Charles.

[5] 1 Thess. 2:12; 2 Thess. 1:5; 15:24,50; Gal. 5:21; *cf.* 2 Tim. 4:1,18. The μετέστησεν in Col. 1:13 is not necessarily proleptic. The kingdom had not come to earth, but the believer on earth was already a citizen of the kingdom that was in heaven. *Cf.* Phil. 3:20. Similarly, the force of καλοῦντος in 1 Thess. 2:12. See also the references given below. 1 Cor. 4:20 evidently refers to the evidence of the believer's participation in the already existing (but not yet visible) kingdom, as seen in the gifts of the Spirit. It is also probably true (with KENNEDY, *St. Paul's Conceptions of the Last Things*, p. 290) that Paul clothed the idea of the kingdom in various guises; *e. g.*, the idea of the family (Rom. 8:17.).

[6] Rom. 14:17; 1 Cor. 4:20; 6:9,10; Gal. 5:21; Col. 1:13; Eph. 5:5; *cf.* Rom. 8:17. It will be noticed that these passages all have an eschatological force. For rabbinic parallels see DALMAN, *Worte Jesu*, pp. 97 f.

Χριστοῦ from βασιλεία τοῦ θεοῦ has already been considered.[1] It is enough here to say that the idea is out of keeping with the entire Pauline scheme. The kingdom of Christ is the kingdom of God in its judicial and punitive period. The work of the Christ is for a definite period[2] and intended to establish the absolute and unopposed reign of God.

4. Between the two ages was to be the judgment established by the Christ as the representative of God.[3] In fact, as will appear later, the entire Pauline soteriology centers around this expectation of the judgment. As with the other Christian evangelists, he endeavored to bring men to repentance by bringing them face to face with the certainty of that dread event of the future.[4] It was then that punishment was to be assigned[5] and rewards given.[6] This judgment was still future and is always conceived of eschatologically in connection with the parousia of Jesus.[7] It is interesting to notice, further, that Paul distinctly states that the saints are to share the work of the Christ in judging the angels.[8]

As in the case of contemporary Jewish thought, Paul sometimes joins to the idea of judgment that of a great struggle which is to precede the final decisions of the messianic conqueror. The idea of anti-Christ does not play

---

[1] P. 77. See, in general, J. Weiss, *Predigt Jesu*, etc. The chief passage is 1 Cor. 15:24-27.

[2] 1 Cor. 15:24.

[3] Rom. 2:16; *cf.* vss. 1-11; 3:5, 6. While it is true that the Christ is represented by Paul as sitting in judgment over all the world, it is clear from such passages as Rom. 2:16; 3:6; 1 Cor. 5:13, that God also is regarded as a judge. There is really no inconsistency in such a duplication, for, it will be recalled, the messianic hope did not distinguish sharply between the work of God and his Christ. The Christ always was doing God's work. See Volz, *Jüdische Eschatologie*, pp. 260, 232-34. Volz (p. 260) declares that the Christ is never represented as the world-judge in the apocalyptic literature, but of angels and devils. The distinction does not seem to me to be vital. *Cf.* Eth. *Enoch*, chap. 62.

[4] Acts 9:20, 22; 13:38-41; 17:31.   [5] Rom. 1:18; 2:8, 9.

[6] Rom. 2:7; *cf.* 8:18-39.

[7] Rom. 3:5, etc.; 2:12; 13:11, 12; 16:3-6; 1 Cor. 3:13; 4:5.

[8] 1 Cor. 6:2, 3.

quite the same rôle in Pauline thought as it does in that of the Revelation of John, but it none the less is present.[1] It is difficult to say whether the reference to the man of Lawlessness is immediately to Rome or to the Jews,[2] but probably it is to the latter.

Similarly, too, Paul agrees with certain aspects of current Jewish messianic hope in believing that the time immediately preceding the beginnings of the messianic age—the last days of the primitive church—that is to say, the actual time in which Paul was living—was to be one of suffering and distress.[3] The coming of the messianic age and judgment Paul certainly believed was to be soon.[4]

Paul was also at one with current expectations in believing that the time of the messianic appearance and judgment was in some way conditioned by the condition of a wicked humanity.[5]

The penalty which was to be inflicted in the judgment was the ordinary one of Jewish expectation—suffering, but more particularly it is negative—death; that is to say, the dead sinner was not to share in the resurrection which was to mark the beginning of the ineffable joy of those who were to enter the messianic age.[6] This matter will be considered later and at length, as it is a central point in the Pauline thought.

[1] 2 Thess. 2:7-9.

[2] *Cf.* Charles, *Eschatology*, p. 383; Thackeray, *Relation of St. Paul to Contemporary Thought*, pp. 135-41; Volz, *Jüdische Eschatologie, passim;* Weber, *Jüdische Theologie*, pp. 365 f.; Kennedy, *The Eschatology of Paul*, pp. 49 f., 215-19; Bousset *Anti-Christ;* and "Anti-Christ" in *Ency. Bib.; Religion des Judentums*, pp. 242-45.

[3] 1 Thess. 3:3, 4; *cf.* Dan. 12:1; Eth. *Enoch*, 48:8, 10; 50:2; *Apoc. Baruch*, 70; *Assump. Moses*, 10; *Jubilees*, 23. All Jewish literature, however, does not join such woes to the age preceding the coming of the Messiah as are suggested in 1 Cor. 7:26. But as to the perils of married women in the time of messianic struggle, see *4 Esdras* 5:8, 6, 21. *Cf.* Eth. *Enoch*, 99:5.

[4] 1 Cor. 7:29; 10:11; 15:51; 16:22; Rom. 13:11; 1 Thess. 4:15; Phil. 4:5. A belief in the speedy coming of deliverance is an essential of apocalyptic, and seems to have been common among the Jews of New Testament times.

[5] 2 Thess. 3:1, 2. [6] 2 Cor. 5:3; Rom. 5:12, 14, 17; 6:23.

5. Paul breaks with Jewish messianism in that he holds that the messianic kingdom is not to be limited to Jews. This is, of course, one of the fundamental points in Paulinism and hardly requires explication. This universalizing habit may in a measure explain why he does not constantly use the term βασιλεία. As has already appeared, the term is no stranger to him, and the concept is to be felt even when not explicitly referred to.[1] The fact that he conceived of Jesus as the Christ carries with it in itself the concept of the kingdom,[2] and the entire Pauline literature is addressed to those who are awaiting the coming of God's kingdom. The apostle's chief purpose is to be seen in his effort to draw out the ethical implication of this element of Christian faith[3] and to meet certain objections which arise on the side of those who would limit the blessings of the new age and kingdom to the Jews. For this reason, as well as for the danger of the misinterpretation of the term as one implying political revolution, Paul is more concerned with the prospect of assuring the followers of Jesus of acquittal at the messianic judgment and of entrance into eternal life than he is with the kingdom itself. At the best, the phrase ἡ βασιλεία τοῦ θεοῦ was Jewish, and liable to perpetuate the struggle in which Paul was for so many years engaged. In this particular we see the general tendency of the New Testament thought inaugurated by Jesus and completed by the Fourth Gospel to divert attention from the kingdom itself to the qualities of life which are demanded of its subjects.

6. The resurrection of those who are to share in the messianic age is perhaps the most striking element in the teaching of Paul. It is invariably placed over against the

---

[1] Cf. TITIUS, Neutestamentliche Lehre von der Seligkeit, Vol. II, p. 32. For a study of the possible influence of the teaching of Jesus upon Paul in this particular, see FEINE, Jesus Christus und Paulus, pp. 170–74.

[2] Cf. Acts 17:7.

[3] See, for example, Rom. 14:17.

unrelieved and miserable state of death which is the punishment of sin.[1] The details of this expectation will be considered presently.

7. Jesus was the personal Christ. He was in heaven,[2] from which he was to come to bring salvation and to establish judgment. Thereafter there would be a messianic reign.[3] The chief argument for believing that Jesus was the Christ is to be seen in his resurrection.[4] Just the course of argument by which Paul found evidence of the messiahship of Jesus in his resurrection, it is at this distance a little difficult to say, unless it be that of Acts, chap. 13.[5] It is to be noticed that this argument does not make the resurrection the origin of the belief in Jesus as Christ. This already had appeared; the disciples believed him to be the future Christ before his death. It does argue, however, that the resurrection would become a support and corroboration of this faith in messiahship. Nothing could be more untrue to the position of the apostle than the speculation that Paul's belief in the resurrection can be reduced to a conviction that God would not let so good a man as Jesus be annihilated. Paul did not believe that Jesus was immortal because he was the Christ, but that he was the Christ because God had raised him from the dead. He was not thereby *made* the Christ; he had been such during his earthly life, and indeed from before time. The resurrection simply exhibited this glorious fact and laid a foundation for the apostle's

[1] Rom. 5:21; 6:20-23. See also Acts 13:46-48; Rom. 2:7; 5:12-21; 6:5, 22, 23; 7:5, 6; Gal. 6:8; 1 Cor. 15; and innumerable other passages. The explicit term ζωή αἰώνιος is used as the supreme good in Rom. 2:7; 5:21; 6:22, 23; Gal. 6:8; 1 Tim 1:16; 6:12; Tit. 1:2; 3:7.

[2] Rom. 8:34.   [3] 1 Cor. 1:15, 24-28.   [4] Rom. 1:4 and often.

[5] The elaborate and ingenious argument of BARTON, "The Spiritual Development of Paul," *New World*, March, 1899 (pp. 111-24), deserves consideration. Its most important element is: The ordinary messianic belief recognized the resurrection only of the righteous and the release from death of such as Enoch, Elijah, and Moses. They would be "children of God" as well as sons of the resurrection (Luke 20:36). Hence Jesus would have had the same experience only on the ground that his claim to messiahship were true.

faith.[1] This resurrection of Jesus will be seen to play a
very large rôle in the Pauline thought.   In fact, from one
point of view, the Pauline soteriology is a generalization of
the experience of Jesus.   In view of this fact, it is idle to
belittle the historical element in Paulinism.

It appears from this comparison that Paul shared largely[2]
in the eschatological messianism of the apocalypses.   When
one comes to consider his views in detail, it will appear
that eschatology is really the center of Pauline thought.
He, like the Christians of Jerusalem, found the beginning of his Christian life in the conviction that Jesus was
the Christ, destined to return from the world of spirits
where he was already in supreme authority, to do the work
of the expected eschatological Messiah upon the earth.
How far he was forced by the facts of the belief of Jesus and
by his own experience to modify the pharisaic messianism,
and to transfer the emphasis from the interpretation of
Jesus to the significance of Jesus himself and to the Spirit,
will appear presently.

II

For in the case of Paul, as in the case of the other New
Testament writers, it would be a serious mistake to overlook
the radical changes which came in the messianic concepts
which he had inherited because of the positive data afforded
him by the historical career of Jesus.   The Christ with
Paul was not a speculation or the product of faith.   He was
real.   Inevitably, therefore, with him, even more than with
the other apostles, the facts connected with the historical

---

[1] The argument of GUNKEL, *Zum religionsgeschichtlichen Verständnis des Neuen
Testamentes*, that the belief in the resurrection of the Christ was included in con-
temporary unofficial messianism, is untenable in view of Gunkel's own statements.
Cf. op. cit., p. 79.

[2] *Cf.* WREDE, *Aufgabe und Methode der sogenannten Neutestamentlichen Theologie*,
p. 66, "There is a Pauline doctrine of redemption . . . . but there is—to speak
cum grano salis—no Pauline angelology and eschatology, but only a Jewish or
primitive Christian." There are both truth and error in the statement.

career of Christ set certain conditions which led to the modification of an *a priori* expectation. The inherited messianic concept was but the starting point of the new Christian thought which Paul inaugurated.

First among these modifications were those resulting from the humiliation to which Jesus had been subjected. The Christ, notwithstanding the fact that he was next in importance to God,[1] had submitted to the humiliations of humanity and had suffered the extremes of suffering, contumely, and death. The doctrinal consequences of this fact are, perhaps, the most profound contribution made by Paul to religious thinking—a contribution which needs only to be estimated in a truly historical light to be recognized as possessing supreme evangelical value. Here, as in so many other instances, Paul was dominated by a reverence for historical facts which some of his modern interpreters might well emulate. And here, too, he was at one with the early apostolic Christianity. There was a mystery in the unexpected appearance of Christ, and there were unanswerable problems from the point of view of Judaism and of philosophy,[2] but in it was limitless help for those oppressed by the problems of human suffering and by the apprehension of death. It was not a mere man who had died; it was the Christ.

A second modification, again already made by primitive Christianity, was the inevitable outcome of the same regard for historical reality. The fact that the Christ had died in no way diminished his messiahship. It rather opened up a more magnificent vista of authority. Dead, he had been raised, the first-fruits of all those in whose life the spirit of God was working. It may well be emphasized that, with Paul, the resurrection of Jesus was a historical fact and not a product of faith. Paul did not come to the messianic

[1] Phil. 2:5-11.　　　　　[2] 1 Cor. 1:23, 25.

conviction as to Christ by precisely the same path as that followed by Peter. The early apostles had believed that Jesus was the Christ by virtue of their association with him, and this conviction had been confirmed by his resurrection. Paul, on the contrary, had found it impossible to believe that the Nazarene who had been crucified was the Christ until the evidence that he had been raised from the dead declared to him that messianic quality.[1] But, if raised from the dead, Jesus was already Christ in the spiritual world. Through the spirit he was already exercising his authority from heaven. Thence he would presently appear to do upon the earth those things which the eschatological expectation of the Christ in a general way prescribed. This expectation of the return of Jesus was therefore in Paul's case, as in the case of the apostles, a corollary of the messianic interpretation. The argument was simple and convincing: Jesus was the Christ; he had not done his messianic work; he had gone to heaven; and therefore he must return to earth to perform his proper work.[2] It was this return and the belief that those who had accepted him as their messianic king would at the Christ's appearance be made perfect members of the messianic kingdom, and so saved, that became one of the dominant elements in Paulinism. Holding fast, on the one side, to the Davidic descent of Jesus,[3] Paul yet saw the real significance of his Lord's work in his future manifestation in the body of the resurrection. The question of the times and the seasons when he should return upon the earth to exhibit the messianic authority and glory he was already exercising in heaven, is one about which Paul does not particularly speculate. He was convinced that it would be soon.[4] In his earlier career he

---

[1] Rom. 1:4.   [2] Phil. 2:20, 21.   [3] Rom. 1:3.

[4] Rom. 13:11; 1 Cor. 7:29; 15:51 (cf. 12:26; 16:22) ; 1 Thess. 4:15; 5:2; Phil. 4:5. See Teichmann, *Auferstehung und Gericht*, pp. 13 f.; Holtzmann, *Neutestamentliche Theologie*, Vol. II, p. 188. The rabbis also believed that the coming of Messiah would be soon. *Cf.* Weber, *Jüdische Theologie*, pp. 334 f. Kennedy, *St. Paul's Conceptions*

evidently expected it to be in his own lifetime. Later this expectation seems to have become somewhat modified by the delay in the fulfilment of his hope, and he seems to have expected that he himself might die before the parousia.[1] But he never abandoned his general expectation that the time was short and that the kingdom was at the door. It was merely a question of his own individual experience — as to whether he would be among those who slept and so be actually raised from the dead, or among those who were not to die, but who "were left,"[2] and were to be "changed."[3]

When Paul came to describe this appearance of Christ and the kingdom, he was without historical data, and the details he gives are probably derived from contemporary expectations both Christian and Jewish. The Lord was to descend with a shout of an archangel at the "last trump."[4] As has already appeared, the apocalyptic hope always implied existing misery quite as much as deliverance. The apocalypses were always the messengers of hope to men in distress. It would be easy, therefore, for those possessed of that hope in the apostolic times quite as truly as in later times to see in any increase of misery, whether or not it was the work of the persecutors, the evidence of the approaching end. Thus Paul explained the appearance of persecution in the Thessalonian church. As has been noticed, he introduced the idea of anti-Christ already engaged in a struggle with the Christ.[5] In view of the fact, therefore,

of the Last Things, p. 163, very properly refuses to hold to developing stages in the Pauline eschatology. CHARLES, Eschatology, chap. 12, certainly fails to substantiate the opposite view. Really to appreciate Paul's expectations of the time of the parousia attention should be given to a great number of passages in which he refers to it and the judgment in a general way. See, e. g., Rom. 8:23; 2 Cor. 5:1-7; Col. 1:22, 28 (παραστῆσαι); 3:4. The hopes of Israel's conversion before the parousia in Rom., chap. 12, are to be interpreted from this point of view.

[1] Rom. 11:25; Phil. 3:11.   [2] 1 Thess. 4:15.   [3] Rom. 14:8.

[4] 1 Thess. 4:16; 1 Cor. 15:51. Cf. 4 Esdr., 6:20-23. WEBER, Jüdische Theologie, p. 369, gives parallels from rabbinic thought. See also KABISCH, Eschatologie des Paulus, pp. 238 f.

[5] 2 Thess. 2:1-10; cf. 1 Cor. 7:26-28

that persecution was coming upon the church because of
its loyalty to the Christ, as well as in view of the evident
struggle of Christ against the demons evinced in the
power of those possessed of the Spirit, Paul was convinced
that he and all those to whom he wrote were living in the
last days.

Paul in speaking of the παρουσία evidently does not contradict the recorded sayings of Jesus, however he may deal
with other matters than those treated by Jesus.   Indeed, in
the light of 1 Thess. 4:15, it would not be impossible to
hold that the apostle's thought was directly affected by
the teachings of his Lord.[1]   Whether or not he derived his
conviction as to the speedy return of Jesus from his Lord's
own words can probably never be satisfactorily answered.
It is not improbable that in some degree the belief did rest
on some of the words of Jesus recorded in Mark,[2] but there is
no absolute need of discovering such an origin.   All apocalyptic hope looked for speedy deliverance, and the Christians
of the New Testament as a class expected the coming of
Jesus within their lifetime.

III

The facts already noticed direct us to the proper point of
approach to Paulinism as a system.   Historical orthodoxy,
as represented by the older Protestant theologians and practically all those of the Roman church, has come closer to
the center of the apostle's thought than those later interpreters who have made the mystical union of the believer
with Christ or faith as an incipient and potential righteousness the center of Paulinism.   Even a superficial study of
Paul's thought will convince one that there is much truth in

[1] But see TEICHMANN, *Auferstehung und Gericht.*

[2] P. 117 above.   Even MUIRHEAD, *Eschatology of Jesus*, 135 f., though explaining
away all personal reference, admits that Jesus expected the fall of the Jewish state
and the introduction of a new age during his own generation.

these later views. The apostle certainly believed in the union of the believer with Christ, and quite as certainly believed faith in Jesus as Christ to be the condition of moral advance. But neither of these two conceptions forms really the center of his thought. Both by his experience and his antecedents Paul could hardly have made anything but eschatological messianism the co-ordinating schema of a system that centered about a belief that Jesus was the Christ.[1] He had been a Hebrew of the Hebrews; a Pharisee, as touching the law blameless.[2] As regards experience, his acceptance of Jesus as the Christ[3] was the turning-point of his career.

Evidently the content of the predicate "Christ" would be a vital element of his new thought. Jesus he had known at least by reputation.[4] Conceptions of the character and office of a Christ he had derived from Judaism. He had but to bring the personage and the conception together, that is, have faith. In this he was at one with the other apostles. He was interpreting a historical character in terms of inherited concept. The faith that Jesus was the Christ was the beginning of the apostle's Christian life. From it followed those deeper experiences which he describes in terms of the Spirit. When Paul came to extend this new faith and this experience into something like a system, his writings at once

[1] It is interesting to notice that in the same proportion as investigators have freed themselves from dogmatic presupposition and have come under the influence of the historical spirit, they emphasize this thought. In his preface to his admirable volume, *St. Paul's Conceptions of the Last Things*, KENNEDY has this significant sentence: "In an investigation of Paulinism, undertaken for another purpose, I had been growingly impressed by the vital bearing of St. Paul's eschatological outlook upon his theology as a whole. His conceptions of the Last Things were manifestly factors of supreme importance in the organization of his religious thought." Kennedy goes on to insist that Paul has no systematic eschatology. In this, as may appear, he is both right and wrong.

[2] Phil. 3:5; Acts 23:6; *cf*. Gal. 1:13, 14.

[3] Gal. 1:15, 16; Acts 9:15; 22:21; 26:17, 18.

[4] 2 Cor. 5:16. However this passage may be interpreted, it is certainly impossible to doubt that he who was persecuting people for accepting Jesus as Christ should have known something about Jesus.

make evident how formative in his thought was his early training. Eternal life, as enjoyed in its initial stages, was co-ordinate with the historical Jesus as a focus of all his thought.

Nor do the Thessalonian letters represent a passing or a local phase of the apostle's thought. Eschatology, buttressed as it was by the historical data furnished by the experiences of Jesus, always conditioned it. All Paul's converts, not merely those at Thessalonica, had been taught concerning the new king Jesus,[1] and had left their former gods or cult to wait for the appearance of God's Son from heaven.[2] To this event, as not only the supreme moment of human history, but also as a supreme motive for right living, Paul repeatedly returns.[3] For that day[4] of the revelation of Jesus Christ[5] with his angels[6] he and all his converts looked, waiting for the adoption, viz., the resurrection of the body.[7] Then was to come the judgment for all men.[8] Then were all things to be tried by fire.[9] Then were to be assigned the two great awards: "vengeance to those who know not God, and to those that obey not the gospel of our Lord Jesus, who shall suffer punishment, even eternal destruction from the face of the Lord and from the glory of his might"[10]— "wrath and indignation, tribulation and anguish;"[11] but eternal life with all the blessings of the resurrection to those "who by patience in well-doing seek for glory and honor and incorruption.[12] To be worthy of the new kingdom then to be established is Paul's repeated prayer for himself and his converts.[13] While in it alone, through the possession of a

[1] Acts 17:7; cf. 1 Tim. 1:1. [2] 1 Thess. 1:10; 2:20; 3:13; cf. Phil. 1:6, 10.

[3] Rom. 8:23-25; 1 Cor. 6:9, 10; 15:23. [4] 1 Cor. 1:8; 3:13; 2 Cor. 1:14.

[5] 1 Cor. 1:7, 8; Phil. 1:6, 10. [6] 2 Thess. 1:7.

[7] Rom. 8:18-25.

[8] Acts 17:30, 31; Rom. 2:6, 16; 1 Cor. 4:5. Cf. Rom. 2:16; 14:10 f.; 2 Cor. 5:10.

[9] 1 Cor. 3:11-15. [10] 2 Thess. 1:8, 9.

[11] Rom. 2:8. [12] Rom. 2:7.

[13] 1 Thess. 2:12 (cf. vs. 10); 2 Thess. 1:5; Gal. 6:7-9; 1 Cor. 15:58.

"spiritual body"[1] was to be ended that struggle between the σάρξ and the πνεῦμα which was the tragedy of the unbeliever, and the cause of continuous discipline and struggle on the part of the believer. And finally, Paul's entire teaching concerning justification by faith is conditioned by this eschatological judgment.

[1] Rom. 8:23-25; 1 Cor. 15:44.

CHAPTER III

THE THEOLOGICAL ASPECTS OF PAULINE MESSIANISM

To ADD an eschatological expectation to an otherwise complete system is one thing; to make eschatological messianism the correlating thought of an entire system is quite another. Recent speculative theology is inclined toward the former treatment of the matter, but Paulinism is an example of the latter. The two great elements of the apostle's thought were, first, as has already been said, the belief that Jesus was the eschatological Christ, and, second, the experience of the Spirit which came in consequence of such belief. All of Paul's thinking was an ellipse about these two foci. How far the messianic scheme controlled his speculations and arguments is now to be considered.

I

With all the early Christian writers, Paul made ethics depend upon religion, and deep within the religious concept was that of rewards and punishment which were to be determined at the judgment.[1]

Paul's starting-point for all his evangelic thinking is that of the prophets—human guilt. Liability to punishment was, however, a matter not of national, but of individual concern. While it is very probably an overstatement to declare that such a concept was a necessity because of Paul's apologetic presentation of Christianity (Wernle), it is none the less apparent from the first chapter of the letter to the Romans that condemnation to punishment was to be

[1] See KABISCH, *Eschatologie des Paulus*, chap. 1; KENNEDY, *op. cit.*, chap. 1; TITIUS, *Neutestamentliche Lehre von der Seligkeit*, Vol. II, pp. 68-70, has a discriminating discussion of the real significance of eschatology in the Pauline teaching.

feared by all. Theoretically, it is true, Paul would recognize the possibility that a man might so live as not to be liable to punishment which came to those who broke God's law, but practically both Jew and gentile were without excuse and in danger of punishment.[1] In this recognition of the finality of moral law he was in advance of most of the Jewish theologians of his day. They were not oblivious to sin or to the "evil impulse," but their profound conviction as to the exceptional favor to be shown the descendants of Abraham tended to add ethnic to genuinely moral estimates of conduct and future conditions.[2]

The origin of sin which brought guilt to the individual can hardly be said to have been discussed by Paul in detail, but the controlling concepts are to be found in his psychology. Untechnical and empirical as it is in its broad lines, it is essentially that of pharisaism. Christian personality included two elements: flesh and spirit. Flesh may be defined in a general way as the survival of animalism in humanity. It includes not only the physical body, but also such impulses and habits as characterize the animal struggle for existence. As physical it is corruptible, and as physico-psychological it is the ready instrument of sin.[3]

---

[1] Rom. 2:1-16.

[2] It is easy to overstate matters at this point and to overemphasize rabbinic minimizing of ethical matters. It should be borne in mind, however, that nationalism with the Jew had in itself ethical elements. The Jew had the Thorah; the gentiles had it not, and were consequently evil. It would be exceedingly difficult to prove that any reputable Jewish teacher seriously held that mere birth, apart from religious and moral relations, was to be a basis of acquittal at the judgment. For the most favorable presentation of the matter of talmudic morality, see LAZARUS, *The Ethics of Judaism*. See also BOUSSET. *Religion des Judentums*, pp. 391-401. The Jewish literature sometimes states the genuinely ethical character of the judgment clearly. *Cf. Apoc. Bar.*, 13:8; (Jer.) *Pea* 2b. On the other hand, some of the later rabbis completely shut the door of hope to the gentiles. See references in WEBER, *Jüdische Theologie*, chap. 6.

[3] 1 Cor. 2:11; 5:5; Gal. 3:3; 4:29; 5:16 f.; 6:8; Rom. 8:2; 9:13. See GUNKEL, *Fleisch und Geist*. For an elaborate lexicographical study of terms, but in which no use is made of anthropology, see SCHOEMAKER, "The Use of רוּחַ and of πνεῦμα in the Old Testament, and of πνεῦμα in the New Testament," *Journal of Biblical Literature*, Vol. XXIII (1904), pp. 13-67. 1 Cor. 15:50-54 shows the corrupt nature

On the other hand, the spirit is that element of man that is not physical and is essentially of the same character as God. It would hardly be safe to deny that Paul conceived of the spirit as in some attenuated way material, or that he believed that it could exist in a bodiless form.[1] Whether Paul would hold that the unregenerate man had a spirit is doubtful. Any final statement seems excluded by the fact that the apostle is chiefly concerned with psychology in its moral and religious sides, and is not in the least interested in it in a purely scientific way. In view of the current anthropology of his day, it might be presupposed that he would hold to a dichotomy of body and spirit (soul). Such a passage as 2 Cor. 7:1, which speaks of the "filthiness of the flesh and spirit," as well as 1 Cor. 2:11, where the "spirit of man" is spoken of in a genuinely psychological sense, argue that Paul did hold that a man before his reception of the Holy Spirit had a spirit of his own.[2] But the apostle never elaborates this view, even if he never actually contradicts it. All but exclusively πνεῦμα is used of Christians, and in such relations as tend to obscure its distinction from the Holy Spirit. Perhaps it could be defined material-

and future of the flesh. See, in general, LÜDEMANN, *Anthropologie des Apostels Paulus*. The distinction sometimes drawn between ψυχή and πνεῦμα is not to be found in Paul except in 1 Thess. 5:23, where the tripartite formula is used in a loose sense. But see DELITZSCH, *Biblical Psychology*, and LAIDLAW, *Bible Doctrine of Man*. See also, CONE, *Paul, The Man, The Missionary, and The Teacher*, chap. 10; PFLEIDERER, *Paulinism*, Vol. I, chap. 1; THACKERAY, *The Relation of St. Paul to Contemporary Jewish Thought*, chap. 2, which gives a number of interesting parallelisms between Paul and pharisaism. On the Jewish psychology see VOLZ, *Jüdische Eschatologie*, pp. 146-48.

[1] *Cf.* "naked," 2 Cor. 5:3; PFLEIDERER, *Paulinism*, Vol. I, pp. 201; KABISCH, *Eschatologie des Paulus*, pp. 113. The current Jewish belief was also dichotomous (Eth. *Enoch*, 108:7 f.). Human personality consisted of body and spirit. The latter is pre-existent and immortal. (See BARTON, *Journal of Biblical Literature*, 1902, pp. 78-91.) The former is corruptible. The two were united at conception, the spirit being brought from the "treasure house" in the seventh heaven by its guardian angel (WEBER, *Jüdische Theologie*, p. 212). They were separated at death. After death souls went to Sheol. For the figure of clothing and unclothing with reference to life and death, see Slav. *Enoch*, 22:8; Eth. *Enoch*. 62:15, 15; *4 Esdras*, 2:39.

[2] So, too, Rom. 8:16.

istically as that portion of the Holy Spirit "given" to each individual Christian; and more psychologically as the moral and religious elements of human personality brought into new consciousness and power[1] through their union with the Spirit of God;[2] or from another point of view, it is God in human consciousness.

Our discussion, however, would not be complete without a consideration of a second line of contrast, viz., between σῶμα and νοῦς. In a general way, this contrast is parallel with that between σάρξ and πνεῦμα, but it emphasizes psychological rather than moral elements. At the same time, Paul regards the νοῦς—at least that of the Christian—as possessed of high moral ideals. It is that which wishes (impotently) to keep the law of God,[3] but is hindered by the body ("members").[4] It is the mind that, when renewed, transforms the entire personality[5] until the will of God is known. On the other hand, its evil transformation affects the personality for evil.[6] One might even define it as reason exercised in and capable of moral distinctions. It would be a mistake precisely to identify νοῦς and πνεῦμα,[7] for in the untechnical psychology of the apostle the two are contrasted according as emphasis is centered upon the work of the Holy Spirit. The spirit may exercise in fullest the divine afflatus, and yet the rational faculties remain unsatisfied.[8] Similarly σῶμα is not precisely the same as σάρξ, for it does not possess those qualities which sometimes might be described as ψυχικός as well as σάρκινος. It is purely physical, destined to disappear at death.

Yet it would be a mistake to draw the line of distinction

---

[1] Gal. 5 : 22, 23.

[2] For approximate parallels see Slav. *Enoch*, 30 : 8; *Wis. Sol.*, 2 : 23, 24.

[3] Rom. 7 : 22, κατὰ τὸν ἔσω ἄνθρωπον, is equivalent to νοός of vs. 23. *Cf.* further Rom. 7 : 25.

[4] Rom. 7 : 23; *cf.* vs. 24.   [5] Rom. 12 : 2.   [6] Eph. 4 : 17.

[7] But *cf.* 1 Cor. 2 : 14 with 2 : 16, and Rom. 11 : 34.

[8] 1 Cor. 14 : 14. Similarly Eph. 4 : 23, although the phrase is difficult.

too sharply when Paul speaks of either σῶμα and σάρξ in relation to sin.[1] The flesh is indeed formally made the opposite of the spirit, and the body (with its members) the opposite of the mind, but the two sets of contrasts are often almost identical.[2]

These two sets of parallel antitheses result from looking at humanity from different points of view, and with two sets of correlated ideas.[3] But a certain area is common to both. Neither "mind" nor "spirit" is a property of the physical nature; both "body" and "flesh" are separable from the non-physical element, and both involve the punishment of sin in the individual, viz., death. In a word, both are mortal, and mortal because of sin. Whatever other matters are connoted by his terms, it is this great difference that controls the apostle's thought.[4]

It follows that perfection is that state of life in which the spirit is freed from the flesh or the body, and lives in a body especially adapted to it, that is, spiritual.[5] Doubtless Paul was confirmed in this position by his knowledge of the resurrection of Jesus.

Christianity, thus, as Paul conceives of it, deals not merely with moral questions, but, if we may use the term, with onto-

---

[1] Rom. 8:9; Gal. 5:24; cf. Rom. 6:6, 13 with Gal. 5:19. See HOLTZMANN, Neutestamentliche Theologie, Vol. II, p. 40; CONE, Paul, etc., pp. 228, 229.

[2] In 1 Cor. 5:3, 4; Col. 2:5 the contrast is made between σῶμα and πνεῦμα, and 1 Cor. 5:5 speaks of the destruction of σάρξ as a condition of the saving of the spirit at the day of the Lord.

[3] Perhaps one might even say that σῶμα and νοῦς were the outcropping of a Hellenistic consciousness; σάρξ and πνεῦμα, of a Semitic. And the two were never systematized.

[4] Cf. the "outer" and the "inner" man; 2 Cor. 4:16; Eph. 3:16; Rom. 7:22.

[5] 1 Cor. 15:44, 46. In this Paul is at one with the Pharisees who are said by JOSEPHUS, Ant., xviii, 1:3; War, ii, 8:14, to hold that the souls of the righteous after death pass into new bodies. Cf. 4 Esdras, 7:75 f.; Eth. Enoch, 46:6; Sanhedrin, 10:1. Jewish eschatology, however, was not unanimous in this particular. Some writers evidently believed in the actual reappearance of the physical body that had been buried; e. g., Sib. Or., iv, 180 f. See WEBER, Jüdische Theologie, pp. 352 f. Apoc. Bar., chaps. 49 and 50, on the other hand, holds that, although, for the sake of preserving and exhibiting personal identity, bodies should be raised with all their peculiarities, those of the righteous would subsequently be changed.

logical as well. Sin worked changes in a man's mode of existence. Salvation also must be concerned, on the one side with a deliverance from death, and, on the other, with the entrance into the larger and higher life possible for those who are not restrained by the flesh. In such a concept as this it is evident that psychological as well as moral considerations are of weight.

Paul does not conceive of the individual as originating sin, but as an unhappy wretch who because of his flesh is particularly liable to sin and its penalty.[1] Rabbinism had within it an element which is here singularly attractive from a speculative point of view, the evil impulse, יֵצֶר הָרָע.[2] This was created by God and existed in all people.[3] It is possible to show that this evil impulse was an element in the pharisaic anthropology, and it would be natural to appeal to it as a means of elucidating the Pauline doctrine of sin. Unfortunately, however, evil impulse, though present, plays no large rôle in Jewish thought contemporary with Paul, and certainly was not so much an explanation as a representation of the fact of evil in men. Nor does it necessarily involve a contrast between body and soul. The apostle's hamartology works along a different line. Sin is the outcome of Adam's disobedience.[4] Sinners were "the children of disobedience."[5] Since Adam's act sin has been a force in the world, working its evil results upon humanity.[6] The law, Paul held, had

[1] The rôle played by Satan, who is identified with the serpent, is seen in 2 Cor. 11:3.

[2] For a discussion of this important element of rabbinic ethics see Weber, Jüdische Theologie, especially pp. 215–18; Bousset, Die Religion des Judentums, pp. 384 f. Especially see the admirable essay by Porter, "The Yeçer Hara," in (Yale) Biblical and Semitic Studies, pp. 93–156.

[3] Sirach, 17:31; 21:11; 15:14; Test. XII Pat. Asher, 1. This relegating of the origin of sin to God was an element of perplexity to the rabbis, but they found some relief in the belief that God had also created the Thorah as a remedy; Kiddushin, 306; Bacher, Die Agada des Tannaiten, Vol. II, p. 337.

[4] Rom. 5:19.   [5] Eph. 2:2; 5:6; Col. 3:6.

[6] For rabbinical views as to Adam's fall and sin cf. Sanday and Headlam, Com. in Romans, pp. 136 f. For parallel between these and Paul's see Thackeray, Relation of St. Paul to Contemporary Jewish Thought, chap. 2.

been given by God's grace in order to show to men what things were sinful,[1] and thus to make it the easier for them to avoid the punishment of sin—a view not unlike that of the rabbis themselves.[2] But men yielded to the force that was working upon their personality seeking through the flesh to control the spirit, and the law given in grace really increased their unhappy lot. Sin became transgression, and a man's punishment was consequently more severe.

In order to appreciate this conception of the working of sin, it is necessary to recall that the Semitic mind was incapable of thinking long with the aid of abstract definitions. Inevitably the most abstract conceptions were to a greater or less degree personified. In the case of Paul it was not merely that he regarded a man as in the midst of a universe filled with superhuman beings seeking to work him harm. Sin, the disobedience of God's law, whether known or unknown, was also endeavoring, like a fearful spiritual monster, to overcome every human being. It worked through the flesh, which in itself is not sinful,[3] but is susceptible to the influence of sin, and incapable of withstanding it or of avoiding its consequences. The working of sin itself is traced by Paul in a variety of ways, but perhaps never more strikingly than in the first chapter of Romans, in which he describes the downfall of the heathen. Ceasing to be obedient to God, and to such knowledge of him as they had, they became vile in every particular and suffered the natural consequences.[4] In his own experience also Paul knew of the tremendous power which sin exerted over a person through the intermediate agency of the flesh.[5] In his "inner man" he wished to obey the law of God, but,

---

[1] Rom. 3:20; 5:13; 7:7 f.; Gal. 3:19 f.

[2] *Cf.* WEBER, *Jüdische Theologie*, pp. 20 f., for references.

[3] Rom. 7:18.   [4] Rom. 1:18-32.

[5] Rom. 7:13-25. *Cf.* WERNLE, *Christ und Sünde bei Paulus*, pp. 100-106.

because of the control exercised over him by sin, he was quite incapable of moral freedom. He was therefore utterly without hope, needing deliverance from the body[1] quite as much as from sin.

II

The punishment which sin brought was death.[2] There has been no small discussion as to just what Paul meant by this term.[3] On the part of those of a speculative turn of mind it has been thought that death was to a large extent a figurative expression intended by Paul to set forth the moral decay of a personality, and the suffering which would therefore ensue. Such a conception is more akin to Greek thought than to Semitic, and there is no clear reason for giving the term such an abstract force. The Pauline conception of death springs from the Pauline conception of the constitution of man. Sin caused the separation of the two elements of personality. Adam had disobeyed. Through his disobedience sin had entered into the world, and physical[4] death through sin.[5] Such a concept as this is not abstract, but thoroughly concrete. The spirit was separated from the body, the body decayed,[6] the spirit remained "naked,"[7] and after the judgment, unless delivered, was to suffer misery as well as deprivation of the joys that belonged to such spirits as were provided with "new" bodies and entered into the enjoyment of the new age. Moral degeneration is implied

---

[1] Note the expression τίς με ῥύσεται ἐκ τοῦ σώματος τοῦ θανάτου τούτου, Rom. 7:24.

[2] Rom. 5:12; cf. Gen. 2:17; 3:19; Rom. 6:14, 23; 7:13; 1 Cor. 15:55, 56.

[3] For the Hebrew idea of death see DAVIDSON, Expositor, Fifth Series, Vol, I, p. 330. See also KABISCH, Eschatologie des Paulus, pp. 86–89.

[4] Rom. 5:14.

[5] Cf. the entire passage setting forth the contrast between Adam and Christ, Rom. 5:12-21. Paul does not expressly say that Adam was immortal before the fall, although such a view is a fair implication from his words. Nor does he discriminate between the death of animals and the death of man.

[6] 1 Cor. 5:5 speaks of the ὄλεθρον τοῦ σαρκός.

[7] In Sheol if, as is altogether probable, Paul shared in current Jewish beliefs.

by mortality,[1] but it is not a part of death. Nor is death annihilation. Death with Paul means simply death—a change in, not a destruction of, personal existence. Life, the opposite of death, is not an abstract or ethical term, but eternal life—that sort of life which Jesus himself actually is living since his resurrection. It has moral qualities, of course, but it is fundamentally ontological. Sin working in the non-spiritual element of humanity made it mortal, corruptible. And this liability to death was humanity's inheritance. Death was already in humanity, and hell with its sufferings for evil doing was awaiting unrepentant humanity.[2]

III

If punishment be something so concrete and unspeculative as that death which so inspired the Hebrews with terror, we should expect that, in the Pauline thought, salvation would be something equally remote from abstract ethics; nor are we disappointed. Σωτηρία is clearly an eschatalogical term which in an inclusive way stands for deliverance from death and all that the guilty man might fear as the result of his approaching condemnation. Positively it also connotes the entrance of the "redeemed," through the resurrection of the body, into that glorious life which was to come to those who believed in the Anointed King.[3] Here, as in

[1] 1 Cor. 2:14.

[2] A similar result is gained by a consideration of such terms as ἀπωλεία and ὄλεθρος. Only by abandoning the entire Hebrew anthropology and by reading into the words Greek abstractions can annihilation be found in them. The entire context, for instance, of the striking passage, Phil. 3:19-21, makes it clear that one element of the ἀπωλεία awaiting those of whom Paul spoke was their non-participation in the resurrection of the body. The force of ὄλεθρος is to be seen in 1 Cor. 5:5. Cf. 2 Thess. 1:9. The contrast between men with two contrasting futures is seen in 2 Thess. 2:10; 1 Cor. 1:18; 2 Cor. 2:15; 4:3; Phil. 1:28. See, further, Menegoz, Le péché et la redemption, pp. 78 f. References to Jewish literature in Volz, Jüdische Eschatologie, pp. 282, 383. ὀργή (θεοῦ) is also an eschatological description of the approaching punishment, but is given a very general force; e. g., Rom., chap. 1.

[3] The passage which is the starting-point for all interpretation is Rom. 13:11, in which salvation is conceived of as future and is evidently correlated with the return

so much else of his messianic thought, one sees how the apostle uses the terminology of the ethnic and national hope to describe the future of the individual. The salvation which the Jews of his time expected was that of a nation delivered from its enemies.[1] With Paul the collective idea is altogether secondary to that of the state of the individual. The church was, of course, to be saved as the body of Christ,[2] but the reward of each believer contributed to the welfare of the social unit.

If we look to the apostle for more express statements as to the content of this messianic salvation, it will at once appear that fundamentally it is from the consequences of sin rather than from sinfulness during the physical life. In fact, Paul nowhere assures the believer of any release from the struggle in his flesh so long as that flesh is existent. His salvation was assured, but for that very reason he must more vigorously enter into those struggles with the kingdom of darkness which evinced the presence of the last days.[3] The seriousness of this conflict was due, not only to the nature of the Christian's enemies, but to the fact that God was working in them[4]—a very expressive paraphrase of the thought of salvation in terms of its "earnest," the inworking of the divine spirit. But salvation was not achieved by the believer, it was granted to those whom God had "elected."[5] Salvation was a gracious gift of God.[6] For

of Jesus. Similarly in 1 Thess. 1:10; 5:8; 1 Cor. 5:5; Phil. 3:20; 2 Tim. 4:18. Gal. 1:14 expressly refers to a deliverance from an evil age. The same thought appears in the synoptists, as, for example, Matt. 25:31, 46.

[1] This appears in the Gospels in the messianic songs of Mary and Zachariah, Luke 1:46-55, 67-79.

[2] Eph. 5:23.   [3] Eph. 6:10-18.   [4] Phil. 2:12-16.

[5] 2 Thess. 2:13. It is not necessary for the purposes of our discussion to consider the questions of predestination which Paulinism certainly involves. This recognition of the supremacy of God it is that gives the great power to the apostle's theology. That there are difficulties therein no one can deny, but no more difficulties than lie in the modern scientific equivalent of election—natural selection; or, for that matter, in any other question of theodicy.

[6] Eph. 2:5, 8.

those who believed in Jesus as Christ there was a "spiritual"[1] body of the resurrection like the body already possessed by Jesus.[2] It was this sort of deliverance for which every Jew with his horror of death, perhaps even more intense than that shared by most other men, had hoped. From death, with its inevitable misery, the Christian was to be delivered through the resurrection, and, on the other hand, the joys which Jesus the Christ was to introduce, the Christian was to enjoy. While salvation in its precise sense could not be conceived of as yet accomplished, all those who were to share in the resurrection and the joys of the messianic kingdom were already saved. They were sure of deliverance from the punishment for sin; they were sure of a share in the messianic glory. It is in this way that the two concepts present in Paul, one expressed by the noun and the other by the verb,[3] are to be harmonized. The apostle is again at one with his Master. As, according to the teaching of Jesus, the kingdom of God was already present in that the conquest of Satan's kingdom was in process, and some of the future members of the kingdom were already known, so in the teaching of Paul was salvation present in the sense that those who were to enjoy it were already in possession of an assurance to that effect. Such a deliverance from the punishment of sin was not the common property of humanity, although Paul called upon all men to enjoy it. The interpreter is, however, taught caution here by Acts 24:15. Only those who actually accepted Jesus as Christ could be counted as

---

[1] σῶμα πνευματικόν, 1 Cor. 15:44, 46. While the term is obviously hard to define positively—as indeed Paul admits—negatively it is not flesh but serves the πνεῦμα in some such way as the σῶμα ψυχικόν had served it.

[2] Phil. 3:20. See also Rom. 8:29, where the ultimate goal of predestination is distinctly stated to be conformity to the image of Christ, "that he might be the first born of many brethren;" i. e., partake in the resurrection and eternal life.

[3] Generally speaking, the verbal form of σώζω is in form or in connotation future; e. g., Rom. 5:9, 10 (10:9); 1 Cor. 3:15; 5:5; 2 Tim. 4:18. Occasionally it is present as in 1 Cor. 1:18; 15:2; 2 Cor. 2:15. It is past only rarely, as in Rom. 8:24; Eph. 2:5, 8.

those who were saved,[1] and the evidence for the fact was very distinct. They had as the first instalment of the heavenly inheritance that Spirit of God which had raised Jesus from the dead and would subsequently quicken their mortal bodies.[2]

It is worth while to notice that the conclusion that salvation involves the renewal of the personality after death is corroborated by the fact that Paul evidently believed that it was not necessary for all men to die. Those Christians who are alive at the coming of the Savior were not to die, but be changed into his likeness.[3] Of the fate of others than Christians Paul does not treat in detail, but such passages as speak of the "faith of Abraham as being counted to him for righteousness"[4] would lead us to infer that he would hold that those who had faith in God before the appearance of Jesus would also share in the Christian's salvation.

Finally, with Paul, as with Peter and primitive Christianity, and with Jesus himself, to be saved is formally to be aquitted at the judgment, and to share in the messianic kingdom. Actually it is to be freed from death, and to share in eternal life. The question of conduct before death is a corrollary rather than a cause of such salvation. The Christian is to be like Jesus on earth because through the gift of the Spirit he is possessed of that higher order of life which is now in its consummate form being lived by Jesus in heaven.[5]

[1] Rom. 3:22, 24. It is perhaps worth noticing that Slav. *Enoch*, 42:2, speaks of the suffering of sinners in the eternal life. Sokolov's text, however, omits the statement.

[2] 2 Cor. 1:22; 5:5; Eph. 1:14.

[3] 1 Thess. 4:15; 1 Cor. 15:51, 52.

[4] Gal. 2:6, etc.

[5] On the entire matter see HOLTZMANN, *Neutestamentliche Theologie*, Vol. II, pp. 106 f. It is gratifying to find so much corroboration for this view in KENNEDY, *St. Paul's Conceptions of the Last Things*, chap. 3.

IV

Thus we are again brought back to the messianic significance of Jesus, and to the meaning to humanity of the actual facts which the messianic conception expresses. It is doubtless true that the center of the Pauline thought is the adjustment of human life to divine conditions so complete as to insure the enjoyment after death of all those blessings which may be summarized in one term, life, and the avoidance of all that misery and checked development which he calls death. But as a historical phase of religious experience Paulinism centers about the Messiah, Jesus. Certain recent tendencies in theology have made it difficult to appreciate the full significance of this fact. There has been a decided effort to strip Christianity of those elements which were paramount in the Pauline thought, and reduce it from a religious to an ethical system. As a necessary element in this plan there has been the elevation of the human side of Jesus, and the strictly messianic qualities ascribed to him by Paul have been ignored, or have been replaced by those derived from a trinitarian theology. The loss resulting has been considerable both for exegetical and practical purposes. Jesus as a mere social reformer or ethical poet is interesting, and the story of his life makes a good basis for rhetorical appeals, but any careful and impartial student of his words and character will say that, if this be all of his significance, he is of no very large importance to modern life. Beautiful and true as his principles are, they have been duplicated by nearly every teacher who has voiced the best conclusions of the moral experiences of any people, and like them would stand in need of authentication. And it is only a natural corollary of this reduction of Jesus to the rôle of example and sage that there should appear the tendency to strip him of something of ethical importance which even the first generation of those favoring this course of interpretation ascribed to him. It is more or less the fashion for the second generation of these destroyers of New Testament ideals to see in his teachings impracticable exhortations, and in his own character serious moral blemishes.

The point of view of Paul is radically different. Christ's [1] moral teaching, difficult as it may be for human realization, is the expression of those great principles of conduct which would assure in the messianic kingdom the ideal social condition. However difficult they may be of realization for men in a lower stage of life, they yet represent that toward which human development which leads to the glorious stage beyond death must tend. Therefore it was that acts, words, and deeds which seem out of place to those who see in Jesus only the apostle of human sweetness and light got value. They are the expression of divine judgment against human sin, no more inconsistent with a supreme personality than are death and suffering and the terrible calamity which fell upon the Jewish state inconsistent with divine sovereignty.

Similarly, too, as regards the pre-existence of Christ. The Jews were, if we may trust the few statements of rabbinic literature, believers in the pre-existence of all souls. From such a point of view, therefore, it would be easy, and for that matter inevitable, for Paul to conceive of Jesus as also pre-existent, and as the pre-existent Christ. [2] His authority would have been from the beginning, when he was

---

[1] Jesus is called by Paul χριστός 382 times. He is also called κύριος. In fact, to confess that Jesus is Lord is made by Paul the specific prerequisite of the Christian life. (1 Cor. 12:3; Rom. 10:9. See also Phil. 2:11; Col. 2:6; 4:1.) It is worth noticing that in 1 Thessalonians the phrase ὁ κύριος ἡμῶν Ἰησοῦς χριστός is very frequent. Altogether he is referred to as κύριος thirty-seven times in this first epistle. The term is applied to Jesus 232 times in the entire Pauline literature. GILBERT, *The First Interpreters of Jesus*, p. 19. Acts 9:22; 17:3; 18:18 are a precise representation of the apostle's center of interest.

[2] Phil. 2:6-8; Rom. 8:3; Gal. 4:4. To the contrary see the summary of arguments by GILBERT, *The First Interpreters of Jesus*, chap. 1, in which the contention is urged that the Christ pre-existed ideally; *i. e.*, as an element in the thought of God. See also STANTON, *Jewish and Christian Messiah*, pp. 129-33.

all but equal with God.[1] What his relations to the universe were before his birth Paul does not discuss except in broad terms; he was the agent of God in creation.[2] However foreign such an expression may seem to those who think of God as an eternal personality permeating a universe which is in constant process, for the Jews it was the one means of describing the pre-historical supremacy of him who was to be supreme in the historical period.[3]

The incarnation was therefore a natural belief of Paul. Only, to be explicit, he speaks of the incarnation of the Christ rather than of the incarnation of God.[4] The Christ is presented by Paul as the eternal son of God,[5] not in any strict sense of parentage but in the sense of Messiah. The incarnation is presented in its simplest form. The Christ took on the form of man[6]—the likeness of sinful flesh[7]—and thus emptied of honor and position, took up an actual life of humiliation and suffering. Such an incarnation would be lasting. The whole Pauline conception of the resurrection of Jesus demands that the Christ who is now exercising his messianic authority in heaven anticipatory to his return to establish his messianic glory upon earth should be the historical Jesus. What may have been the mode of his existence before the incarnation Paul never describes, but the mode of his existence after death is sharply fixed in his mind. He has been raised from the dead and in the body of the resurrection.[8] Yet Paul never describes particulars.

---

[1] Phil. 2:5 f.   [2] Eph. 1:10; 1 Cor. 8:6; Col. 1:16, 17.

[3] *Cf.* The relation of wisdom to the world and God in Proverbs.

[4] Gould, *Biblical Theology of the New Testament*, pp. 96–99, argues that Jesus was the incarnation of the Spirit.

[5] The full term υἱὸς θεοῦ occurs only in Rom. 1:4; 2 Cor. 1:19; Gal. 2:20; Eph. 4:13; but he refers to him as the Son of God thirteen times also. The idea of Messiah embodies the primary conception.

[6] Phil. 2:7.   [7] Rom. 8:3.

[8] Phil. 3:21. This position clearly lies behind the apostle's doctrine of the resurrection.

The vision at Damascus apparently gave him no view such as that which is reported to have come to the other disciples. But Jesus appeared to him; and in such a way that his description of the body of the resurrection must be regarded as in some way its result. Jesus was the firstfruit of those who slept; those who believed were to be like him; and therefore to describe them is in some secondary way to describe him. Here again do we see the importance of the historical element in Paulinism.

The relation of this eternally incarnate Christ to mankind as a race is not discussed by the apostle. Of the seed of David according to the flesh,[1] Jesus was no typical man. Paul does, indeed, speak of him as "the last Adam," or "the second man,"[2] but it is untrustworthy exegesis that sees in such terms a rehabilitation of some Alexandrine or rabbinic philosophy.[3] Paul does not draw the parallel between Adam and Christ except to show the relations of a primal individual to a social group. In the case of Adam the social group is humanity; in that of Christ it is the body of believers. The further analogy is wholly conditioned by this general relationship. The result of disobedience on the part of Adam was the death of mankind; the result of the obedience of Christ was the life of the believers. To find in this striking parallelism a general philosophy is to miss the point of the entire passage.

What should be the final position of the Christ, Paul does not discuss in detail. His eschatology is singularly sane in that it rests upon the historical facts connected with the risen Jesus rather than upon Jewish speculation. And

---

[1] Rom. 1:3.   [2] 1 Cor. 15:44-49; cf. Rom. 5:12-21; 1 Cor. 15:20-22.

[3] Cf. G. F. MOORE, Journal of Biblical Literature, Vol. XVI (1897), pp. 158-61, who shows how late are the rabbinic passages that speak of the Messiah as the Second Adam. SCHIELE, "Die rabbinischen Parallelen zu 1 Cor. 15:45-50," Zeitschrift für wissenschaftliche Theologie (1899), finds the origin of Paul's expression in Philo. SOMERVILLE, St. Paul's Conception of Christ, elaborates this view into a theological treatise.

yet in the same proportion as Paul moves away from facts into the region of implication from facts do we see the influence of his inherited hopes. It would not be safe to say that he believed in a millennium, but he clearly does hold to the belief in a messianic reign of limited duration. After Jesus as the Christ has put all enemies under his feet, he is to give up his messianic reign and transfer all authority to God the Father that God may be all in all.[1] Until his Appearance he was exercising messianic rule over the church, his body, caring for its organization and supplying its members with his Spirit.[2]

V

It is from this point that we must approach the apostle's teaching concerning justification, that is to say, acquittal at the coming judgment.[3] Obviously that great good is one not of experience, but of anticipation and hope. The judgment has not taken place, and yet the Christian was assured that he was to be acquitted when he appeared before the bar of God. Paul taught that the basis of this acquittal was in no way Judaism. The Jew as well as the heathen was without hope of acquittal. He had kept the law no more than had the Greek.

In speaking of justification it is to be borne in mind that, as in the matter of salvation, Paul does not deal with the removal of sin, but with the removal of guilt; that is, the liability to punishment.[4] It is also to be borne in mind that his entire doctrine is in the apologetic spirit against the claims of the Jew and of the Jewish Christian. And, in

---

[1] 1 Cor. 15:24-27. [2] Eph. 4:7 f.; 1 Cor. 12:11; Rom. 12:3, 6.

[3] The act of acquittal is δικαίωσις; the declaration of rightness, δικαίωμα: the state of those δικαιόμενοι, δικαιοσύνη.

[4] Rom. 3:20, 21. The much-discussed phrase of Rom. 1:17, δικαιοσύνη θεοῦ, is most naturally translated "a state of acquittal given by God," not "righteousness of God." The context makes it evident that the contrast is not between moral states, but between guilt and acquittal. See Sanday and Headlam, Commentary on Romans, in loco.

the third place, it should be borne in mind that justification was not a matter of experience, but of assurance. The believer is assured of the fact that he is not to be condemned but is to be delivered at the approaching world-judgment. In this sense he *is* justified.

It was this latter fact that lay behind the great discussion between Paul and the primitive church. In each alike there was the hope of acquittal at the messianic judgment. But in Paulinism the assurance of such acquittal was complete without recourse to supplementing virtues of Mosaism. Men were justified by faith and by faith alone.[1]

What, then, was this faith on the basis of which the judge would acquit the believer? The answer which Paul gives is exceedingly simple: the acceptance of Jesus as Lord — that is, as Christ — involving as it did the belief that God had raised him from the dead.[2] That this initiatory acceptance of Jesus at the messianic valuation would grow richer and more inclusive is beyond question, but there was no condemnation for the man who had so accepted Jesus. Faith is therefore with Paul not a matter of mysticism; neither is it that which is something exclusively religious. It is the yielding of one's entire life to an interpretation of the historical Jesus. Strictly speaking, its ethical content is derived from the character ef Jesus. He who believed that Jesus is the Christ first of all needed to repent from his sins, and, in the second place, found in Jesus' own life, both on earth and in heaven, the basis of moral control. In the same proportion as one's interpretation of Jesus grew richer would his personality and the bearing of the facts of his life upon conduct grow more intense. But this larger faith was with Paul a matter of Christian growth, due to the inworking of the Spirit. And in this spiritual life lay the

[1] It is unnecessary to give references here in detail. The teaching of Paul is on nearly every page of his letters. Gal. 2:15-21 is a good summary of his position.

[2] 1 Cor. 12:3, and particularly Rom. 10:9, 10.

ground for assurance that the day of judgment was not to disclose disappointment. All those who had accepted Jesus as Christ and had been given the spirit were already treated by God as members of the messianic kingdom. So much was the indubitable evidence of their Christian experience. They had the Spirit of God, the same Spirit that had been in Jesus himself. It was inconceivable, therefore, that they could be treated by God at the judgment as other than members of the messianic kingdom. They could rest in peace as they anticipated that great day of the Lord.

Thus back of the messianic schema at its most vital point is seen the evidence of the religious life.[1] The judgment day was inherited from Jewish messianism; justification was also; but the assurance of such justification was not an inheritance—it was born of the conscious life of the Christian. Again we are face to face with a fact and an interpretation. Only in this case the interpretation, when confronted with the fact, gave rise to a problem.

VI

There came from the junction of the indubitable facts of Christian experience and the Jewish conception of Jehovah as a God of law, a difficulty. The Christians were convinced that they had been sinners, and that they were still doing those things that were wrong; and Paul, on his part, was convinced that such a liability to sin was to continue as long as men were possessed of the flesh. And yet over against this consciousness of continued desert of punishment was the assurance of acquittal at the coming judgment. Had then God become indifferent to his own moral requirements? How could he have been just in declaring that the soul that sinned should die, and yet permit certain sinners to overcome death? How could he at the same time prescribe death as

[1] Gal. 3:1-6; *cf.* Rom. 8:33-39.

a punishment and also make it a release from evil conditions and the entrance into ineffable blessings?

To this question, characteristic only of minds filled with the survivals of Mosaism, Paul replied by an appeal to a historic fact. As messianic expectation had given rise to the problem, so the messianic faith gave its answer. And this answer was very simple. Jesus died, not as an ordinary martyr, but in his capacity as Christ. Any act, whether or not technically messianic, when performed by him obtained supreme value from the fact that the Christ performed it.[1] Now the Christ had died; that is, he had himself endured that change which the law had declared should come as punishment for sin. As the Christ he had not himself committed sin.[2] The penalty of sin, therefore, death, came upon him vicariously. As the head of a kingdom composed of all those who accepted him as Christ, he could be regarded as representing his subjects. Such a representative and vicarious relationship[3] would have been familiar to all those who recalled the history of punishment inflicted upon the king of rebellious subjects.[4] Now, those who had accepted Jesus as Christ are evidently treated by God as members of his kingdom, for they had been given his spirit. As therefore the king might bear the penalty for his subjects, Paul argued that God could be just while acquitting those who accepted Jesus as the Christ. The law that sin should bring death was vindicated in that the Christ himself, "in the likeness of sinful flesh"[5] the just for the unjust, submitted to

[1] This enables us to appreciate the significance of Paul's conversion. He did not believe Jesus was the Christ because he had been killed. No such element lay in the Jewish messianism of his day. But when convinced by the "revelation" of Jesus that the Crucified One was Christ, he had in the events of Jesus' life material for the construction of a new theology and for the solution of questions arising from systematic treatment of the religious consciousness.

[2] 2 Cor. 5:21.   [3] 1 Cor. 11:24; 2 Cor. 5:15; Rom. 5:6-8; Gal. 1:4.

[4] In the case of the Jews the punishment inflicted upon Aristobulus by Pompey must certainly have not quite passed out of mind.

[5] Rom. 8:3.

it. At the same time God would be free to express that love which wished to see all men saved rather than to see them perish. Evidently, therefore, the basis for the acquittal which the believer confidently expects, and the blessings which he already in part enjoys, is not the individual's righteousness, but the love of God as expressed in the death of Christ as his representative and as the representative of those who hold him to be the messianic king. In this sense the death of Jesus was a part of the great plan of God to deliver men from the death brought upon them by sin.[1] Jesus was the Redeemer;[2] and, with a striking use of the sacrificial figure, the propitiatory sacrifice of the world.[3] This crucified and risen Mediator Paul made the center of evangelization.[4] The Christ had not been forced to death by divine decree. He had freely submitted to incarnation and its consequent humiliation and sufferings.[5] The blessings of divine acquittal came to a man, not because he was incipiently righteous, but because he had accepted Jesus as Christ. The death of Christ did not make God gracious, but exhibited his right to be gracious.[6] A man was not to be saved because he was good, but he was to be good because he was to be saved—in fact, was already saved.

How thoroughly forensic this conception is has been recognized by all interpreters who have not preferred to find in Pauline thought more modern and less figurative elements.[7] The origin of the concept has not so generally been recognized. *Why* the death of Christ was necessary Paul never

---

[1] Eph. 1:4; Rom. 8:29.   [2] Gal. 3:10, 13.

[3] Rom. 3:21-31; discussed by DALMANN, *The Words of Jesus*, pp. 124-35.

[4] 1 Cor. 1:17, 18; 2:2; Gal. 3:1. Whether Paul made the *doctrine* of the atonement central in his evangelization is doubtful. It seems rather to belong to Christian "edification." And even in his letters Paul's references to the matter are more by way of allusion than by discussion. Compare his treatment of the atonement with that he gives the resurrection of the believers.

[5] Rom. 8:32.   [6] Rom. 3:26.

[7] As, for example, GOULD, *Biblical Theology of the New Testament*, pp. 66-79. See also RITSCHL, *Justification and Reconciliation*, especially pp. 38-85 and chap. 8.

discusses. He had the *fact* to use in the interest of Christian hope and life. He did not and could not have reached his doctrine of the atonement *a priori*. The modern mind, which does not think of God's relation to the world in monarchical and judicial terms, is naturally perplexed when it attempts to reconstruct this section of Pauline teaching. But it will be a sad mistake, if, because we recognize the fact that the problem came from a controlling thought that has passed away, we should ignore the Pauline teaching. The problem to which Paul set himself is one which is much greater than that particular form given it by the messianic schema of thought. It is the everlasting problem of the relation of the God of law to the God of love. In particular it is the question of the meaning of death and of the possibility of some sort of advance through death. Whether one may or may not correlate the dissolution of personality with evil conduct of Adam or of one's self, the fact remains that it is the great enigma of human existence, for the modern man as well as for the primitive Christian. And for both there is hope in the death of Jesus. It is not merely that, in the same proportion as one gives Jesus a higher value, he finds encouragement in the thought that he submitted to inevitable death without abandoning his faith in God as father. That in itself is inspiration. But a far larger truth lies in the fact that by submitting to death he has shown to the world by his resurrection that, through the love of God, to a life like his own, death is a step toward something larger and happier. To such a life death is transformed into an element of a beneficent teleology—one had almost said a beneficent evolutionary process. The Christ who had taken on the form of sinful flesh, *i. e.*, had assumed the dual personality of humanity—had, by virtue of the power of his spirit[1] been released from the flesh and, sharing in

[1] Rom. 1:4.

the new life of the "spirit," is the first fruits of all those who, though in a less degree, honestly attempt to live the sort of life which he lived. They too are to be freed by death from the "flesh" to live in the "spirit" and the "spiritual body." They too like him will experience the joy that springs from the release of the spirit from the body, and its rehabilitation in a higher mode of existence. It is this that is set forth in messianic terms when Paul says that if the believer was reconciled by the death of Jesus, much more will he be saved by his life.[1] In this sense Jesus was the new Adam. As Adam had been the first of a race of living souls, raising his descendants above the beasts though also bringing upon them death; so Jesus, by his resurrection and by the revifying power of the spirit ($\pi\nu\epsilon\hat{\upsilon}\mu\alpha$ $\zeta\omega\sigma\pi\sigma\iota\hat{\upsilon}\nu$) which he gives to men, is the first of a race of "spiritual" personalities—the inaugurator of a new stage in human existence superior to that of merely physico-psychical humanity.[2]

Justification and the atonement are the messianic forms taken by truths which are capable of any philosophical interpretation which correlates their content with a belief in the historical Jesus—truths which make it possible for any man, whether or not he be controlled by the messianic apperception, to believe that the God of love is the God of law, and that the God of law is the God of love. And this belief comes through a knowledge of the death and resurrection of Jesus.[3]

VII

If we pass to the details of the Pauline forecast of eschatological salvation, we are at once struck with the fact that it is a generalization of his Christology. The immortality of

---

[1] Rom. 5:10. This of course is his glorified life, not that lived in the flesh.

[2] 1 Cor. 15:22, 45.

[3] For a popular presentation of current theological thought on this subject see *The Atonement in Modern Thought*, by a number of leading theologians.

the entire personality had been assured by the experience of Jesus. That for which the believer waited was not merely the triumph of right over wrong; it was such a change in his own personality as would make it possible for him to live like the risen Christ, freed from the flesh, from attacks of sin, and from suffering and death. To be "justified" was to live in the joyous assurance of the certainty of this glorious mode of personal existence revealed by Jesus.

Paul never shows himself more thoroughly sane than in his discussion of the details of the Christian's future. It is not difficult to see here the influence of the positive historical data which were furnished by the resurrection of Jesus. The apocalypses of Judaism never shrank from the wildest sort of imaginations concerning the future. As a result they were very often absurd. It would be hard, indeed, to bring, for instance, the expectations of the Enoch literature into line with facts made known to us by scientific investigation. While it would be presumptuous to say that there is no difficulty in correlating the Pauline expectation of the spiritual body with scientific facts, it must at the same time. be admitted that there is nothing absurd in his positions. He distinctly[1] claims to be ignorant of just how the body of the new life differs from the physical body. Resurrection is certainly not re-animation. His controlling conviction is that it belongs to a new order of life; it is "spiritual" whereas the body that is separated from the spirit at death is "psychical," i. e., animal. As stars differ in glory, so the body of the resurrection will differ from the body that dies.[2] No man can read the Pauline forecast of the future, as we find it, in his letters to the Corinthians, without sharing in the enthusiasm with which he looks forward to the great change which is to come to all men, either by death or by miracle. And

[1] 1 Cor. 15:30.
[2] See the discussion in 1 Cor., chap. 15, and 2 Cor. 5:1-10.

for the man whose apperception is controlled by evolutionary hypothesis, strangely enough, nothing seems more familiar. It is the everlasting process of life from order to order that Paul here recognizes. The life that he lived, according to the intimations of the Spirit of God, will find itself passing on to a higher form of existence in which the animal survivals are wanting and the spirit is supreme.

And the basis of his recognition, and that which gives it value above all apocalyptic expectation, is that it is built upon the historical experience of the Christ. Christianity as Paul presents it is something more than a religious philosophy. It is a generalization of certain distinct facts. It is not merely a product of religious experience; it is also the source of religious experience. If it be replied that such an interpretation puts the gospel at the mercy of historical facts, the only reply is that to Paul's mind it was these historical facts that constituted it the gospel. If Christ were not raised from the dead, then nobody was raised from the dead, and the whole world was still liable to the results of sin. The Christian himself was of all men most miserable, because he had not only lost the hope of salvation, but he had made God a liar, by asserting that God had raised Jesus from the dead.

Dominated by this element of fact, the eschatological forecast of Paul was of necessity conservative. It is noteworthy that he does not attempt any elaborate discussion of the judgment, or of the condition of those who die before the coming of the Lord, or of the reason for the Christ's delay, or of the New Jerusalem, or in fact of most of those matters about which Christian curiosity has always been so keen. Paul was not a sensationalist in religion, nor was he interested in satisfying the curiosity of humanity. He knew that the future was dependent upon a man's relation to God. He did not know exactly what the future life was to be, but he did know that the man who had placed himself in the right relation with God would find it blessed and like that already enjoyed by Jesus.

Various attempts have been made to extract from scattered sayings and words of the apostle more precise details as to the future. What, for example, is the relationship between the body of flesh and the spiritual body? Some have detected inconsistencies[1] in the various answers which Paul gives to this question. On the one side he apparently speaks of the physical body as being transformed by the spirit so as to pass into a new body.[2] On the other hand he speaks of the body which is already prepared for the Christian in heaven,[3] into which the permanent element of the personality, after having left the physical body, will enter and be clothed upon by the spiritual. If, however, one refuses to push these various expressions into a system, this inconsistency does not appear very great. In either case they are phases of the common belief upon which Paul does not dogmatize, that the personality continues, and that a spiritual body replaces the physical, the struggle between the flesh and the spirit is ended, and, through the power of God, the believer lives in a new, a higher, and a more joyous order of life.[4]

So too as regards the condition of those who die. Do they immediately take on the body of the resurrection, or do they remain in an intermediate state awaiting the coming of the Lord? Here again there is no express uniformity of expression, but nothing of sufficient importance to warrant one's believing that Paul's opinions went through radical stages. Bearing in mind the fact that he expected that the coming of Jesus would be soon, the matter was one of no

---

[1] So, e. g., CHARLES, *Eschatology*, chap. 11, especially p. 399.

[2] Rom. 8:11.　　　　　　　　　　[3] 2 Cor. 5:1-8.

[4] 1 Cor. 15:46 and indeed the entire chapter as well as 2 Cor. 4:7—5:10.

particular importance, except as it involved the actual resurrection of the dead. Evidently his position was different from that of those who have come to believe that this so-called intermediate state might continue for hundreds, if not millennia, of years. In view of Paul's relationship to current Jewish thought in general it is probable that, as he was convinced that flesh and blood could not inherit the kingdom of God,[1] he must have believed that the dead Christians were with all the rest of the dead in Sheol, whence they would be called at the coming of the Lord; they would be raised literally, not from the grave, but from the underworld.

Again as regards the question of the fate of the wicked, there have been those who have found in Pauline expressions ground for holding that all those who are evil would be annihilated, that the reign of Christ might be supreme. No man can come to the Pauline thought from the study of its Jewish antecedents and share such a view. Annihilation is not to be found in the Jewish thought. The destruction and loss which the wicked enjoy is that of the body, and of the blessings of the messianic reign. So far from being annihilated they remain in Sheol suffering punishment. Paulinism involves a limitation of the resurrection, but there is not one element in it that can legitimately be urged to favor the annihilation of the wicked.[2]

And, finally, the Pauline picture of the consummation of all things is drawn with but a few lines. Here, as everywhere throughout his teaching there is the reticence which is born of a regard for facts. The messianic age proper was

---

[1] 1 Cor. 15:50.

[2] On the other hand, attempts have been made to show that Paul expected that all men would be saved. Such a view rests on Rom. 5:1; 1 Cor. 15:21, 22, 28; Eph. 1:10; but is contradicted by the entire scope of the Pauline thought. The universal admission of the lordship of Jesus in Phil. 2:9–11 proves nothing to the contrary. Even enemies would be forced to admit the messianic conquest. The πολλοί of 1 Cor. 15:21, 22 marks simply the distinction between Adam and the Christ on the one side and the social results of each one's act on the other. See good discussion in KENNEDY, *St. Paul's Conceptions of the Last Things*, pp. 309 f.

to pass over into the great period of God's absolute supremacy, and with this the apostle rested content.[1] With the assurance of release from the flesh, from guilt, from punishment, from sin, from suffering, and from death, the future held for him only an eternity of joy. Salvation was more than a theological term, it denoted an actual condition and mode of life into which he who had received the spirit of God was to enter. Death had been overcome; had been swallowed up in victory. The believer was saved, not partially, but as a complete personality.[2]

VIII

It therefore appears that eschatological hopes centering in Jesus were dominant in Paul, and that in so far as the apostle was without actual historical data to force modifications, these hopes were essentially the same as those of the general apocalyptic movement. It also is apparent that the exposition and development of those elements of Paul's thought that rested wholly upon the inherited messianic interpretation will be really of power only in those ages in which the religious apperception to which the gospel appeals is the same as that to which Paul himself appealed. Speaking roughly it may be said that this religious apperception continued with unimportant modifications until modern times. Recently the rise of an entirely new conception of the universe through the philosophy born of the new physical sciences is rapidly removing this apperception. The question, therefore, as to whether Paulinism has any message to the religious thought of today is one of critical importance.

[1] 1 Cor. 15:23-25. In my opinion it is idle to attempt to build up a complete chronological program of the future from the words of these verses.

[2] Was then this glorious heavenly kingdom to be on earth? There is no evidence that Paul so expected unless we determine a priori that his silence is to be filled with the vocalizations of contemporary thinkers, e. g., Eth. Enoch, 72:1, or make central such a passage as Rom. 8:18-23.

Any answer to this question must consider those elements in Paulinism which are the outcome not of the inherited messianic concept, but of the actual facts of Christian experience. Such facts rather than their interpretations can certainly be correlated with other facts of any age whatever its temper, and it is to these that we should now give attention. For as in the teaching of Jesus a life of love and faith in God was superior to messianic conceptions, and as in primitive Christianity the acceptance of Jesus as the Christ of eschatological hopes led to new spiritual enthusiasm and deepened religious experiences; so in Paulinism the acceptance of Jesus as Christ was but a forerunner of the reception of the Spirit of Christ.

CHAPTER IV

THE NEW LIFE IN CHRIST ACCORDING TO PAUL

ESCHATOLOGY, central as it is in Paulinism, is a hope. Except in so far as it was a generalization of the experiences of Jesus it was only a hope. We have seen to what extent in the case of Paul this hope was a representation of the inherited faith of his people, and the question immediately arises as to the meaning of his thought to those who do not share in such an inheritance. The answer to this question has already been incidentally stated repeatedly. Eschatological messianism is not the material but the form of Paulinism. Face to face with the questions with which men of all times have grappled, he found his answer not in the speculation of the apocalyptic writings, but in two great groups of facts. On the one side was Jesus with his life and teaching and resurrection; on the other was Christian experience. The kingdom had indeed not appeared, but eternal life was a fact. It is to this second element that any student who attempts a systematic presentation of Paulinism must give large attention. For as "salvation" was a completion of life, so before the consummation he expected one was to live the sort of life he awaited.

I

Attention has already been called to the fact that the certainty of justification at the coming judgment is a matter of inference from the fact of Christian experience. It is not to be confused with the eternal life. The actual relation of a justified man and God is described by Paul without recourse to forensic analogies in two ways. In the first place, starting from the idea of the enmity which existed

206

between the sinner and God during the time when the former was liable to divine punishment, Paul describes the new relation of the two as one of reconciliation. Which of the two parties is conceived of by him as taking the initiative he does not state explicity, but probably, it would be most in accord with his thought to think that the love of God seen in the death of Christ had removed all obstacles,[1] to the establishment of friendship between God and man which sprang from the sovereignty of God. In such case God may very properly be said to be reconciled to men, and the apostle conceived of as being intrusted with the ministry of reconciliation whose message would be a plea that men be reconciled to God.[2] At the same time, this reconciliation would not be consummated until the man repented and became a member of the heavenly kingdom through faith. And it is never conceived of by Paul as merely figurative. It is genuinely vital, the establishment of actual personal relations between God and man. It is not an external affair; it is as truly an interpenetration of personalities as is friendship, and even more pregnant with results. He who is reconciled is "in Christ."

It is easy, therefore, to understand why Paul should speak of the new relation of the Christian to his God as one of adoption or sonship, υἱοθεσία.[3] He is doubtless here affected by two contemporary concepts: On the one side there is the Roman adoption by which one who was not an actual member of a family became such by the act of the *paterfamilias;* and on the other hand he is in accord with the Jewish idea by which members of the kingdom of God were spoken of as sons of God.[4] But this filial relationship is a reality of experience. It springs from the new

[1] 2 Cor. 5:18.   [2] Rom. 5:11; 2 Cor. 5:18-20.

[3] Eph. 1:5; Gal. 3:7, 26; Rom. 8:29. See Ramsay. *Hist. Com. on Galations*, on διαθήκη in Roman and Syrian law.

[4] *Pss. Sol.,* 17:30; *cf.* Rom. 9:4.

indwelling of the spirit of God—the realization of God in consciousness. It is the spirit by which both Jew and Gentile cried "Abba Father,"[1] and lead a Godlike life. Indeed, Paul never utilizes the general philosophical thought of the universal sonship of God to which he refers in the speech at Athens.[2] Sonship with him as with Jesus is a genuinely religious concept, and one that involves the resurrection of the body. Men are sons of God in that they are to be saved; *i. e.*, through having the Spirit they are to be transformed into a mode of life that is like God's, holy and independent of the flesh.[3]

This twofold exposition of the relation of the believer in Jesus and God is not inconsistent. Its two phases but accent the fundamental element of salvation, the realization of supreme personal welfare after death in a dual personality (spiritual body and spirit) resulting from the working of God in the personality before death. From this conception of personal well-being and the possibility of eternal development, the approach to a genuine and peculiarly Christian ethics is easy. Ethics becomes a formulation of directions for the ever more complete adjustment of one's person and conduct to the new element of consciousness won through faith in Jesus as Christ—God.

Before discussing the center of the Pauline teaching as to life and conduct, it will be advisable first of all to recall distinctly the fact that while faith according to Paul is, in its first exercise, the acceptance of Jesus as the Christ of the apocalyptic hopes, the life of the believer was fundamentally moral. Ethical ideals were inseparable from his hope. "The word of the Lord" was as imperative now that the Lord was Jesus the Christ as when the Lord had been

---

[1] Rom. 8:14, 15; Gal. 4:6-15. [2] Acts 17:28.

[3] Rom. 8:19-23, 29. Sonship was a familiar way of expressing moral likeness, *e. g.*, υἱοὶ τῆς ἀπειθείας, Eph. 2:2; 5:6; υἱὸς διαβόλου, Acts 13:10; υἱὸς ἀπωλείας, John 17:12; υἱοὶ φωτὸς καὶ υἱοὶ ἡμέρας, 1 Thess. 5:5; *cf.* John 12:36.

Jehovah. Indeed nothing could be more contradictory than to suppose that the very people who saw in Jesus the supreme representative of the sovereign God should hold that his teachings as regards conduct were without authority. The fact that Paul does not often quote these teachings of Jesus or refer to them should not blind us to the fact that they were in possession both of himself and of his churches.[1] His failure to appeal to them was undoubtedly intentional, and due to his attitude toward law as a means of achieving acquittal in the day of judgment, but really to believe in Jesus as Christ was inevitably to undertake to live according to his teaching. An unrepentant man could not believe in Jesus, and a believing man would try to be good. Thus faith, even in its inceptive form, presupposed and involved morality. It was not only an intellectual conviction that Jesus was the Christ; it was also to *live* as if he were the Christ.

The first Christian community was made up almost exclusively of those who had been associated with Jesus during his work in Galilee. Therefore, however heartily they accepted him as the one who was in the future to fulfil their hopes of the Messiah, they must also have been affected to a considerable extent by his religious instruction. To think of them in any other way would be contrary to every probability. It would be a most extraordinary contradiction if those who preserved the tradition of the life and words of Jesus should have been utterly unaffected by his teaching. In accepting Jesus as Messiah they had passed through a moral crisis, in the midst of which they had dedicated themselves unreservedly to the service of their brotherhood, their Master, and their heavenly Father.

During the life of Jesus this dedication on the part of the group of men and women who constituted the nucleus

---

[1] For a discussion of this matter in detail see FEINE, *Jesus Christus und Paulus.*

of the Jerusalem community had taken the form of an abandonment of daily occupation, if not of wealth, and some attempt was made at rectification of wrongs done in earlier days.[1] In any case, none would think of denying that the acceptance of Jesus as Christ was accompanied by a moral renewal. From the days of John the Baptist, preparation for the coming judgment and the heavenly kingdom involved a moral change that could find its guarantee in works of mercy and righteousness. The first recorded message of Jesus as he took up the work of the Baptist was the same call to repentance. Faith in the new preaching was the very antipodes of cold, intellectual assent. Indeed, Jesus was eager to rid himself of men who were without this moral renewal.[2] Apostolic preaching like that of John and Jesus made repentance the first requirement of the convert. Peter and Paul were here at one. Moral revolution was indispensable for acceptance both in the kingdom and in the church.

In the apostolic age, faith in Jesus was uniformly followed by spiritual ecstasy and other striking experiences, concerning which many questions naturally arise. If we waive them for the present, the mere fact itself grows in significance. The initial experience of this sort is represented in Acts as having occurred seven weeks after the resurrection which finally fixed the apostolic faith in Jesus as Messiah. But it is to be remembered that, according to the same authority, Jesus was occasionally with the disciples during forty days of this interval. Their complete possession by the conviction of his final disappearance into heaven, that is, of his complete messiahship, was therefore practically contemporary with the beginning of new experiences. In the

---

[1] Thus in the case of Zacchæus (Luke 19:8), though he never became one of the intimate friends of Jesus.

[2] Compare the remarkable instance in the sixth chapter of the fourth gospel, as well as Jesus' explanation of his use of parables in Mark 4:12.

case of those who subsequently believed, these spiritual phenomena followed immediately either the beginning of faith itself or the act of baptism or the first laying on of hands.

Thus from the beginning of Christian history Christian experience was the accompaniment and result of Christian faith.   The two were mutually supporting, and both were elements of messianism as it appeared in apostolic Christianity.

It was characteristic of the new community that their new experiences should have been given a messianic explanation.[1] It was not enough simply to recognize the new impulses born of a new and confident approach to God.   Centuries before, the prophets had foretold that then God would pour out his spirit upon all men.   This prophecy Peter and the other disciples saw fulfilled in their new enthusiasm and ecstasy.[2] The Christ was, indeed, absent, but they had not been left comfortless.   During these days in which they awaited the return of their Lord they had been given the Spirit, the first instalment of their future inheritance.[3]   From Pentecost the reception of the Spirit was an integral part of the new messianic hope.   It was not only an argument for the newly acquired authority on the part of Jesus; to possess the Spirit was the one indubitable evidence of one's justification by God, and of one's certain membership in the coming kingdom.[4]

[1] How generally a revival of prophetism was expected in the messianic period may be seen possibly in the general hope of Elijah's coming, in the expectation of some prophet (1 Macc. 4:46), and quite as plainly in the fact that the various popular leaders of the first century presented themselves as prophets, e. g., Theudas (JOSEPHUS, Ant., xx, 5:1), and the Egyptian (Ant., xx, 8:6); cf. GUNKEL, Wirkungen des heiligen Geistes, pp. 53-56.

[2] Acts 2:14-36; 3:21.

[3] Cf. Eph. 1:14 and Acts 20:32.

[4] Acts 10:44-47; 11:17, 18; cf. 15:8, 9; Gal. 3:2.

II

In Pauline teaching and practice the elements of this messianism of the primitive Christians are clearly evident: the one formal and interpretative, derived from current messianism; the other experiential, the result of the religious trust and consequent divine renewal induced by the acceptance of Jesus as the fulfiller of messianic hopes. The distinction is fundamental in Paul, for with him the appeal to spiritual experience is final. In his own case this experience had been revolutionary. He had been "apprehended" by the Christ, and in the change from his old to his new life lay the subject-matter for much of his teaching. His conversion had consisted in the substitution, not of one theology for another, but of one life for another. Reduce this experience and its implications to words, and there is obtained one of the two great foci of Paulinism: the new life of the believer, due to the presence of God.

It would be a grievous misinterpretation of the apostle's thought if one should at this point identify the regenerate life itself with the so-called "gifts of the Spirit."[1] The psychological conceptions of early Christianity are farthest possible from those of today. The air that covered the flat earth was full of bodiless spirits, some good, some evil, but all, though especially the latter, liable to enter into men. Demoniacal possession was, however, no more accepted as a true explanation of phenomena like epilepsy, hemorrhage, deafness, insanity, and boils, than the coming of God's Spirit was believed to be the explanation of certain other phenomena quite as remarkable, if less painful. We are too far removed from the first generation of Christians, and the data at our disposal are too vague, to warrant a very confident constructive statement as to what these "gifts" may

---

[1] See the elaborate article by SCHMIEDEL in *Encyclopædia Biblica* on "Spiritual Gifts."

have been, but we may confidently infer from the apostle's words what they were not.   When one sees the final editor of Acts himself somewhat at a loss to understand "tongues," if one were to judge from his description of the phenomena of Pentecost, caution grows all the more imperative in explaining the gifts of tongues, interpretations, miracles, and prophesying so familiarly discussed by Paul in his correspondence with the church at Corinth.   Yet, however one may confess his ignorance in the matter, however one may speculate as to their precise symptoms, as to whether they were pathological, as to whether they are properly to be considered as permanent elements of Christian experience, one thing stands out with perfect distinctness: Paul regards them only as secondary and inferior evidences of the new life.   The least valuable of them all—"tongues"—was unfitted for "edification;" while the most desirable— "prophesying"—was itself far inferior to the "more excellent way" of brotherly love.[1]   In other words, Paul regarded the work of the Spirit in human life as essentially moral. God's life in those who had chosen Jesus as Christ, and who were seeking to live according to his teaching, was destined to produce moral change and growth; not sensational actions. It was a source of character, not of omniscience.[2]

Paul treats this new life from two points of view: (1) It is conceived of eschatologically as the earthly counterpart and beginning ($\zeta\omega\grave{\eta}$ $a\grave{\iota}\acute{\omega}\nu\iota os$) of the ideal proposed by his messianic hopes.   In the resurrection of Jesus Paul saw something that was to be enjoyed by all believers.   The Christ had but anticipated his kingdom, and the time was soon to come when all those who had accepted him were to put on immortality and enter upon an eternity of righteousness made possible by the end of the tyranny of the body.[3]

[1] 1 Cor. 12:1—14:39.   [2] 1 Cor. 13:9-12.
[3] See Phil. 3:21 and the entire argument in 1 Cor., chap. 15.

During the brief period[1] of waiting for this deliverance, the Christian was to endeavor to live the sort of life which was to be his in the new kingdom. Here is evidently a formal ethical ideal which, though somewhat indistinct, has yet an appreciable content for the believer in the risen Jesus. Paul constantly uses it as a basis of ethical appeal. "If ye are risen with Christ," he urges the Colossians,[2] "think the thoughts that pertain to things above where Christ sits." He tells the Romans to subordinate physical pleasures, on the ground that the kingdom of God is not to be characterized by eating and drinking, but by love, joy, and peace in the Holy Spirit.[3] And, perhaps as striking as anything. he repeatedly urges that, as the Christian is a citizen of the new kingdom, he is to live as if he already possessed the privileges of that kingdom. His citizenship is in heaven.[4] For the one who does so live, beating down his grosser nature, living according to his future, reward is certain. He who lived to the flesh was to die, but he who lived according to the Spirit was to live the son of God, fellow-heir with Christ, the future possessor of the redeemed body.[5]

But (2) the new life is also morally dynamic, and the basis of the Christian's ethical imperative. He is not wholly dependent upon the presentation of a heavenly ideal. Incomplete though it was, the life to be lived in the full presence of God had already begun in the believer. Due as it was to divine influence, it was to be supreme in all his conduct. Paul here carries to its legitimate ethical conclusions the doctrine of the Spirit's presence. His approach is, as always, through his eschatology; the Spirit is the first instalment of the inheritance awaiting the members of the coming kingdom. Through him it was that "gifts" came to men, it was the Spirit that directed the church, that

1 Rom. 13:11–14; *cf.* 1 Thess. 4:15–17; 1 Cor. 15:51.
2 Col. 3:1.   3 Rom. 14:17.
4 Phil. 3:20.   5 Rom. 8:12–25; *cf.* vss. 29, 30.

reinforced the believer's spirit in its desperate struggle with the "flesh," that pleaded with God for erring men, that helped men's infirmities, that would later quicken their mortal bodies into likeness with that of Jesus.[1]

It is at this point that we see Paul in his profoundest and most influential mood. He shared to the uttermost in the ethical passion of the Pharisees. Life with him, as with them, got its full meaning in that completion which was to be the outcome of the judgment day. Morality was, therefore, not a matter of speculation as to the origin of the moral sense, but one of determined endeavor to embody the will of God in one's personal relations. The method by which the Pharisee would accomplish this righteousness, or at least acquittal, is well known. The judge who was to determine the eternal destinies of mankind had graciously given to the Jew his Thorah. He who kept that law would live; and he who did not keep its provisions was already cursed. Theoretically, therefore, the matter was very simple: determine what the law demanded and meet its demands. "The oral law" of the scribes was the result.

In their zeal to elevate Christian teaching, it has been usual for Christian scholars to belittle the pharisaic and rabbinic teaching at this point. It is, of course, possible to adduce sentences from the Mishna, and especially from the later rabbinic writings which are absurd and trivial, but he is a poor interpreter who is content with an over emphasis of such minutiæ. Once grant pharisaism its great premise that a man's eternal destiny is set by his observance of the Thorah, and its attempt to extend the principles of that law in minute regulations is not only inevitable, but it is beneficent. If it is necessary, for example, for a man to observe the Sabbath by not working, it is certainly necessary for him to know when the Sabbath begins, and what is work and

---

[1] See admirable brief discussion in SABATIER, *Religions of Authority*, pp. 305 f.

what is not work. For such a necessity there is no act in life which must not be defined as either permissible or forbidden. The fact that the attempt so to "build a hedge about the law" resulted in a mass of rules and regulations which taxed beyond endurance memory and logical acumen is not to be given undue weight. If the principle be final that a man must do right because he is commanded to do right, the Talmud is the gospel of heteronomy.

Further, the Pharisee just as truly as Paul saw the impossibility of keeping all the rules which were implied in the law of Moses, and attempted to meet this difficulty by anticipating the Roman Catholic doctrine of supererogation. The absolute conformity to law being impossible, morality became a matter of accounting. If a Jew's good deeds exceeded in number his evil deeds, especially if he had seen suffering, the God of Israel could be trusted to let him enter the heavenly kingdom. If he failed of the balance of good deeds demanded, the excess virtues of Abraham and the Patriarchs might be counted to their descendants to make up the requisite proportion.[1] Such a morality is evidently unsatisfactory from both the theoretical and the practical point of view. Yet it contains in it a suggestion of an element which Paul himself appropriated, namely, the grace of God. Only in Paul's case the fundamental principle of the Pharisee was attacked. The acquittal could not come from keeping the law, and must come in another way. This acquittal we have already seen came to those who accepted Jesus as Christ and so were treated even before the judgment as members of the messianic kingdom. The ethical question which remained may be stated baldly thus: Why should a man be good who no longer was afraid of death and hell? In other words, what is the great moral imperative?

[1] See WEBER, *Jüdische Theologie*, chap. 19.

Paul's significance as an ethical teacher lies in the fact that he denied the finality of statutory law. Confronted with the question as to the seat of moral authority, he replied: It is God as he is known in the believer's life. It is not merely personality that Paul thus makes the moral autocrat; it is the Spirit—that element of the human personality in which the human is surcharged with the divine.[1]

Paul's position at this point explains why he does not appeal more strenuously to the teaching of Jesus. Having abandoned his earlier hope of winning an acquittal at the messianic judgment by conscientious observance of the law, he would be the last man to replace the Thorah with a new series of rules, either of his own devising or derived from the words of Jesus. That would be to discredit faith, and by faith, as he told the Corinthians in one of his most strenuous passages, the Christian stood.[2] As long as one was true to the faith he had professed in Jesus as the Messiah of the future kingdom, he was beyond the reach of even apostolic authority. At the same time, however, Paul gave his judgments as one who had obtained mercy of the Lord to be worthy of trust,[3] and these "judgments" may very well have been understood as authoritative advice regarding the form and direction in which the new life of the Christian should be given expression. Paul further magnified his official position in matters in which the religious element was at a minimum, and did not hesitate to deliver over to Satan an evil-doer for the destruction of the flesh, that the spirit might be saved in the day of the Lord Jesus.[4] None the less, however, even to the recalcitrant Corinthians he protests that he was but a master-builder who laid foundations, and that he and Apollos and Peter were but the stewards of

---

[1] The Christians in this sense are πνευματικοί; 1 Cor. 2:13-15; Gal. 6:1. So, too, the body is to be πνευματικόν after the destruction of the σάρξ; 1 Cor. 15:44, 46. *Cf.*, for general statement, Eph. 1:3; Col. 1:9.

[2] 2 Cor. 1:24. [3] 1 Cor. 7:25. [4] 1 Cor. 5:1-5.

the Christ to whom all believers belonged.[1] The gospel was not a new law, and the life of faith was not to yield to a new legalism. It is "a perfect law of liberty" of which even James speaks.[2]

But even in the case of Christians Paul seems never to have abandoned the idea of the judgment. For them as for the angels it was inevitable. The presence of the Spirit argued that Christians would be acquitted, but they were not to be excused. They themselves because of their faith in Jesus were to be saved — possibly "as by fire" — but their works if unworthy of the Spirit were to be destroyed.[3] However obscure such a distinction may appear, it is clear that Paul did not teach that the Christian was outside the region of moral law. Liberty was not to be an opportunity to the flesh.[4] Morality was not a negative matter, but positive, and in the same proportion as one followed the Spirit would he be kept from yielding to the flesh, and live the life of love.[5] And this consideration brings us to the heart of the Pauline ethics.

Once strip off Paul's peculiarly Jewish terminology, and he is the very Coryphæus of ethical autonomists. How otherwise could one designate the man who declared law had no more control over the Christian, whose letter to the Galatians is a veritable declaration of moral independence,

[1] 1 Cor. 3:5, 8, 23; 4:1. The entire argument as to the apostolic prerogative in 1 Corinthians is well worth consideration upon this point.

[2] James 1:25; 2:12.

[3] 1 Cor. 3:13 f.; cf. Test. Abraham, 93:10; Apoc. Bar., 48:29.

[4] Gal. 5:13.

[5] It is noteworthy that, although Paul apparently does not conceive it possible that one who has once believed upon Jesus as Christ would be condemned at the judgment, the later New Testament writers are not possessed of the same assurance. The writer of the Epistle to the Hebrews believes that it is impossible to renew one who sins wilfully after receiving a knowledge of the truth; for him there is no forgiveness, but a certainty of judgment, fierceness of fire; Heb. 10:26, 27. Perhaps the basis of this is the author's belief that it is impossible to renew through repentance those who fall away after having once partaken of the Holy Ghost, and tasted the good word of God and the powers of the age to come; Heb. 6:4, 8. 1 John 1:19 charges apostasy to hypocrisy.

and who believed that the Christian had the mind of Christ?[1] It is one of the curiosities of today's ethical thought that he who even more distinctly than Plato magnified the necessity of "walking in the Spirit" should have been utterly overlooked or relegated to the mercies of dogmatic theology. The neglect is, of course, due in large measure to the modern sensitiveness over appeals to rewards and punishments; but even more, one cannot help believing, to the unwillingness of ethical thinkers to accord religion any determining place in morality. To such philosophers Paul, with his insistence upon the active presence of God in a man's life, can hardly fail to be of little importance. Yet we venture to believe that Paul is near the heart of things when he insists upon the moral results of the interpenetration of the divine and the human personalities. If there be a personal God, it is hard to see how he can be excluded from personal relations; and why from such relations should there not result, as Jesus and Paul taught, a new moral life due to the effect of God's Spirit upon man's spirit?

The danger here clearly is that one who looks thus to God for moral assistance should become morally inert. Paul, however, avoids this danger by his recognition of the distinction between influence and compulsion. Impulses the religious soul must receive from God, but as the plant is influenced by its environing sunshine. To make these impulses of moral worth, they must be followed and thus incorporated through volition into one's own personality. The non-moral "charismata," like tongues and miracles, are of value only when morally practiced.[2] By following the impulses received from one's approach to God through faith, the believer becomes ethically a new man; old things

---

[1] 2 Cor. 1:22; 5:15; Rom. 8:23; Eph. 1:14. See also the profound discussion in Rom. 8:1-13.

[2] 1 Cor., chap. 13.

pass away, all things become new.[1] As Paul said so strikingly, the new life he lived by faith was Christ living in him.[2] The ethical imperative becomes therefore clear: from one point of view it may be expressed, "Grieve not the Spirit;"[3] from another, "Walk in the Spirit;"[4] from still another, "Stand fast in the liberty wherewith Christ has set you free."[5] Or, in un-Pauline words: Realize the new self made possible by the new life with God. Such a self might be described in non-messianic language as characterized by faith in a loving God, free from fear or future ill, self-sacrificing like Jesus, masterful over the animal instincts, brotherly and serviceable, full of love and joy and peace.

It is characteristic of the apostle that he conceives of all this strictly religious experience under the personal messianic formula: The believer is in Christ and Christ is in the believer.[6] It is noteworthy that he does not use the unofficial name Jesus. 'Εν Χριστῷ expresses, not a friendship between individuals, but the dependence of a subject upon a king. Baptism symbolized something more than an ethical resurrection. It portrayed the change in the believer's personality by which he was assured of the resurrection—i. e., of an experience like that of his Christ.[7] He was in Christ in the sense that he had entered into the "spiritual" as distinct from the "fleshly" life,[8] was redeemed,[9] and was already a subject of the heavenly king. The relation was, therefore, less mystical than quasi-political.[10] It was mystical only in the sense that the Christian life as a whole was mystical, i. e., dependent upon the interpenetration of the human and the divine spirits. For the expression represents a fact of the Christian experience.

---

[1] 2 Cor. 5:17. [2] Gal. 2:20. [3] Eph. 4:30.

[4] Gal. 5:16 f. [5] Gal. 5:1. [6] The classical passage is Gal. 2:20.

[7] Cf. Rom. 6:3-9. [8] 1 Cor. 3:1; cf. v. 3. [9] Cf. Rom. 8:24.

[10] Rom. 12:5. Cf. the figure of the Church as the "body of Christ" with individuals as its members, 1 Cor. 12:27. See also Gal. 3:2, 5, 14; Rom. 5:5; Eph. 1:13.

Christ was in believers in the sense that the Spirit of Christ
—*i. e.*, sent by him—was in them.[1]   The apostle had "the
mind of Christ" in the sense that God had revealed "wisdom"
to him through the Spirit.[2]   Indeed, Paul mostly uses ἐν
Χριστῷ as a sort of qualifying term expressive of the
believer's new relations in general.[3]

But no one can fail to appreciate the reality in the
Pauline conception of salvation and the achievement of the
eternal life.   Eternal life was, it is true, the supreme good
of the pious Jew,[4] but in the usage of Paul and all the New
Testament writers the term, like its correlate "kingdom of
God," was filled with a new and non-national content.   It
was a state of the individual similar to that enjoyed by the
Christ after his resurrection, and waiting for those who had
been delivered from that death which was the result of sin.[5]
It was due ultimately to the realization of God in consciousness—a fact far above any philosophy by which it may be
expressed or interpreted.   The acceptance of Jesus as the
supreme revelation of God contributed to such a new state
of consciousness, and in this sense as truly as in any other
he is Mediator.   But any exposition must here be but relative to the age which begets it.   This highest good to which
the believer looked was not born of Jewish messianism, however much it may be colored by messianic hopes.   Nor was

---

[1] The two expressions are identical in Rom. 8:9-11. The whole passage 8:1-17 is
of first importance in this connection.

[2] 1 Cor. 2:10-16. Paul carries this thought a step farther in 1 Cor. 3:1 f., when he
declares that the Corinthians are only "babes in Christ" in the sense that they were
"carnal."

[3] Thus in Rom. 9:1; 15:17; 16:3, 7, 9, 10; 1 Cor. 1:2; 4:10, 15; Eph. 1:3. For a
somewhat different view of this entire matter see Sanday and Headlam, *Commentary on Romans*, pp. 162-66.

[4] Mark 10:17; Matt. 19:16; Luke 10:25. Bousset, *Religion des Judentums*, p. 399,
denies, but too absolutely, that Jewish ethics were controlled by eschatology. For a
truer statement see Volz, *Jüdische Eschatologie*, pp. 326 f., 368, 369. *Cf. Pss. Sol.*,
14:10; Eth. *Enoch*, 37:4; 62:16; 65:10; Slav. *Enoch*, 42:3 (text of Sokolov); *4 Esdras*,
7:48; *Apoc. Baruch*, 54:12; 57:2; 85:10; *Berachoth*, 28b; *Pirqe Aboth*, ii, 7 f.

[5] Rom. 6:23.

it the child of Greek philosophy, an abstract hope of ethical victory. Nor is it born of a modern evolutionary philosophy. Ζωὴ αἰώνιος with Jesus, with Paul, and with the modern man describes a fact of consciousness, a generalization of historic phenomena. It is at bottom not moral, but ontological with moral corrollaries. It is *life*—life in the fullest sense in which the present dualistic personality is preserved, but stripped of those animal survivals that pull men back to the beast. The flesh is to be forever gone—nay, one should already live as if it were dead.[1] Holiness is involved in such a life, but no more truly than is a process of development we can only call hyper-physical.[2] And this highest good, anticipated in part in the moral and religious growth of the Christian, is the ground of obligation.[3] The Christian is a new creation[4] due to the transformation by the Lord's Spirit.[5] He is therefore to live as if already risen with Christ.[6]

III

Thus one comes to see more distinctly the relations existing between Pauline and pharisaic messianism. The one is undoubtedly derived from the other; but that which was the essence of the older has become the interpretative medium of the newer hope. It was the regenerate life, the new religious dynamic born of the religious experience induced by the acceptance of Jesus as Christ, that distinguished Christianity from pharisaism, and which has given it historical vigor and pre-eminence. Paulinism as a fulfilled pharisaic messianism might have had vast influence among

---

[1] Rom. 8:12-17.

[2] So, too, TITIUS, *Neutestamentliche Lehre der Seligkeit*, Vol. II, p. 76: "Es ist nicht eine rein etisch-religiöse, sondern eine zugleich hyperphysische Auffassung des Lebens, die er [Paul] in der Mittelpunkt gestellt hat." I am indebted to Titius for the term "hyper-physical."

[3] In general see SOKOLOWSKI, *Die Begriffe von Geist und Leben bei Paulus*

[4] 2 Cor. 5:17.   [5] 2 Cor. 3:8; Rom. 8:9-11.   [6] Col. 3:1-17.

the Jews, proselytes, and "devout" gentiles of Palestine and the empire at large; but Paulinism as the exposition of the meaning, the blessings, and the ethical and ontological possibilities of a life of trust in a loving heavenly Father is bounded by no age or place or archæological knowledge. It is the veritable Christianity of Jesus himself.

As a teacher of such a life, dynamic because dependent upon God, Paul has yet to come to his own. The historic theologies have, it is true, never neglected it: but they have made it secondary to an exposition of justification, an all but universally admitted forensic element in the apostle's thought, and one clearly derived from pharisaic messianism. Historical exegesis will increasingly reverse the process, and see, not in the survivals of pharisaism, but in the new life— the eternal life of Jesus—the permanent and all-inclusive element in Pauline teaching. Messianic faith led to a life regenerated by God himself. To trace the apostolic exposition of the ethical and social implications of this new life is, therefore, to set forth essential Paulinism. But it is also to do something far more important: it is to make easy the process by which apostolic Christianity may be accurately re-expressed in our own day. For this "life of the Spirit" is interpreted, not caused by the Pauline philosophy and world view. It will continue and will be experienced by those who have faith in Jesus, whether they fail or succeed in mastering the apostolic exposition.[1]

---

[1] It has not appeared necessary to preface the discussion of Paulinism with any general critical statement. Notwithstanding the tangential criticism of Van Manen and his school, the above discussion has used without question Romans, 1 and 2 Corinthians, Galatians, 1 Thessalonians, 2 Thessalonians, Philippians, Colossians, Ephesians, and Philemon. There are still questions of details connected with all of this literature, but not sufficient to warrant hesitation in its use as genuinely Pauline. The question of the Pastoral Epistles may still be regarded as open, but with a tendency toward the recognition of a strong Pauline element.

CHAPTER V

THE MESSIANISM OF POST-PAULINE CHRISTIANITY

The history of Christianity after the death of Paul is in deep obscurity. That churches were founded everywhere about the Mediterranean is beyond question, but of their founding we know practically nothing. So, too, as regards the literature of the time. External as well as internal evidence forces us to assign a number of writings, mostly anonymous, to the fifty years succeeding the death of Paul, but it is as impossible to tell exactly the date of their composition as to decide precisely as to their authorship.

To this group of literature belongs a number of the most important writings in our canonical New Testament; among them those now to be considered: the Synoptic Gospels (in their present form), Hebrews, the Fourth Gospel and the three epistles ascribed to John, the epistles of Jude and Peter.

I

In treating the teaching of Jesus it was shown that our synoptic gospels are the result of combining various groups of early collections of the words and the deeds of Jesus. At that time a distinction was drawn between these original materials and the present completed works. We have now to consider the gospels in their present completed form as indicating in themselves the general tendencies of the messianic hope in the early church.

It is impossible to state with precision the exact time of composition of the synoptic gospels.[1] Specific external

[1] See in general JÜLICHER, *Einleitung* (English translation, *Introduction*) and the article by SCHMIEDEL, "Gospels" in *Encyclopædia Biblia*, as well as the parallel articles in HASTINGS, *Dictionary of the Bible.*

evidence is wanting till the middle of the second century, and the critic is dependent, on the one side, upon quotations and "echoes," and, on the other, upon the internal evidence of the gospels themselves. Such data do not give us a definite *terminus ad quem*, but make it probable that all three[1] of the synoptic gospels reached their present form subsequent to the destruction of Jerusalem, 70 A. D. As they now stand, they are finished compositions in which the original material has been subjected, not only to editorial selections, but to other editorial treatment.

From the critical point of view, the strictly editorial material in the synoptics falls into three general classes. First, there are easily recognizable editorial additions in the way of comment or explanation.[2] In the second place, there are variations in numerous sayings the original form of which can approximately be determined by a comparison of the various sources.[3] And, third, there are details which are added to the original statements of Mark[4] or material which is substituted for sections of such material.[5]

In considering this material it is to be borne in mind that it springs from the second generation of Christians. The original materials of the gospels, as we have already seen, may be accepted as the work of the disciples of Jesus himself, but the synoptic gospels, as completed literary units, represent to a considerable degree the point of view of the church during the last quarter of the first century. Pauline literature antedates the synoptic gospels in their present

[1] This is generally admitted in the case of Matthew and Luke. Mark 13:20, to my mind, is conclusive also as to Mark. In this connection it is also worth while comparing Mark 13:14 with Matt. 24:15. In both cases the reference is most naturally seen to be to Titus's profanation of the temple. Luke 21:20, however, though equally historical in its references is less objectional to a Roman world looking for evidence of *lèse majesté* in Christians.

[2] As Mark 7:19; 3:30.

[3] As in Matt. 16:16; Luke 9:20; *cf.* Mark 8:29.

[4] As σωματικῷ εἴδει in Luke 3:21. *Cf.* Mark 1:10.

[5] As Luke 5:1-11 for Mark 1:16-20.

form, and its influence can hardly have been small. But the general point of view of the synoptic gospels is that which we have already seen in primitive and Pauline Christianity. God's will was being done in heaven, but not upon earth. Jesus was reigning as Christ in heaven, but was not supreme yet over men, and death had not yet fully been conquered, although the beginning of his new authority had been established by the Spirit in the hearts of Christians. They must maintain the strenuous struggles against the enemies of the new kingdom, whether superhuman or human.[1]

The synoptists, therefore, came to all the sayings of Jesus with a serene faith as to the final outcome of the conflict with the powers of evil. To a considerable extent they are interested in adjusting historical events to the general scheme of God's conquest over his enemies. These enemies are three: First, the devil, and supernatural beings. As Jesus himself had pointed out, the conquest over them was already in process, as indicated by miracles. Second, the Jews. The conquest of the kingdom over them is seen in the destruction of Jerusalem. Third, death, which, as Paul said,[2] was to be the last enemy overcome, was not yet subdued, but would be at the resurrection.

These three enemies are not always specifically referred to in the gospels, but constitute the elements in the point of view from which the synoptists approach the interpretation of the personality of Jesus. At the distance of a generation the perspective of his work shaped itself more plainly and his significance became more sharply defined. Whatever he had done gained value because it had been done by the Christ.

1 If J. WEISS be correct (*Reich Gottes*[2], p. 97), this point of view appears clearly also in Rev. 12:7 f. Michael is there represented as having conquered the dragon in heaven, but the dragon had been cast on earth, where he was making trouble.

2 1 Cor. 15:26.

The general tendencies of this synoptic interpretation, whatever its critical form, are varied.

1. There is, first, the tendency toward messianic precision. Thus, the work of John the Baptist is more distinctly seen to have been of messianic significance. Not only is his preaching regarded as the beginning of the gospel,[1] but his birth is described as involving miracles of various sorts, indicating his future mission,[2] and he himself, it is stated, was regarded by the people as a possible Christ.[3] His preaching is summarized by Matthew as a message concerning the coming of the kingdom of God,[4] rather than the more generically ethical call to the forgiveness of sins, contained in Mark. He is, furthermore, distinctly identified as Elijah.[5]

Similarly in the case of Jesus we learn from the later form taken by the gospel narrative that he was recognized even as a babe as the future Christ,[6] and that he was born in Bethlehem in accordance with prophecy.[7] In the account of the shekel found in the fish's mouth[8] we have additional material intended to enforce the independence of the Christ, and in that of the dead saints who rose at the time of Jesus' resurrection an even later addition, originally probably in the form of a gloss, intended to illustrate the power of the Christ over the dead.[9] There are a number of cases in which the evangelists in reworking Mark have made slight changes to call attention to the real messianic significance of Jesus.[10] Perhaps most noticeable of these changes are the addition of the terms "Son of man," "Son of God," and other expressions intended to relate Jesus with God in the

---

[1] Mark 1:1 f.   [2] Luke 1:5–25, 39–56, 57–80.   [3] Luke 3:15.

[4] Matt. 3:2, a rewriting of Mark 1:4.

[5] Matt. 17:32. The identification is not in the original, Mark 9:13.

[6] Luke 2:21–39.   [7] Matt. 2:1-12.   [8] Matt. 17:24–27.

[9] Matt. 27:52, 53. Is this in some obscure way connected with the preaching to the spirits in prison of 1 Pet. 3:19?

[10] Matt. 4:23; *cf.* Mark 1:39. Luke 5:43; *cf.* Mark 1:38.

account of Peter's confession at Cæsara Philippi,[1] the reference of the "sign of Jonah" to the three days in the tomb[2] the substitution of a question concerning the parousia of Jesus for one concerning the fall of Jerusalem,[3] and the more precise form of the cry of the people at the triumphal entry,[4] to which reference has already been made.[5] Distinct references to the dependence of Jesus upon the Spirit are also occasional.[6] The primitive christology is to be seen in the explanation appended by Mark to the section on the unpardonable sin.[7] There are to be seen, also, frequently slight editorial changes which can hardly be assigned to any definite motive, but which would be very natural in the case of those writing after Christian history had fairly begun, and the messianic importance of Jesus had become a fundamental element in Christian hope.[8] Luke also adds material[9] emphasizing the messianic significance of both Jesus and the authority of his representatives.

2. There is further to be seen, especially in Luke, the substitution of a somewhat more miraculous for a simpler account, as for example, in the narrative of the baptism,[10] and that of the call of the four.[11] While it is easy to lay too much stress upon this characteristic of the third evangelist, just as it is also easy to overemphasize his ebionitic and universalizing tendencies, it is undeniable that the general attitude of mind of early Christianity was favorable to receiving miraculous narratives as supplementary to the original record of the gospels. The *Protevangelium* and

---

[1] Mark 8:27 f.; Matt. 16:13 f.; Luke 9:18 f. For other instances of the addition of the term "Son of man," see Luke 17:8b; Mark 10:45; Luke 19:10.

[2] Matt. 12:40.   [3] Matt. 24:3; *cf.* Mark 13:4.

[4] See Matt. 21:9 and Luke 19:38; *cf.* Mark 11:10.

[5] Pp. 98 f. above.   [6] As Luke 4:14.   [7] Mark 3:30.

[8] For example, the origin of the word "apostle," Luke 6:13; *cf.*, Mark 3:4; the additional clauses in the Lord's Prayer, Matt. 6:10; the generalizing of the precise formula, "Ye are Christ's," Mark 9:45, to "the name of a disciple," Matt. 10:42; the attribution of Judas's wrongdoing to Satan, Luke 22:3.

[9] 22:28-30.   [10] Luke 3:21.   [11] Luke 5:1-11.

the entire mass of apochryphal gospels dealing with the infancy and boyhood of Jesus illustrate this tendency clearly.

3. There is further evident the desire in Matthew to establish the messiahship of Jesus on the basis of an appeal to the Old Testament. The passages to which appeal is made are not those commonly used by the rabbis, but are clearly suggested by various events in the life of Jesus himself. These events are said to have occurred in order that certain prophecies might be "fulfilled,"[1] but in not a few cases the force of the argument is quite lost for the modern interpreter.[2] These passages disclose the general apologetic and interpretative purpose of all the canonical gospels. Even Mark, though without formal statement, may be seen to be built up about the purpose to exhibit the gradual revelation and apprehension of the messianic character of Jesus.[3]

4. The chief interest of the synoptic writers is eschatological. That to which they looked forward is the return of the absent Christ for the purpose of judgment and salvation. Writing, as they do, subsequent to the destruction of Jerusalem,[4] their faith in the speedy return of their Lord is quickened by that terrible event. From this point of view, the difficulties which lie in the thirteenth chapter of Mark, which has been used by both Matthew and Luke, to a considerable extent vanish. That chapter, as has already been pointed out, seems to be a combination of a group of

---

[1] Matt. 1:22, 23; 2:5, 6; 2:15; 2:17, 18; 2:23; 4:13-16; 8:17; 12:17-21; 13:35; 21:4, 5; 27:9. In addition there is in Matt. 13:14, 15 the change to the result of the telic form of Mark 4:12, and Matt. 9:13 is added to Mark 2:17.

[2] See TOY, *Quotations*, and, for the contrary view, JOHNSON, *The Quotations of the New Testament from the Old, passim.*

[3] See WENDT, *Lehre Jesu*, Vol. I, and J. WEISS, *Das Marcusevangelium*, and *Das älteste Evangelium*, pp. 99-109.

[4] Mark 13:14, which lies back of Matt. 24:15 and Luke 21:20; Mark 13:20.

prophecies concerning the fall of Jerusalem,[1] and another group of prophecies concerning the coming of the Christ. Despite the objections of Wendt,[2] both may safely be considered as coming from Jesus himself. That he expected the fall of Jerusalem is beyond question,[3] and it has already appeared that he regarded his return as in some way susceptible to interpretation by apocalyptic figures. The critical difficulty has always lain in discovering the motive for the origin of the Jerusalem doom and for the combination of these two sets of material in Mark, chap. 13. Is it only an apostolic mistake? If so, it is difficult to account for. Beyond this passage there is no evidence that the early church[4] saw in the destruction of Jerusalem evidence of the messianic parousia. If, however, the two sets of prophecy are genuine—and who would quite like to say so keen a mind as that of Jesus would have failed to forecast the inevitable outcome of the revolutionary Zealot messianism we have seen characterizing so influential a section of his people?—an explanation is not altogether beyond our reach. Its key lies in a comparison of the pronouns ταῦτα in vs. 30 and ἐκείνης in vs. 32. The two contrasted pronouns refer respectively to the fate of Jerusalem and the parousia of the Christ, and suggest that the two sets of material are in such a relation that the one gives a basis for

[1] Mark 13:7, 8 (9a), 14–20, 24–27, 30, 31 refer to Jerusalem, and the rest of the passage, vss. 4–6, 9b–13, 21–23, 28, 29, 32–37, to the messianic consummation, according to Wendt. In my judgment vss. 24–27 should be transferred to the second source.

[2] *Lehre Jesu*, Vol. I, pp. 10 f.

[3] Luke 19:41–44. This passage may have been sharpened up by Luke, but such a hypothesis is really gratuitous. Any picture of the doom of a city might easily run into the conventional particulars of a siege. See also Matt. 23:37–39 (Luke 13:34, 35). Compare also his doom of the Galilean cities (Luke 10:13–15).

[4] Yet see RUSSELL, *The Parousia;* WARREN, *The Parousia.* See also SCHWARTZKOPFF, *The Prophecies of Jesus Christ,* etc.; BEET, *The Last Things;* WEIFFENBACH, *Die Wiederkunftsgedanke Jesu;* BRIGGS, *The Messiah of the Gospels,* pp, 132–65; HAUPT, *Die eschatologischen Aussagen Jesu, passim.* A good summary with literature is the article by BROWN, "Parousia," HASTINGS'S *Dictionary of the Bible.*

confidence in the other.[1] The destruction of Jerusalem showed the accuracy of Jesus' authentic forecast of its approaching punishment. The judgment had begun with the house of Israel, the second group of enemies of the Christ. Such precise and terrible fulfilment of his prophecies regarding Jerusalem argued an equally certain fulfilment of his prophecies of messianic glory. Further, the persecution Jesus had said[2] would come upon his disciples just before the coming of their salvation was already being suffered under the Roman state. It might also be trusted to presage the coming of the Son of man.[3] Thus the parallelism led to faith in the speedy establishment of the messianic kingdom. The generation within which all "these" events—i. e., the political—were to take place had not yet quite passed from the earth, and the woes which, as appears from Jewish and Christian literature, were expected to precede the coming of Christ, had already begun. Sustained by these fulfilments of Jesus' words as regards Jerusalem and their own persecution, the Christians who "read"[4] might well "understand" and rest in supreme confidence that Jesus' prophecies of the coming of the kingdom would also be fulfilled. "These things"—the destruction of Jerusalem —had, as foretold, come to pass before the generation who heard Jesus' words had disappeared. As to the coming of "That Day" Christians might be in ignorance, but they were always to await it.[5]

[1] This view is involved in the double question of the disciples, When will Jerusalem be destroyed, and what are the signs of thy coming? in Matt. 24:3. In Mark 13:4 both questions refer to Jerusalem. Matthew has given the second question the definite messianic form.

[2] Vss. 9–13.

[3] Vs. 29 (ταῦτα γινόμενα) makes the siege of Jerusalem the sign of this greater event. Cf, also the pronouns in vs. 24.

[4] Vs. 14.

[5] This interpretation would make it more natural to regard vss. 24–27 as belonging to the apocalyptic rather than to the political group of sayings, as in the analysis of Wendt.

5. There are to be seen also traces of the evangelist's general belief in the vicarious and sacrificial death of Jesus. The passages referring to the death of Jesus as a ransom[1] may possibly be a comment from the evangelist similar to that concerning the "cleansing of all meats."[2] The words of Jesus at the Last Supper are given distinctly mediatorial reference by Matthew.[3]

Just how far this insistence upon the vicarious nature of the death of Jesus was due to the influence of Paul must always be a matter of discussion, but the antecedent probability of such influence is considerable. John Mark was one of Paul's companions,[4] and his gospel was written after the Pauline doctrine had been widely disseminated.[5] At the same time, it would be a mistake to hold that every such similarity between the evangelists' interpretation of the death of Jesus and that of Paul was due to the direct or indirect[6] influence of the latter. As has already appeared, the germ of this interpretation lay in the Christian faith of the earliest period.[7]

6. As regards the personality of Jesus, two of the synoptic gospels represent a point of view which is less strictly messianic than that of Paul. Both Matthew and Luke[8] prefix to the Markan gospel, accounts not quite consistent, of the birth of Jesus. The christology of the original gospels, as

1 Mark 10:45.

2 Mark 7:19. But see WENDT, *Teaching of Jesus*, Vol. II, pp. 227 f.

3 Matt. 26:28.

4 Acts 13: 5, 13; 15: 37, 39; Col. 4:10; Philem. 24; 2 Tim. 4:11. HOLTZMANN, *Neutestamentliche Theologie*, Vol, I, p. 424, note 2, criticises Holsten's extreme position on the point. See J. WEISS, *Das älteste Evangelium*, pp. 94 f., for discussion of entire matter.

5 That Paul used the Markan gospel seems apparent from 1 Cor. 7:10, which finds a parallel only in Mark 10:12.

6 For example, through 1 Peter.

7 It would be a mistake to regard all additional matter in Matthew and Luke as mere reflections of the evangelist's own faith. Much of it is clearly that of Jesus himself. Compare, *e. g.*, the words of Jesus to Peter in Mark 8:32 f.; Luke 12:49 f.

8 Matt. 1:18-25; Luke 1:26-56; 2:1-20.

has already appeared, is exceedingly simple. Jesus was the Anointed One; the Spirit of God came upon him at his baptism. In the new form taken by the synoptic material in Matthew and Luke this experience of the baptism is retained, but another explanation of the personality of Jesus is found in the miracle wrought by the Holy Spirit in causing his birth without a human father. The figure of unction is thus replaced by that of paternity. The messianic quality is further said to have been recognized in Jesus while he was yet an infant.[1] In the Matthean account of the baptism there is introduced[2] a conversation between John and Jesus which brings the two concepts together. John recognizes Jesus as one not in need of baptism, and Jesus receives the rite as a means of fulfilling all righteousness.[3] Further than this there is no attempt in either Matthew or Luke to adjust the two explanations of the divine character of Jesus, if indeed it is fair to say that even this addition of Matthew is such an attempt. In other material prefixed by Luke to Mark,[4] Joseph and Mary are said not to understand the reference which the boy Jesus made to God as his Father.

Yet it would be hardly safe to argue that for these reasons we are to declare off-hand that these early chapters are late and legendary. No reference is, indeed, made to their content throughout the New Testament, but at the same time these sections contain messianic psalms which cannot be referred to Christian influences. The songs of both Zacharias[5] and Mary[6] are thoroughly Jewish and represent a messianic concept which it is quite impossible to derive either from the facts of the career of Jesus or from the early Christian hopes, but which is precisely what might have been expected of their authors at the time they are declared to have been

---

[1] Luke 2:21-29; Matt. 2:1-23.　　　[2] Matt. 3:14, 15.

[3] The *Gospel of the Hebrews* represents Jesus as hesitating to seek John's baptism because of his ignorance of any sinfulness in his life.

[4] Luke 2:41-50.　　　[5] Luke 1:67-79.　　　[6] Luke 1:46-55.

uttered. The critic, therefore, finds himself in difficulty in seeking to arrive at any final opinion as regards these infancy sections. From the point of view of strict messiahship, they are not needed to account for the personality of Jesus and are not used by the writers of the New Testament, or indeed by the early Christian writers before Ignatius.[1] At the same time, it is difficult to discover any motive for inventing their strong pre-Christian coloring. Possibly their origin may lie in the evangelist's desire to explain the term "Son of God" which in Paul is used as equivalent to Messiah, but which in the Græco-Roman world might more naturally be interpreted from the point of view of current beliefs in divine paternity. Possibly, also, these section may be the outcome of an attempt to emphasize the actual rather than the merely apparent humanity of Jesus. In any case whether they are to be treated as resting upon safe critical foundations or not, they represent a phase in the development of the messianic interpretation of Jesus which does not appear in primitive Christianity or in Paul.

7. A somewhat similar difficulty meets the student as he compares the Pauline doctrine of the resurrection with the material in Matthew and Luke dealing with the appearances of Jesus. Mark, it will be recalled, contains no story of the appearances of Jesus. His gospel closes with the terror of the women to whom angels have brought the news that Jesus was risen.[2] This abrupt ending can be accounted for only by the destruction of the original ending of the gospel. In Matthew and Luke, however, we have two independent cycles of narratives dealing with the resurrection, one locating the event in Galilee,[3] and the other,[4] in the vicinity of Jerusalem.

---

[1] See HOBEN, *The Virgin Birth.* May there have been some reference to them on the part of the heretic Cerinthus ?

[2] Mark 16:1-8. All that follows Mark 16:8 is now admittedly an addition by some later Christian.

[3] Matt. 28:1-20. [4] Luke 24:1-53.

In both cycles are materials which it is difficult to harmonize with the Pauline dictum[1] that flesh and blood cannot inherit the kingdom of God. The Christ who visited the disciples in the upper room[2] had flesh and bones and could eat solid food. The Matthean cycle records that the disciples took hold of Jesus's feet.[3] Yet at the same time there is other material in Luke which is in accord with the Pauline concept. The Christ suddenly appeared[4] and vanished[5] before his disciples. In view of these inconsistencies, one is forced to recognize the possibility that the second or third generation of Christians sharpened up certain elements in the accounts of the appearances of the risen Christ as they increasingly emphasized the reality of the resurrection. As apart from these particular narratives the historical resurrection of Jesus is sufficiently attested, it would be unwise to dogmatize concerning their details. But the reference to the flesh and bones of the risen Christ introduces problems, both critical and philosophical, which are very perplexing; and yet which are more or less involved in the datum of the empty tomb. For our present purpose final decision is not demanded. Whatever position one takes as regards the authenticity of the details of these accounts, it is indisputable that they indicate the belief of the early church in the continued incarnation, if one may use the expression, of the Christ. The risen Jesus is not diffused through the universe, as is the Spirit, but, as Paul and Peter insist, is in heaven, whither he had gone by the ascension.[6] And the Christ who went to heaven disappearing in the clouds was not a mere spirit; he was a real personality possessed of spirit and some sort of body.

It cannot have escaped notice, however, that in these expositions and reworkings of the evangelists, no attempt

[1] 1 Cor. 15:50.   [2] Luke 24:36-43.   [3] Matt. 28:9.

[4] Luke 24:36.   [5] Luke 24:31.   [6] Luke 24:51; Acts 1:1-11.

—except in the case of the infancy sections—is made at adjusting the strictly messianic interpretation of Jesus to other than the strictly messianic apperception. Such readjustment was inevitable and appeared in several of the most important of the later books of the canon.

II

All questions as to the authorship of the epistle to the Hebrews are confessedly open, yet it bears unmistakable trace of the influence of Paul. Without the ordinary salutation to be found in letters,[1] it is also anonymous. Who could have written it has been a favorite subject of speculation from the days of Tertullian, who ascribed it to Barnabas.[2] This view has obtained general acceptance in modern times. Clement of Alexandria and Origen conjectured that its ideas were from Paul and the composition from a disciple, possibly Clement of Rome or Luke[3]—a position that was given weight by the Textus Receptus and passed over to orthodoxy. Other conjectures have been Clement of Rome, Luke (as independent author), Apollos, Prisca.[4] But no choice can be more than tentative. The noble writing continues to raise the perplexing question: How could so great a man as its author must have been become unknown to the early Fathers? and to suggest caution in denying culture to the Christians of a period about which we evidently know so little.[5]

The general purpose of Hebrews is apologetic.[6] The new Christian hope is restated from the point of view of ritualis-

[1] That it is none the less an epistle seems clear from 6:10; 10:32-34; 13:7, 9, 18, 19, 23, 25.

[2] De Pudicitia, 20.

[3] Eusebius, Hist. Eccle., iii, 28; vi, 25.

[4] Harnack, Zeitschrift für die neutestamentlische Wissenschaft, Vol. I (1900), pp. 16 f.

[5] In general see Jülicher, Einleitung; and art. "Hebrews," Encyclopœdia Biblica.

[6] Bruce, art. "Hebrews" in Hastings, Dictionary of the Bible.

tic Judaism, yet it distinctly presupposes that those to whom it is addressed are Christians who should be well grounded in the first principles of their religion: repentance, faith, baptism, laying on of hands, resurrection, and judgment.[1] Back of these "first principles" are to be seen further the controlling concepts which we have already traced as they have passed from Judaism into early Christianity.

1. To the writer of Hebrews, as well as to other messianists, time fell into two great divisions. Although he does not use the expression "this age,"[2] his eye is constantly setting up "the age to come."[3] Living himself "at the end,"[4] during the consummation of the ages,[5] he looked forward to that glorious sabbath rest which was drawing near,[6] of which Jesus was the High-Priest.

2. The power of Satan in the present age is to be inferred from the fact that he has the power of death.[7]

3. The kingdom of God was still future,[8] although in a sense already possessed by those who awaited its coming.[9] There is in the book absolutely no suggestion of any coming of the kingdom through social evolution. It cannot come until the cataclysm prophecied by Haggai is past.[10]

4. The judgment is always before the mind of the writer and is that for which all men are to prepare. Indeed, with repentance it is one of the first principles of the Christian faith.[11]

5. The Jews are those to whom the letter is especially addressed, and they are evidently conceived of as the true members of the kingdom. Israel is the οἶκος Θεοῦ to which

---

[1] Heb. 6:1, 2.   [2] ὁ κόσμος, however, occurs in Heb. 11:7, 38; 10:5.

[3] Heb. 6:5; cf. 9:11, 15.   [4] ἐπ' ἐσχάτου τῶν ἡμερῶν, Heb. 1:2.

[5] Heb. 9:26. This expression is interesting in its bearing upon the belief in the speedy coming of the Christ.

[6] Heb. 4:9; 10:25, 36–38; cf. καιρὸς διορθώσεως, 9:10.

[7] Heb. 2:14.   [8] Heb. 13:14.   [9] Heb. 12:28.

[10] Heb. 12:26, 27; cf. Hag. 2:7.   [11] Heb. 6:2; see also Heb. 9:27; 10:26, 31.

the author and his fellow Christians belonged.[1] Christ assists not angels, but Jews,[2] and the New Jerusalem is the New Zion.[3] At the same time, there is in the letter no retrogression toward primitive Christianity, only belief that Israel can partake of the heavenly calling,[4] and the letter appeals quite as strongly to gentiles as to Jews. The extra-canonical literature of early Christianity shows plainly that even in the gentile churches the method of exposition followed by the book would be thoroughly satisfactory. Early Christian writings, like *1 Clement* and *Barnabas*, which closely resemble Hebrews in many ways, appeal more constantly to the Old Testament and the fulfilment of prophecy than they do to peculiarly Christian literature.[5]

6. The resurrection of the Christ is constantly referred to, and in a certain way is made a type of that of the believers.[6] But no detailed reference is made to a general resurrection, and belief in it does not belong to the "wisdom of the perfect," but rather to the first principles[7] presupposed on the part of those to whom the letter is addressed.

7. The Messiah is the central point of interest in the epistle. He is in heaven on the right hand of God,[8] but was pre-existent,[9] and above the angels in that he was Son rather than a servant.[10] He is to appear again unto the salvation of those who wait for him.[11] Hebrews, however, shows clearly the beginnings of the third stratum of early Christian thought. Paulinism had systematically treated the impli-

---

[1] Heb. 3:2-6.   [2] Heb. 2:16.

[3] Heb. 12:22.   [4] Heb. 3:1; 4:14; 13:10-12.

[5] To this may be added the entire contrast drawn between the old Hebrew kingdom and that of the new dispensation.

[6] Heb. 6:20; *cf.* also 10:32-38, where the Christians are urged to endure persecution because of the coming reward.

[7] Heb. 6:2.   [8] Heb. 8:1, 2; 12:2.

[9] Heb. 1:2; *cf.* 1:9. There is no reference here to a miraculous birth.

[10] Heb. 1:1-14; 3:6; 5:8; 7:28.

[11] Heb. 9:28. It is interesting to notice that in Heb. 13:20 Jesus is described in conventional messianic terms as the shepherd of the sheep.

cations of Christian faith in its relation to Hebrew religious philosophy. Hebrews begins the process of finding and defending interpretations of Christian theology in other than messianic terms. Messianism is indeed in the background, but the main purpose of the writing is twofold, viz.: to show how the Christ fulfils the types of sacrifice and High-Priest as they exist in the Old Testament, and to encourage the early Christians to larger faith and hope in the midst of persecution.

In treating of the Christ as an anti-type of the temple worship, the author distinctly asserts that Jesus was not a High-Priest in the Old Testament sense. If he were on earth, he would not be a priest, since he was not of Aaronic descent,[1] but rather after the fashion of Melchizedek.[2] At the same time, he insists that the priesthood of the old dispensation was the forecasting of the actual deeds of Jesus who by dying went behind the veil, after having offered himself as a sacrifice.[3] It is natural, therefore, to find the vicarious character of the death of Jesus strongly emphasized in Hebrews.[4] By it there was established a new covenant easily understood, written in men's hearts rather than upon statute-books, and thus superior to that of Moses, which was provisional.[5] Jesus was the priestly mediator of this covenant, his historical appearance marking the pre-messianic age at the end of which the writer conceived of himself living.[6] Just what that covenant is in particular the writer of Hebrews does not say, but[7] it is evidently the promises which they have received, which include the entrance into the sabbath rest[8] and the resurrection of the body. Indeed, it is

[1] Heb. 8:4; cf. 7:25.　　　[2] Heb. 7:5 f.
[3] Heb. 8:1-13; chap. 9, especially vss. 23 f.; 10:1.
[4] Heb. 2:9; 5:7-9; 9:11, 15; 10:11-18.　　[5] Heb. 7:18, 22; 9:19-22; 12:24.
[6] Heb. 12:24.
[7] Cf. Heb. 13:20, where the risen Christ establishes a διαθήκην αἰώνιον.
[8] Heb. 3:7—4:10.

possible to argue that, like Paul, the author of Hebrews saw in the death of Christ the promise of the conquest of the spirit over the flesh, not only in his case, but in that of all those who believed.[1]

Obviously this interpretation of Jesus as the great High-Priest is not derived from, but is superimposed upon his messianic significance. Another tendency in the Christology of the epistle is even more remote from messianism. It is the epistle's metaphysical valuation of the personality of the Christ. This concept, as has just appeared, is in the term "Son." The method followed by the writer is worth consideration. Instead of proceeding from an assumption as to the nature of the pre-existent Christ to the historical person Jesus, he argues backward from the (historical) elevation of Jesus to the messianic dignity to the original nature which he must have possessed in order to have made such exaltation possible. That is, the metaphysical Sonship is an inference from the messianic power now exhibited by the historical but risen Jesus. How great he must have been to have achieved such supremacy! The thought is not developed far, but is obviously on the way to Nicea.[2]

An important characteristic of the epistle is, therefore, its general tendency to present Christianity systematically from the point of view of a reinterpretation of the messianic estimate of Jesus. The original material, so to speak, from which Christian thought is drawn is that common to primitive and Pauline teaching, but the mind of the writer, obviously under the influence of the Alexandrian school of

---

[1] Heb. 5: 7-9, 14.

[2] ἀπαύγασμα τῆς δόξης; χαρακτὴρ τῆς ὑποστάσεως αὐτοῦ (1:3) remind one of Alexandrine modes of thought as well as *Wis.*, 7: 25, 26; BRUCE, "Hebrews," in HASTINGS, *Dictionary of the Bible*, Vol. II, p. 335; *cf.* RHIEM, *Lehrbegriff des Hebräerbriefs*, pp. 409-14. This metaphysical tendency is more clearly shown at the beginning of the epistle than in its later chapters; *cf.* especially chap. 1. WEISS, *Biblical Theology*, Vol. II, p. 189, note, very properly says: "On these expressions . . . . Beyschlag's attempt is irredeemably wrecked, to understand the pre-existence of Christ as that of an impersonal principle."

thought, is not content to leave matters where Paul left them. He is dealing with a different theological apperception. Jesus and Peter and Paul brought the gospel into relations with essentially and all but exclusively Judaistic thought. The author of Hebrews has another audience, and consequently another problem. The Hellenistic Judaism and Christianity of the time demanded that Christian "first principles" should be restated and recombined, and subjected to new inductions. Hebrews does not mark the reworking of these "first principles" from the genuinely Hellenic philosophy, but it does mark the same method. Messianism now appears in the process of passing into theological equivalents. It is a point of departure, not, as in earlier Paulinism, a final interpretation. The incarnation of the Christ is given a new value, although one already presaged in Pauline teaching. It is something more than an incident in his humiliation and re-exaltation. It is a part of a general philosophy. The Christ became incarnate as a part of his messianic preparation. He became incarnate and suffered that he might become thoroughly in sympathy with humanity.[1] His offering of himself as the Sacrifice was through the Holy Spirit,[2] which is also in the believer. By virtue of his incarnation he was liable to, and was subjected to, temptation, but by virtue of his Sonship he did not, like the priest of the Mosaic covenant, commit sin.[3] Thus perfected through the experience of humanity, and through humble trust in God,[4] the Christ became not only the High-Priest raised from death to the heavenly kingdom, but the great Inspirer and Captain of all those who believe in him and receive his Spirit.[5]

It is on this basis of a conviction grounded in this high-priestly interpretation of the Christ that the writer incites

---

[1] Heb. 2:9-18; 4:15; 5:7-9. [2] Heb. 9:14. [3] Heb. 4:15; 9:14.
[4] Heb. 2:13. [5] Heb. 2:10; 12:2, 3.

his readers to endure persecution, holding fast to the faith which is theirs, and of which Jesus is the great Captain.[1] In the interest of stimulating this consistency, he introduces the noble list of martyrs who, although they had not received the promise, yet preferred holding to such faith as they had, to saving their lives or the lives of their friends. The reward is so certain for the Christian as to make persecution endurable.[2] The very Christ had to suffer in order that, like humanity, he should be made perfect through suffering.[3]

As a corollary of this generalizing and equivalenting process is the epistle's teaching as to faith. It is no longer so much the acceptance of Jesus as Christ as "faith toward God."[4] Those who, like the Old Testament saints, "had not received the promise"—i. e., participation in the historical revelation of the messianic salvation—believed God quite as truly as those to whom the letter is addressed.[5] While Paul had anticipated this conception in his references to the faith of Abraham, he had not elaborated its religious and generic elements, but had rather confined it to the messianic definition. Hebrews in some degree turns back to the more general thought of Jesus himself, and treats faith as an attitude of trust in God and a self-sacrificing devotion to moral ideals. In this, as in the reinterpretation of the messianic idea itself, there appears a step toward the dejudaizing of the definitions and concepts intended by Christianity. The eternal value of Jesus was thus set forth in terms and by methods already dominating the minds of those to whom the exposition was made. Christian theology, like Paul, is thus seen becoming Grecian to Grecians as it had been Jewish to Jews.

It is perhaps inevitable that, because of the strong emphasis laid by the epistle upon Jesus as an example and

[1] Heb. 13:1.　　　[2] Heb. 10:32-38.　　　[3] Heb. 5:7-9.
[4] Heb. 6:2.　　　[5] Heb. 11:39, 40; cf. 6:2.

upon the generic character of faith, the Spirit should be less prominent. To a considerable extent Hebrews, like James, represents Christian "wisdom." Conduct is made more dependent upon one's own volition than upon the following of the better spiritual impulses due to the conscious presence of God. None the less back of the "wisdom" of Hebrews as back of the forensic theology of Paul there is the experience of the Spirit. Through the Spirit Jesus had been raised from the dead;[1] from the Spirit the believer had received "gifts,"[2] and the worst of all sins was doing despite to the Spirit of Grace.[3] But farther than these hints at the great presupposition of Christian life the author does not go. His aim is too philosophical, too ethical, and too apologetic. He would convince his already Christian readers as to the significance of their Christ; he is content to trust their new conviction to express itself in moral endeavor.

III

The Johannine literature includes the Gospel according to John and the three epistles ascribed to the apostle. Of these four writings the second and third epistles are very brief, and for our present purpose are of comparatively small doctrinal importance.[4] The first epistle and the gospel exhibit, however, a phase of Christianity which has always appealed powerfully to the religious consciousness of the church. The critical questions concerning this literature are well known, and have been for two generations the source of an almost boundless literature.[5] While it would be unsafe to say that any unanimous decision has yet been

[1] Heb. 9:14; cf. Rom. 8:11.   [2] Heb. 2:4.   [3] Heb. 10:29.

[4] 2 John, vs. 7, defines antichrist as one who denies that Jesus Christ "comes in the flesh."

[5] See Introductions by HOLTZMANN and JÜLICHER. A good brief statement will be found in BACON, *Introduction*, and from a more conservative point of view in DODS, *Expositor's Greek Testament*, Vol. I. The article by REYNOLDS in HASTINGS, *Dictionary of the Bible*, is also valuable.

reached regarding its authorship, the limits of the problem are very much more distinctly seen today than ever before, and there is a tendency toward a compromise view which harmonizes the data upon which opposing schools have based their conflicting conclusions. Without entering into any detailed criticism, it may be said that it is impossible to believe that the author of the Epistles of John was any other than the author of the last chapter of the Fourth Gospel; but just as certain does it seem that the author of the Fourth Gospel in its present form, could not have been the apostle.[1] He was rather a sympathetic expositor of material which came from the apostle.[2]

Whether or not one agrees with this particular critical position, there is no gainsaying the fact that the Fourth Gospel represents a different type of exposition from that of the synoptists. And this peculiar type is due to the evangelist rather than to a change in the teaching of Jesus. He has so reworked and discussed the teaching of Jesus as to make it something very different from the pregnant pictorial words of the synoptist. Yet, notwithstanding its change of form, one would hesitate to say that it is any less true to the teaching of the Master, either in the words of Jesus it records or in its much larger element of comment and exposition. It has proceeded farther even than Matthew along the road of apologetics and theology, but its representation of the gospel, so far from being untrue, is rather an attempt at adjusting the teaching and life of Jesus to a different order of thought from that of the Jew. Eschatology and the eschatological salvation are fundamental to it.[3] In fact,

---

[1] John 21:22-24 clearly implies that the death of John preceded the writing of this chapter.

[2] See pp. 59-61 above, and Burton, *A Short Introduction to the Gospels*.

[3] John 5:19-21, 22-29; 6:40-58 deal with the contrast between life and death, notably that of the resurrection. The judgment is treated in 3:17; 5:22, 23, 27; 9:39; 16:47. Salvation is spoken of as opposed to perishing in 3:17; to being judged, 3:18; 12:43, 50; and the wrath of God, 3:36. Flesh and blood cannot enter the kingdom of God, 5:6; and a man must be born again—*i. e.*, by the resurrection?—to enter the kingdom of God, 3:?

as far as we are able to distinguish the editorial material from that which is unquestionably from Jesus, we see how true the author is to the purpose he himself states. The book was written that men might believe that Jesus is the Christ, the Son of God, and believing, have life in him.[1]

The life to which the evangelist refers is, of course, the eternal life, which we have seen already to be the center of the Pauline thought and the supreme good in the teaching of Jesus. This eternal life is certainly something more than a merely ethical matter, however much it may involve moral qualities. Wherever it is mentioned it is introduced with an eschatological connotation, often as a contrast with punishment which is inclusive of death.[2] It unquestionably therefore refers to that new and completer life that awaits beyond death the personality in which the Spirit is working. It is in this sense of an actual experience of God through a moral life in accord with a supreme definition of Jesus that the evangelist speaks of eternal life as a knowledge of God and of Jesus Christ.[3] Faith in the Fourth Gospel, as with Paul, is, in the first instance, the acceptance of Jesus as Christ, and results in eternal life.[4] In fact, the general plan of the gospel centers about such a confession. Its various sections, which were very probably originally independent treatises, have as a general plan an incident in the life of Jesus which leads up to a discussion which results in the hearers of Jesus taking a decided position relative to him, either accepting him or rejecting him as the Christ. If we had only the Fourth Gospel, it would seem as if the chief thing which Jesus endeavored to accomplish was to have men accept him as the Christ.[5]

[1] John 20:31.

[2] John 3:16, the opposite of perishing; 5:24 (the words of Jesus), 5:26, 29, where the reference is that by the evangelist to the resurrection; cf. 11:25; 12:50.

[3] John 17:3. For a non-biblical, pantheistic conception that approaches this of the evangelist, but minus the expectation of personal immortality, see PICTON, *Religion of the Universe*, pp. 303, 304.

[4] John 1:50; 4:39; 6:29; 9:22; cf. 12:42.   [5] Cf. John 7:25-29; 10:22-39.

This point of view is certainly not that of the synoptic gospels, but it is precisely that of a devoted disciple, who, looking back upon the career of his Master through the course of years, would be quick to see how constantly Jesus was in reality presenting himself as a subject of definition. There is nothing impossible in the statements that the people[1] and the Pharisees were in perplexity concerning him, and there is everything in favor of the correctness of the interpretation given by the evangelist to Jesus' attitude toward this perplexity.

The Fourth Evangelist, however, is not content to have human destiny determined by what might be interpreted, however incorrectly, as an act of mere intellectual assent. The acceptance of Jesus as Christ is fundamentally a moral act and expressive of a moral state. It was a moral criterion. If a man came to the Light, it was because he was doing truth; if he turned from the Light, it was because his deeds were evil.[2] Even the miracles of Jesus would have no meaning to those who could not see in them "signs" of the divine love.[3]

But this reverting to fundamentals, this effort to adjust the new faith of the Christian to the philosophical rather than the Jewish attitude of mind, is carried farther by the evangelist. It extends to an accommodation or redefinition of messiahship itself.

How far removed the readers of the gospel must have been from unalloyed Jewish or primitive Christian messianism is to be seen in that the author translates the word Messiah for their benefit.[4] But such interpretation is of slight importance compared with that larger purpose to revalue the messiahship of Jesus in terms which would

---

[1] John 7:25-27, 40-44.   [2] John 3:18-21: cf. 1 John 1:6.

[3] See in particular chap. 6 entire.

[4] John 1:4; 4:25. Cf. his similar explanation of other Jewish terms, like "rabbi," and customs, like those of the feast and defilement.

make it intelligible to the religious consciousness of the non-Jewish philosophical world.

All critics are agreed that the work was written at the very end of the first or at the beginning of the second century, and was intended for those who were not controlled by those concepts which prevailed in the primitive Christian communities. The Prologue to the gospel[1] seeks to discover a point of contact between the new faith and the current Logos philosophy. It is here that the gospel comes close to the modern mind. The Logos of the later Greek philosophy was strikingly like that half-personified Law that plays so large a rôle in today's religious and philosophical thought. For the Logos was God conceived of as intelligible revelation, sometimes cosmic, sometimes more individually. It would not be correct to say that the Johannine Logos was derived from that of Philo. As has been repeatedly shown,[2] there are decided differences between the two. At the same time, it would be just as incorrect to say the Johannine Logos philosophy was an independent development without genetic relations with the general concept that had become socialized by Stoicism throughout the world quite as truly as by Philo in Alexandria. The Fourth Gospel is the outcome of a desire to present the significance of Jesus as the Christ to those people who were dominated, not by the messianic, but by this Logos concept. It was the Logos rather than, as in Paulinism, the Christ that was incarnated.[3] Just as in Hebrews there is an importation of a metaphysical divine sonship into the messianic designation of Jesus, so in the Fourth Gospel the messiahship of Jesus as presented to the gentile world includes elements not derivable from pharisaism. At the same time, he is still called

[1] John 1:1-18.

[2] For a brief summary see HARNACK, *History of Dogma*, Vol. I, pp. 109-28.

[3] John 1:14.

the Christ, and there is no attempt to substitute the term "Logos" for the term "Christ." A new significance and a new content are simply given the later term.

Similarly, in the first epistle of John there is a development of the broader and more philosophical implications and relations of the original Jewish faith. The reality of Jesus is assumed and vigorously affirmed to be a source of the believer's hope and his new sense of fellowship with the Father,[1] but the ultimate significance of this historical person, although it still includes the chief elements of the messianic concept, is enlarged to something that moves on beyond even the cosmic significance as ascribed to Jesus in the Pauline letters of the imprisonment. Whoever denies that Jesus is the Christ is a liar,[2] and whoever denies the Father and the Son is an Antichrist, and the reason for this severe judgment lies in the entire philosophy of the epistle and of the Fourth Gospel.[3] The Christian partakes of the divine nature,[4] and this divine life is genuinely ethical, expressing itself not merely in protestation of the love of God, but also in the actual love of man.[5] As a life it is derived from the indwelling of the Spirit,[6] sent by God to those who believe Jesus to be the Son of God.[7] As in Paul, this eternal life, which is the result of the union of the human and Holy Spirit, reaches its consummation in a new mode of life at the time of the reappearance of the Christ, when all those who have the spirit and are the children of God are to be like their Christ.[8] This future life, already possessed in part, furnishes a basis for Johannine ethics as truly as for the Pauline.[9]

[1] 1 John 1:1-4.   [2] 1 John 1:22.   [3] John 3:18-21.

[4] 1 John 3:9, 10.   [5] 1 John 3:15-24.   [6] 1 John 3:24; 4:12-16.

[7] This concept furnishes a new confirmation for the interpretation given above of the significance of the Pauline expression "in Christ," as equivalent to having the Spirit which Christ had sent.

[8] 1 John 3:1, 2.   [9] 1 John 3:3; 5:5; 4:15-21.

The advance that the epistle makes toward a later formulated theology is further to be seen in the incidental reference to the threefold witness of the spirit, the water and the blood.[1]

IV

No one can pass without a sense of retrogression from the magnificent Johannine literature, with its profound appreciation of human motives and of religious dynamics, to the last two books of the canonical collection, the Second Epistle of Peter and the Epistle of Jude.[2] In them we have an echo of that fierce chiliasm which dominated a certain section of the church of the second century, and which found more satisfaction in the Jewish elements of Christianity than in its fundamental character as a religion of the spirit made possible through the revelation of God in Jesus and the incoming of God himself into human life. In this literature we see something of the same temperament, world-view, and even personages[3] which are to be found in the slavonic *Enoch*, the *Shepherd of Hermas*, and those other and even cruder apocalypses of early Christianity and rabbinism. Far more than in any other portion of New Testament literature do these writings exhibit the desire for the punishment of the enemies which marks the Jewish apocalyptic literature as a whole.[4] In them, further, do we see that marked tendency of history to emphasize as literal truths the apocalyptic eschatology of Christian hope.[5] Far more than in the case of the Johannine or Pauline literature, or the Epistle to the Hebrews, does the Christian hope become unworldly, and gloomy,

[1] 1 John 5:8.

[2] See especially HOLTZMANN, *Einleitung;* HARNACK, *Chronologie* etc. A good summary of the discussion relative to the interdependence of Jude and of Peter will found in BACON, *Introduction*, pp. 166-74.

[3] Jude, vss. 9, 14.   [4] Jude, vss. 11-16; 2 Pet. 2:1-22.

[5] See, *e. g.*, 2 Pet. 3:10-13.

while the disappointment and doubt resulting from the failure of the Christ to appear during the lifetime of his generation are met by recourse to a forced exegesis which made a day with the Lord as a thousand years.[1] Yet the fundamental elements of Christian life born of the experiences of the Holy Spirit, are not quite overlooked,[2] and the hope of eternal life is as always an incentive to holy living.

V

Thus in the later phases of the New Testament teaching we find, as in Paul, the emphasis upon the messiahship of Jesus and the implied elements of the future messianic age side by side with the equally clear recognition of eternal life, the result of the believer's actual possession, though normal spiritual processes, of the life of God. We see further, the beginning of that steady process of accommodation of messianic values to the needs and preconceptions of a non-messianic philosophy. How far this revaluation was to proceed, any student of Christian thought can testify. Nicæa and Chalcedon are far enough removed from the elemental Christology of the Jerusalem community but they were implicit in more than one of the later New Testament books. But Christian theology, however complete its subjection to a contemporary metaphysic, has never quite failed to see that the end of faith is something other than faith itself, and that the most rigorously logical creed is only a means of bringing men to God and God to men. Jesus, however interpreted, has been a Mediator and a Savior. But early Fathers, like Tertullian and Justin Martyr, even the unknown author of the exquisite *Epistle to Diognetus*, make less edifying teachers for today than the New Testament writers. And for this reason: they were too much

1 2 Pet. 3:3-9.　　　　2 Jude, vss. 20, 21; 2 Pet. 2:4-11.

given to edifying their own unmodern contemporaries. Far enough they seem from our way of thinking. The later New Testament writers, to some extent, share in this remoteness, but in inverse ratio to their emphasis of the facts of the gospel and to the new life of the spirit. With them, even with Paul, began that struggle of this inner life *to* which God came, with those current ways and norms of thinking *through* which God came. Christian faith is fundamentally a means of life with God; theological philosophy, in so far as it did not further that life, checked it.

To this struggle between an inherited messianism and eternal life, as it is recorded in the pages of the New Testament, we must now give consideration.

PART IV

CHRISTIAN MESSIANISM AND THE CHRISTIAN RELIGION

CHAPTER I

THE MESSIANIC FRATERNITY

CHRISTIANITY has never been merely a philosophy; it has always been, as its earliest adherents held, a Way—that is to say, a Life. And life means history. Any study of the New Testament would be incomplete that did not trace the faith and the experience of the early churches in their relation to the larger life of that society in which they lived. To treat New Testament Christianity as anything other than a life dominated by a belief and by a hope would be a serious error. Especially is this true in any attempt to distinguish between the formal or inherited and the essential elements of early Christianity. It has been repeatedly urged in the preceding pages that the apostles, while thoroughly believing in the messianic character of Jesus, regarded the actual regenerating experience of God induced by accepting Jesus at the messianic valuation as the fundamental element in their gospel. We are now to see that the same results come from the study of the life of the Christians in their social relations. After all, the test of Christianity was, in apostolic days as it always has been, its capacity to produce lives filled with love and goodness. It will appear from the study of the social expression of Christianity that strictly messianic elements were so far from being essential as to have been hardly more than economic. They furnished the point of contact for converting the world, but they also to some extent checked the expression of that regenerate life which came from the believer's experience of God. To a considerable extent, consequently, they passed into desuetude. The Christian church, beginning as a sect of the Jews, during the New Testament times developed into a cosmopolitan movement, but it did not break with the messianic movement from which it developed. Brought into touch with a world which was only partially under the Jewish influence, it yet held to the Jewish messianic expectation in so far as it lived again in the Christian teaching, but accommodated itself as best it could to the various social environments in which it found itself.

I

Judaism was the social apperception—if one may use such a figure—to which the Gospel appealed. Without the Jew it is hard to see how there could have been a Christian; without the Jewish Dispersion it is hard to see how there could have ever been a Christian empire.

Yet the presence of the Jew throughout the Roman empire was but one expression of that flood-tide of cosmopolitanism of which the new faith took fullest advantage. Among all the striking phenomena that accompanied the evolution of the Roman empire, none is more marked than the migration of different cults. Generally speaking, these cults were national or ethnic, and their diffusion was the natural outcome of the new commercial conditions that led to a widespread immigration of oriental peoples into the western parts of the empire. With the Egyptian immigration went the worship of Serapis, Isis, and Osiris; with the Phrygian, that of Sabizius (Bacchus) and Cybele; with the Persian, that of Mithra with its fascinating mysteries.[1] By degrees these oriental faiths spread over the entire empire, and, as inscriptions testify, had their temples and devotees from the Tigris to the Atlantic and from the Rhine to the African desert. Their success was due, not merely to their

---

[1] This was by far the most important rival of Judaism and Christianity to the Roman empire. CUMONT, *The Mysteries of Mithra* (see abstract of his *Textes et monuments relatifs aux mystères de Mithra*), *Open Court*, 1903. In general, see the excellent chapters (4–6) of DILL, *Roman Society from Nero to Marcus Aurelius*.

novelty, but to their undoubted moral and religious superiority to classical heathenism. The culture of the period had long since outgrown mythology, and readily welcomed the more or less absolute monotheism which was the common property of the invading cults. Quite as potent in their spread, also, was their insistence upon morality as inseparable from religion. Sin and repentance, punishment and forgiveness, were integral parts of all these oriental cults, and those who would accept them and be initiated into their mysteries were subjected to rigorous probation and highly dramatic initiatory rites. The ethical neutrality of the Roman and Greek mythologies could not for a moment survive before the moral passion, however distorted, of men who would submit to the bloody baptism of the taurobolium. If one recalls that in addition these new cults regarded the individual as something more than a member of a nation, and made immortality, with its rewards and punishments, central in all their teaching, their success is easily understood.

It was characteristic of these religions that their followers should form communities. The vocabulary that is being discovered by the study of papyri[1] is rich in words dealing with such groups of coreligionists. Their members were "brothers" (ἀδελφοί); they had their mysteries, their passwords, prophets, sacraments, common meals, their priests and "elders."[2] Between scattered fraternities there sprang up correspondence, bits of which have survived, while their members were always certain of a hospitable reception from their brethren in whatever city they might chance to arrive as travelers or pilgrims.

The Jewish Dispersion was, therefore, by no means unique in an age of interpenetrating peoples and religions. Possibly

---

[1] See, for instance, DEISSMANN, *Bible Studies*, pp. 87, 88.

[2] DEISSMANN, *Bible Studies*, pp. 233–35 (pp. 368 f.). He even finds an inscription in Caria throwing light on the white robes and palms of Rev. 7:9 f.

it was the most widespread,[1] but from some of the evidence at our disposal it would seem as if it were by no means the most prosperous or possessed of the greatest contemporary influence. In Græco-Roman society the emigrant Jew, though exceptionally favored by the empire, was an object of no small hatred and derision.[2] His unwillingness to eat food highly prized by heathen epicures, his refusal to work upon the sabbath, his apparent readiness to traffic in miracles, his religious pride, all served to remove him from the easy-going toleration of the current religious eclecticism. Yet Judaism was by no means without its influence upon the society into which it had penetrated.[3] The same readiness to accept a monotheistic religion promising forgiveness of sin and a blessed immortality which made the non-Jewish oriental cults popular throughout the empire, led many persons, and that too by no means exclusively from the uneducated and lower classes, to become followers of Moses. In addition to such proselytes, there were many gentiles over whom Judaism exercised a greater or less influence. The Judaism of the Dispersion was less rigorous than that of Palestine, and was ready to tolerate, if not to encourage,

---

[1] Yet one must make large allowance for exaggeration in the words of Josephus, *Against Apion*, ii, 39.

[2] See, for instance, Horace, *Satires*, 1:4, 142 f.; Persius, *Satires*, 5:178–84; Juvenal, *Satires*, 3:12–16; 14:96–106. On Jews as exorcists see Gebhardt and Harnack, *Texte*, VIII, last part, 107; Justin Martyr, *Apol.*, 26; *Trypho*, 31. On the anti-Semitism of Alexandria see von Dobschütz, *American Journal of Theology*, October, 1904.

[3] The influence of Hellenism on Judaism is just now a rather favorite subject of study. Pfleiderer (*Urchristhenthum*[3]) has discussed the matter in detail, and Gunkel has published the brochure already referred to, *Zum religionsgeschicht-lichen Verständniss des Neuen Testaments*, in which the results of his earlier studies are concentrated upon this particular thesis. The works of Bousset and of Bacon (*The Story of Paul*) may also be mentioned. In my judgment, however, little has resulted as yet from these investigations which would justify one in magnifying the Hellenistic influence in the case of Paul. With Philo it is, of course, very different. But Pharisaism, in its broadest sense, best accounts for those phenomena of the apostle's thought which are not derivable from the evangelic facts. When we enter the second century, and especially when we meet Gnosticism, the case is radically different.

those who would accept its teachings as expressing a new religious philosophy, while refusing to become completely identified with it as a cult. Thus around the "community" or "synagogue" of the Jewish colony in the various cities there sprang up two groups of non-Jewish converts: the proselytes and "those who feared God"[1] and observed the general Mosaic regulations for keeping the sabbath and maintaining ceremonial purity.

Nor was the religious influence of Judaism restricted to these limits.[2] Even if one be indisposed to accept seriously the belief of some of the Jewish writers that Plato drew his teachings from Moses, there can be no doubt that the strong morality and uncompromising monotheism of Pharisaism was felt throughout the Græco-Roman world quite outside the limits of those who were even loosely connected with the synagogue. Otherwise it would be hard to understand the literary warfare, offensive and defensive, carried on by Josephus and other Jewish apologists against heathen opponents, and quite impossible to give proper credit to the literary output of Philo and the Alexandrines.[3] Even more perplexing would be the observance of the sabbath in different parts of the empire by gentiles presumably not connected with the synagogue.[4]

It is this widespread influence of Judaism that explains

---

[1] They are termed φοβούμενοι τὸν θεόν in Acts 10:2, 22; 13:16, 26; σεβόμενοι τὸν θεόν in Acts 13:43; 16:14; 18:7; JOSEPHUS, Ant., xiv, 7:2; or briefly σεβόμενοι as in Acts 13:50; 17:4, 17. The expression of Acts 13:43, σεβόμενοι προσήλυτοι, is unique and cannot be said to vitiate the above interpretation. See for full treatment (including discussion of parallel expressions of the inscriptions) SCHÜRER, Geschichte des jüdischen Volkes (3d ed.), Vol. III, pp. 122 f., esp. n. 66, and his essay, "Die Juden im bosporanischen Reiche und die Genossenschaft der σεβόμενοι τὸν θεὸν ὕψιστον ebendaselbst," in Sitzungsberichte der Berliner Akademie, 1897, pp, 200–225; RAMSAY, Expositor, 1896, pp. 200 f. Yet contra see BERTHOLET, Die Stellung der Israeliten und der Juden zu den Fremden, passim.

[2] See the article on "Proselytes" in HASTINGS, Dictionary of the Bible.

[3] Cf. PHILO, Vit Mos, 2:4; JOSEPHUS, Against Apia, 2:29.

[4] See SCHÜRER, Geschichte der jüdischen Volkes[3], Vol. III, p. 116, n. 45. In general see BERTHOLET, Die Stellung der Israeliten und der Juden zu den Fremden; FRIEDLÄNDER, Das Judenthum in der vorchristlichen griechischen Welt.

in large part the rapid growth of Christianity during the apostolic period. When brought face to face with a heathenism unaffected by Jewish thought, the promise of an aquittal at a coming world-judgment, the story of a risen Jesus who was the first-fruits of all such followers of his who should die before the establishment of a glorious but un-political kingdom, made but little impression.[1] To appreciate Jesus as Christ it was first necessary to have some knowledge of what the Christ should be, and this, at least in the Dispersion, could be gained only through a knowledge of pharisaic messianism.[2] As Acts and the Pauline literature make clear, the original members of the Christian communities were almost exclusively Jews, or gentiles who had either come under the influence of the Judaism of the synagogue or through the diffused influence of Jewish thought had a predisposition to the messianic program. The first great problem faced by the new faith was its relation to Judaism as a whole, notably to the observance of the Thorah; the second was that of adjusting a faith in Jesus as the Christ soon to establish his kingdom, with the various non-Jewish or but semi-Jewish religious conceptions that obtained in Asia Minor and those cities of Europe in which oriental mysteries and cults had begun to regulate religious philosophy. This difference in apologetic and exposition is plainly seen by a comparison of Paul's letters to the Galatians and the Colossians, but it is even more pronounced when the Revelation of John is compared with the prologue of the Fourth Gospel. Patristic theology shows similar con-

---

[1] Compare the reception of Paul's preaching by Athenians, Acts, chap. 17. It is hard to see why one should be forced to regard this speech as untrue to Paul's thought. Even if one were to rewrite history on *a priori* methods, what other kind of speech would the uneven spread of messianic Judaism make probable?

[2] This statement is not intended to imply that there were no differences between the messianism of the Dispersion and that of the "Hebrew" Jews. But the evidence to be found in *Sib. Oracles* and the early Christian "Visions" make it evident that it was pharisaic rather than Zealot hopes that were to be found in the Dispersion.

trasts, but throughout its earlier phases its apologetic consists largely of arguments showing that Jesus as Christ fulfils the prophecies of the Hebrew Scriptures.[1] It was only when Christianity passed into the hands of professional philosophers and men of their spirit that its Jewish relations and heritage were neglected and replaced by the generalizing methods of the schools.[2]

The importance of the preparatory rôle played in apostolic Christianity by pharisaic Judaism is evidenced by what the author of the letter to the Hebrews calls "the matter of the beginning of the Christ," or "the foundation,"[3] viz.: repentance from dead works and faith upon God, the teaching concerning baptism and the laying on of hands, the resurrection from the dead and the age-judgment. Quite as plainly does it appear in the references in the Pauline literature to the initial acts of those who formed the new communities. All such had abandoned evil courses to wait for the coming of God's Son and his kingdom.[4] The faith that introduced the convert into the new relationship with God was thus easily formulated; it was the acceptance of Jesus as the one who should do that expected of the Christ by Judaism, in so far as this expectation was not modified by the actual experiences of Jesus. In a word, the Christian churches were composed of those who sought justification— acquittal in the approaching messianic judgment—by faith —i. e., accepting Jesus as the eschatological Messiah. And this is no more true of Pauline churches than of the church

[1] See, for instance, the crude arguments of *Barnabas* and the elaborate treatise of Justin Martyr thrown in the form of a dialogue with a Jew Trypho.

[2] On this in general see WERNLE, *The Beginnings of Christianity*, Vol. II, chaps. 7 and 8; HARNACK, *History of Dogma*, Vol. I, Bk. i, chap. 3.

[3] Heb. 6:1, τὸν τῆς ἀρχῆς τοῦ Χριστοῦ λόγον.

[4] In particular see 1 Thess. 1:10; 2:20; 3:13; Phil. 1:6, 10; Acts 17:7; Rom. 8:23-25; 1 Cor. 1:8; 3:13; 6:9, 10; 15:23. Jews were undoubtedly members of these "gentile churches;" Gal. 2:9. *Cf.* the account of the founding of various Pauline churches in Acts.

at Jerusalem. Its members also sought "salvation" by repentance and the acceptance of Jesus as the Christ who would admit them into his kingdom.[2]

It is not difficult, therefore, to realize the character of the first Christian communities. They were composed of those who believed in the necessity of being acquitted in the coming judgment, who had repented of their sins, who had accepted and professed Jesus as the founder of the coming kingdom, who attempted to embody in daily life the principles believed to dominate that kingdom, who had received new spiritual experiences, and who had joined themselves together into little communities in which the new spiritual gifts and capacities might better express themselves.

II

In a way the church in the apostolic teaching is an equivalent of the non-eschatological conception of the kingdom of God, held by Jesus, although this equivalence is not formal or recognized. Historically the church of the centuries is the perpetuation of that little band of disciples gathered by Jesus in Galilee. This group of disciples must have carried over—actually did carry over—into their new brotherhood the ethical and religious, as well as the eschatological, teaching of their Master. They endeavored to live in his spiritual companionship as they had lived in his bodily presence, and their very meals were made sacred by the memory of a glorified Master and the thought of his unity with themselves. They were those who were to be saved—the members of the approaching kingdom. Their bond was one of a

---

[1] Here again the demands of the historical process give new credibility to Acts. The early chapters of the book in the main express precisely what would be expected of persons under the influence of messianism. Whatever allowance one may make for redaction, it is impossible for one acquainted with Judaism to accept the dictum that a belief in justification by faith is an unfailing evidence of Pauline influence. If faith in Jesus did not help one past the coming judgment, for what conceivable reason should a Jew have accepted him as Christ?

common hope, a common enthusiasm, and a common experience of God. As the older messianists had expected that Israel under the Messiah would be a chosen people, an instructed nation, a holy community, and a God-fearing generation,[1] so the Christians became a community of those who were eternally to be with the Christ—the true Israel.

Yet Jesus himself cannot be said to have originated the term "church." The Greek Old Testament had long before given it currency as the one word that represented the Hebrew people in its mingled aspects of nation and worshiping congregation. After the rise of scribism the word became a part of the vocabulary of Judaism. Evidently its content was very vague. In some general Jewish sense of "community" must Jesus have used the word, if, indeed, it ever passed his lips.[2] He had, in fact, very little use for it. His group of disciples were not a congregation to be removed from the world; they were inceptively a new humanity. It is doubtless the fact that Jesus did not use any special word for his band of disciples except the "kingdom of God" that accounts for its absence in the vocabulary of the earliest Christian community. So completely were the apostles possessed of the eschatological conception of the kingdom as never to use it to denote their community, and for a short time the new movement seems to have lacked any recognized name. The disciples were first called Christians at Antioch;[3] at Jerusalem, during the first months of the new movement's life, they were not spoken of as a congregation, but, if any word was used except "they,"[4] they were styled "brethren,"[5] "they that believed,"[6] "the company,"[7] "the disciples,"[8] as "those of the Way."[9] Soon, however, the need of some self-designation made itself felt, and

[1] *Pss. Sol.*, 17:32-42; 18:7-9; *Eth. Enoch*, 39:6; *Sib. Or.*, v, 431.
[2] Matt. 16:18; 18:17.　　　[3] Acts. 11:26.　　　[4] Acts 1:23, 26; 2:1, 4.
[5] Acts 1:15.　　　　　　　[6] Acts 12:44.　　　[7] Acts 4:23.
[8] Acts 16:1.　　　　[9] Acts 9:2. This term was never abandoned; *cf.* Acts 19:9.

it was but natural that ἐκκλησία—"the community"—should have suggested itself. At all events the word appeared, though innocent of its later content. The Christian brothers still thought of themselves as a religious community, though not as one distinct from Judaism. They still worshiped in the temple, still attended synagogues, still kept the law. Anything like a distinctive organization, except for purposes of charity, was at first not needed. The Christians were Jews who had added to their Judaism a belief that Jesus was the Christ and saw in that fact no reason for abandoning, in any particular, their old life. Their common meals, their sharing of property with the poor, their devotion to the "apostles' teaching," were wholly consonant with the loyalty to their older cult.

The rise of this undifferentiated group into a social institution distinct from Judaism can be accounted for only by the success of Christianity in cities outside of Palestine. The church, like Pauline Christianity and the New Testament canon, was the product of missions. As long as they were hemmed in by Jewish environment, the "brethren" from the point of view of Judaism were but Sectaries. Out in the great Græco-Roman world they were forced into a process of social evolution, and they were Christians. When, as always, the synagogue in which some apostle had first preached was closed to his converts, it was but natural that they should meet in some house or public lecture-hall for the social worship and instruction.[1] There again they adopted Jesus' word and were disciples or brothers. As the brotherhood in Jerusalem resembled in some particulars Jewish societies, so elsewhere it was superficially[2] not unlike the fraternities among the lower classes of the Roman empire which met regularly for various purposes, notably for the maintenance

[1] Acts 19:9.

[2] This modification is decidedly important. The similarities between the two sorts of fraternities may easily be over-emphasized.

of a burial fund. Each fraternity of this sort would have had a fraternal meal, and some more or less rudimentary initiation.[1] The Christians had this memorial meal and their initiatory baptism. But the Christian brotherhood was vastly different from those it superficially resembled. Although later it apparently found legal protection as a burial society, during its first years it was exclusively a religious fraternity composed of men and women who had accepted Jesus as the Christ, and who met to recall his death and his promises of speedy return. Their meetings, if one may judge from the words of Paul, Pliny, and even of Justin Martyr, were not mere banquets, but for religious purposes. Nor were the churches rigidly organized. Once gathered, the brothers seem to have been under no ritualistic bonds, but each was at liberty to express the new life of the spirit according "as God had given to each man a measure of faith." Nothing could have been more informal—one singing, another exhorting, another prophesying, another interpreting the otherwise unintelligible utterances of a brother "with a tongue." Indeed, there was even danger that such meetings should become a babel, and Paul never showed clearer administrative sagacity than when he advised that all religious gatherings should be carried on decently and in order.[2]

It would be a serious mistake, however, to think of the Christian fraternity, or ἐκκλησία, as having no more organic unity than a neighborhood prayer-meeting. As an actual group of men and women it antedated its assemblings. In this it more closely resembled the communities of the Jewish and Syrian dispersion than the burial fraternity. The com-

[1] On the churches as *collegia* see RAMSAY, *The Church in the Roman Empire*, pp. 431 f.; BOISSIER, *La Religion Romaine*, Vol. II, pp. 338 f.; RENAN, *Marc-Aurèle*, pp. 375 f.; SCHILLER, *Geschichte der Römischen Kaiserzeit*, Vol. II, pp. 447 f. DILL, *Roman Society from Nero to Marcus Aurelius*, chap. 3, gives a good general account of the *collegia*.

[2] See this discussion in 1 Cor. 14:26-40.

munity existed even when dispersed, and its members were always to live as the followers of their Christ, the fellow-heirs of his glory.

By origin, therefore, social, it was inevitable that social evolution should have soon begun within a church. As the fraternity grew, the need of officers was felt, and, under the guidance of the apostles, the fraternity undertook to supply its need. With the exception of the shadowy attempt to maintain the number of the Twelve by the choice by lot of Matthias, in the entire differentiation of the officials of the different fraternities there was no appeal to any directions of Jesus. To make such an appeal to authority would have been contrary to the spirit of Paul, but not to that of the Jerusalem church, and it is therefore safe to say that Jesus had left no directions for church polity. The little congregations were free to organize as fast and as far and in such ways as they saw fit. This absence of specific directions from Jesus accounts for the course taken by the organization of the various Christian groups. In the church at Jerusalem, dissatisfaction with the apostles' administration of charity funds led first of all to the choice of seven men whose duty it became to attend to such matters. They, however, like the apostles, soon preferred preaching to charity work, and a few years after their appointment we find the "congregations" of the Christians organized like the synagogue "congregations" of the Jews, with an executive committee known as the "elders." In other words, left by Jesus without any specific directions for organization, the early Christians followed the natural course, and turned to the synagogue as a model. The "elder" was the characteristic officer of the East, whether one looks to Egypt[1] or Judea; but in Judea especially was he an official with distinct ad-

---

[1] *Cf.* HATCH, *Organization of the Early Christian Churches*, pp. 55 f.; DEISSMANN, *Bible Studies*, pp. 154 f., 233-35.

ministrative functions. Nothing was easier, therefore, than for the Jewish Christian fraternities to appoint their elders, and to model the order of service in their meetings after that of the synagogue. Among the gentile Christians the reasons for the appearance of elders is not far to seek. In most Græco-Roman cities the governing body was known by some word implying seniority, and similar terms were applied to teachers of philosophies and probably to the heads of various heathen fraternities. If we add that the gentile churches were commonly founded and organized by Jews, it is not difficult to see that among them also the body of elders would be the administrative organ most to be expected.

Difficult as it is to trace church organization in the later New Testament books, we can still see that by the time the letter to Philippi was written it had evidently proceeded some distance toward its later form, for we find bishops[1] and deacons.[2] In the Pastoral Epistles, although new officials are not clearly named, there is evidence of marked advance in the precision with which the duties of the various officials are described.[3]

Just what functions the elders or bishops performed is apparent from a number of statements in the New Testament. They had the general superintendence, they were the ἡγούμενοι of the churches; in the Pastoral Epistles at least they were teachers; but most of all were they the pastors of the flocks God had intrusted to their care.[4] Such a union of responsibilities made toward officialism, and even in an apostolic father like Clement the presbyter and bishops are of recognized rank, and to reduce them to the plane of the ordinary church member warranted serious expostulation.[5]

---

[1] The ἐπίσκοπος, among the Greeks, was a communal officer, who (at least in the case of Rhodes) held a religious office; DEISSMANN, *Bible Studies*, p. 230. It would be natural for it to come into use among Greek Christians as πρεσβύτερος did among the Jewish.

[2] Phil. 1:1.

[3] For instance, 1 Tim. 3:1f.; Tit. 1:7.

[4] See 1 Pet. 5:1; 1 Tim. 3:8.

[5] *1 Clement*, chaps. 1-3.

But the elders were but one class of officers in the early church. Then, as always, there was a constant tendency toward a division of labor along the same lines as later marked the cleavage between the laity and the clergy, the secular clergy and the monks. As the apostles had preferred the ministry of the word to the ministry of tables, and as Philip the administrator of charity became Philip the evangelist, so the elders seem to have gradually delegated their charity work largely to deacons. But they were not the only persons who ministered to the churches in spiritual things. Alongside of the executive committee of the Christian congregation were many men—and some women—whose duty it was to exercise their "charism" and to prophesy, to teach, to catechize, and to provide in various ways for the religious life of the community. It is impossible to say when such classes of workers first appeared, but doubtless almost from the start, for in Paul's letters to the Corinthians we find them catalogued at length. Thus clearly was Christianity from the start constructively social.

Such an evolution of an organization by the differentiation of officers is certainly a common enough phenomenon, and might very well be dismissed thus summarily, were it not for the interpretation given it by Paul. He sees in it all something more than mere utilitarianism. It is all the work of the Spirit, in other words, of the new life of the individual believers. The unification of believers in any city was not the only expression of the Christian life; besides it there was the distribution of χαρίσματα. By one classification[1] there were accordingly apostles, prophets, teachers, miracle-workers, healers, helpers, administrators, those who spoke with tongues; by another[2] and simpler, apostles, prophets, evangelists, pastors, and teachers. This distribution of gifts, however, Paul insists was economic,

[1] 1 Cor. 12:28.　　　　　　[2] Eph. 4:11.

intended, not for the happiness of those who possess them, but for the building up of the church. He even carries his thought farther, and not only sees that all the χαρίσματα —of wisdom, knowledge, faith, gifts of healing, working of miracles, prophecy, discerning of spirits, tongues and interpretation of tongues[1]—the work of "the one and the same Spirit," are given for "ministration," but also declares that apart from love they are worthless. Thus with him, as with Jesus, the final test of life is not its ability to receive, but to confer, benefits. It is no mere happy coincidence that in his words to the Ephesian elders he used an otherwise lost saying of the Master: "It is more blessed to give than to receive."[2]

III

It is from the point of view of the church as a corporate expression of the regenerate life influenced in its organization by its environment, but not by messianism, that we can best appreciate the further teaching of Paul concerning the church as—with excuses to the sociologists—an organism, or, to use his own word, a body. In this conception there is to be seen something like a development in the Pauline thought. In the Roman letter, while he is especially swayed by his messianic predilections, he insists mostly upon the individual believer's functions, not so much as a member of a social group as one who is presently to be granted the completion of his hopes in the resurrection of the body and the entrance into the heavenly kingdom. Yet even there is to be seen in a summary form the conception of the church as the body of Christ. "As we have many members in one body, and all members have not the same office, so we, who are many, are one body in Christ and severally members one of another."[3] This analogy he had previously elabo-

---

[1] 1 Cor. 12:7-11.   [2] Acts 20:35.   [3] Rom. 12:4, 5.

rated most strikingly in his letter to the Corinthians.[1] The Christian community, he says, is the body of Christ—*i. e.*, that within which the Spirit of Christ dwells; but a body is a unity only in the sense that it is a combination of members, each of which performs its own and indispensable functions. So is it with the individual in the church: his function, be it apparently never so humble, is legitimate, and therefore the individual himself is needed for the efficiency of the body of which he is a member. The very bread and wine of the memorial meal, he reminds the Corinthians, are symbols of, or rather the means of maintaining, the common life of individuals with their Lord.[2] This may appear culpable high-churchism on the part of the apostle, but he has something more advanced to teach. This union with Christ through the church is no mere rhetorical matter; it is as real as the living of a man with a prostitute.[3] Of isolated Christians, of unattached Christians, of Christians who would willingly give up their fellowship—κοινωνία—with their brethren, the apostolic age could not conceive. To cast a member forth from the body of Christ was to turn him over to Satan for the destruction of the flesh.[4] Later, unless we quite mistake Paul's views, in the letters of the imprisonment, this ecclesiastical thought became even more prominent. As the messianic kingdom was the mediating concept by the aid of which Paul arrived at his conception of the atonement of Christ, so the church became almost exclusively the mediating concept by which he arrived at his thought of the relation of the individual Christian to Christ as a matter of actual life.[5]

If this be the thought in the more messianic epistles, one is justified in expecting that it will be all the more

[1] 1 Cor. 12:12-27.　　[2] 1 Cor. 10:15-17.　　[3] 1 Cor. 6:15.
[4] 1 Cor. 5:5.　　[5] Eph. 1:23; 4:1-16; 5:29-32.

prominent when the apostle writes under the influence of Judaic-Grecian philosophy. Nor will such expectations be disappointed. The transition has been made almost unconsciously from the consideration of the separate churches scattered over the empire, each with its own peculiar χαρίσματα, to the genuinely Greek conception of the generic church involved in the various local bodies. The Church has supplanted the churches. But the figure—if one may, indeed, call it a figure—of the organism is also carried to its inevitable completion. As the individual Christians constitute the body of the local church, so now they form the Church universal, and Christ is now head, not of the individual man, as in 1 Cor. 3:1, but of his body, the Church.[1] From this the step was easy to the thought of the church as essential to the Christ. It was his "fulness." Yet still the economic idea is maintained. God again spoke through prophets that men may be "edified." The church shared in the life of the Christ only that it may more perfectly carry on his work. And this work, it will be recalled, was itself organized, different individuals performing the various functions allotted them by the Spirit. Thus Christ worked through the social unity resulting from Christian life in different individuals. It is this thought that is expressed in perhaps the boldest expression of the thought of a social organism ever given by any writer—the prayer of Paul for the churches to whom the Ephesian epistle was written. He prays that they may "grow up in all things into him who is the head, even Christ, from whom all the body, fitly framed and knit together through that which every joint supplieth, according to the working in due measure of each several part, maketh the increase of the body unto the building up of itself in love."[2]

[1] Eph. 5:23.
[2] Eph. 4:15, 16.

IV

A fact of the first importance here comes into light. This social organism, composed of regenerate men each performing his special function under the direction of the Spirit, is not human society as a whole, but the church, a community within society. The relation of the church to society at large was one of election for salvation. It was indeed a community whose real interests were "other worldly." God had graciously selected them from the world. For the world at large was evil. It had lost its God,[1] and in consequence was full of vices.[2] The nearest approach Paul makes to a general social philosophy, however, is here. The fact of sin leads him away from individualism to a generic human solidarity. Humanity as a unit sinned in Adam; and in Adam all died. Characteristically, too, Paul makes sin the socialized result of the prostitution of the religious nature. The heathen world entered upon the hideous conditions portrayed in the opening chapter of the letter to the Romans by turning from a knowable God to idols. Every other sort of prostitution followed. To reverse this condition of affairs, to reinstate the religious nature to its normal position, is the work of Christ. But despite certain of his expressions that sound contradictory, Paul teaches that the new society formed by Christ is not composed of all men and is not created *en masse*. It grows, as has already appeared, through individuals as such assuming through faith in Jesus the proper relation with God ($\kappa\alpha\tau\alpha\lambda\lambda\alpha\gamma\acute{\eta}$) and, in obedience to the new life, joining one another in a social group in which the new life in Christ finds its expression.

Such a philosophy immediately carries a modern thinker across to the hope of a gradual transformation of society by this new and evidently dynamic group. But apostolic Christianity never took the step. The church was not conceived

1 Eph. 2:12.   2 Rom. 1:19-23, 24-32.

of as a source of social transformation.   It was itself "an
elect race, a chosen priesthood, a holy nation,"[1] but it was
not the salt of the earth.   In the apostolic literature one
will look in vain for a single injunction to convert the
world, or to save the world.   Individuals were to be saved
from the world and enter the new kingdom when it should
appear; but the world itself was lost.

[1] 1 Pet. 2:5-9.

CHAPTER II

THE MESSIANIC FRATERNITY IN AN EVIL AGE

WHEN one considers in more detail the relations of the new Christian fraternity to the age and society in which it lived, the contrast between inherited messianism and Christianity as a life becomes even more evident.

I

It is only what might have been expected both from the temper of Jesus and from their own insistence upon the eschatological kingdom of God, when we find the apostles possessed of a conservatism in social matters amounting almost to indifference. The early church was not a society for ethical culture, much less a society for social reform. It was a body of religionists devoted to their faith in a revealed plan of God for their salvation, who were awaiting the coming of their salvation from the "flesh" and death and sin, and were endeavoring in an evil age to live as if citizens of heaven. As such its members at times ran dangerously near to antinomianism, and at other times to legalism, but always because of their devotion to their religious convictions. Throughout the apostolic age Christian morality was the outgrowth of religious faith, and social duties were therefore derivative rather than primary.

But morality was by no means secondary. Repentance was as truly demanded as faith. A bad man could not be a Christian, and a Christian ought to be a good man. The prophecies had been fulfilled; the law had been superseded; the new life begotten of faith in God's love was now to be lived. Therein lay the supreme duty of the Christian while he waited for the appearance of the kingdom.

From this point of view one appreciates both the genetic and the fragmentary character of the apostolic teachings upon matters of conduct and social convention. They are not a new legal code, or speculations upon the social bearings of the new faith; they are solutions of definite problems with which early Christianity was confronted. As in the case of the churches of Thessalonica, Galatia, and Rome circumstances forced Paul to develop the theological content of the new messianic faith, so in the case of these and every other church the necessity of actually living in accordance with a faith in the messiahship of Jesus led the apostles to point out the ethical and social principles it involved. Throughout Paul's correspondence his instructions constitute less a system or program than the advice of a practical man based upon the teaching of Jesus and his own spiritual illumination.[1] His temper of mind is the farthest possible from that of a social doctrinaire. He was not endeavoring to reform society, to legislate for all time, or to champion a paper utopia. He was simply endeavoring to make plain to men and women who had but recently shared in the practices of the heathen society of which they were still members, the lines of conduct consonant with their new life and their faith in a rapidly approaching kingdom. One may, indeed, be even more specific: the social ethic of the apostles, and especially of Paul, consists in directions as to how a member of a Christian church should live in the various cities of the Roman empire during the first century of our era, that life which he expected to live in the coming kingdom. To understand such teaching one must understand the actual historical conditions it was intended to meet.

The problem before the student, therefore, is quite as much historical as exegetical; or, rather, just because it is exegetical it is historical, and any complete presentation of

[1] *Cf.* 1 Cor. 7:10 with 12, and see also 1 Cor. 7:25, 40.

the apostolic thought must rest, not upon a collection of detached teachings, but upon a careful estimate of such teachings in the light both of the apostolic messianism and of the social environment of those to whom they were addressed.

As soon as one takes this historical point of view, one characteristic of the apostolic teaching becomes apparent. So far from resembling the efforts of many others who have attempted to induce men to adopt the same standards of life, it favored no eccentricity, it proposed no revolution. The kingdom of God, with its regenerate institutions, was in heaven and not on earth. The apostolic ethics, in so far as it concerns social relations, is always formulated with the intent of preserving Græco-Roman society as far as possible. If we except the church itself, neither Paul or any other apostle introduced a new social institution. The early Christians, so far as we know, were born, married, toiled, and were buried as were their fellow-citizens of the empire. Like their master, the apostles were constantly on their guard lest their converts should mistake enthusiasm to reform other people for Christian character. Such an attitude of mind was not only the outcome of that indifference to existing evils born of their belief in the speedy coming of Christ. It was undoubtedly that in large part, but it also involved an appreciation of the actual situation in which the Christian communities found themselves. The Roman empire looked with increasing suspicion upon fraternities of all sorts —barring perhaps burial fraternities—and Paul especially knew only too well the danger which lay in any social extravagances. He would not even consent to destroying such conventionalities as the length of a Christian's hair, or a woman's wearing of a veil.[1] Above all, he tried to keep his converts free from even an appearance of social unrest.

1 1 Cor. 11:14-16.

"Let each man abide in that calling wherein he was called," he told the restless Corinthians. "Wast thou called being a slave? care not for it. Was any man called being circumcised? let him not become uncircumcised. Hath any been called in uncircumcision? let him not be circumcised. Art thou bound unto a wife? seek not to be loosed. Art thou loosed from a wife? seek not a wife. The time is shortened, that henceforth both those that have wives may be as though they had none; and those that weep, as though they wept not; and those that rejoice, as though they rejoiced not; and those that buy, as though they possessed not; and those that use the world, as not using it to the full; for the fashion of this world passeth away."[1] And all apostolic teaching was to the same effect. "Be subject to every ordinance of man for the Lord's sake," "Let no man suffer as a meddler in other men's affairs,"[2] are hardly the words of an agitator. Even when an outraged heart breaks forth in apocalyptic visions foretelling the doom of the beast whose number is 666—the Roman empire itself[3]—there is no call for revolt, but rather a eulogium of the martyrs who cry to God from beneath the altar.[4]

It would be a misinterpretation of early Christianity, however, if at this point we should declare with Paulsen[5] that the early Christians belittled courage and opposed aggressive struggle with enemies. Such a position has, it is true, a superficial justification in the maxims of Jesus against contests, and in the well-known willingness of the Christians

---

[1] 1 Cor. 7:18-24, 27-31. And yet PAULSEN (*Ethics*, Eng. trans., p. 66) declares that "true Christianity may always be recognized by the fact that it seems strange and dangerous to the world." See also the even more exaggerated statement of LESLIE STEPHEN, *Social Rights and Duties*, Vol. I, p. 22.

[2] 1 Pet. 2:13; 4:16.

[3] CLEMEN, "Die Zahl des Tieres, Apoc. 13:18," *Zeitschrift für die neutestamentliche Wissenschaft*, 1901, pp. 109-14. For a curious error in this article, which, however, hardly affects its main position, see *Biblical World*, Vol. XVIII (1901), p. 76.

[4] Rev. 6:9; 13:18.   [5] *Ethics*, Eng. trans., pp. 69 f.

to suffer martyrdom. But courage, or, better, virility, is something other than militarism, and in its moral sense is the constant watchword of the New Testament writers. "Quit yourselves like men,"[1] "fight without beating the air"[2] "put on the whole panoply of God"[3]—these are certainly not the words of a man who could suffer and submit, but nothing more. The difference between the Greek and the Christian courage is not so much in the attitude of mind as in the enemies one must withstand. The Greek or Roman found his enemies in the enemies of his state; the enemies of the Christian were just as real, but they were not flesh and blood, but angels and devils and evil passions.[4] It was against these, and not against an existing society in any of its phases, that the early Christians struggled. They could die for their faith, but they would not draw the sword for its defense. The Lord with his kingdom was at hand to destroy the lawless one with the breath of his mouth[5]

II

It was wholly consonant with this anti-revolutionary attitude toward society, the invariable accompaniment of apocalyptic messianism, that one chief aim of the apostolic ethics was to preserve as pure as possible the new life which had been awakened in the Christian. As may well be imagined, innumerable dangers threatened Christian morality from its social environment. Græco-Roman civilization in Paul's day had not, it is true, reached its period of decadence, nor were its morals quite as dark as Seneca and the satirists would have one believe; yet it was by no means calculated to help one live the life of the spirit. Animalism was either magnified or treated as morally neutral by men not at all vicious, and in every city the masses almost inevitably grew

---

[1] 1 Cor. 16:13. [2] 1 Cor. 9:26. [3] Eph. 6:11 f.
[4] Eph. 6:12. [5] 2 Thess. 2:8; *Cf. Pss. of Sol.* 17:39.

debased. Today's society threatens strikingly similar dangers to Christian idealism, but never were programs more opposed than that of the twentieth-century reformer and that of the apostles. The modern reformer endeavors to make honesty, purity, and other Christian virtues more easily realizable by changing the social environment in which men struggle. As Jesus might have said, he seeks to increase the harvest by improving the earth in which the seed of the kingdom is planted. But this recourse to a regenerated society as an aid to the individual Christian, Paul and the other apostles never made. As far as we can learn, no one of them ever proposed to make Christian morality more practicable through the destruction of the evils to which it was exposed. There was to be no compromise with the world, but neither was the world to be converted.

Yet asceticism, the last resource of pessimistic righteousness, was never urged upon the struggling Christian communities. It is, indeed, rather common to find the opposite asserted,[1] but at the expense either of a definition of asceticism or of a true exposition of apostolic thought. The point of view of the apostles was not that of those who regard misery as the royal road to holiness, or of those who would have men leave social life in order to live to God; but rather that of those who have adopted a new standard of values. For them that alone in life is of importance which was to extend over into the heavenly kingdom. The application of such a standard will give results which superficially resemble asceticism, but which are really nothing of the sort. For instance, it is not an injunction to asceticism to tell a person who knows the moral impulses that come from religious experiences and whose highest ethical imperative is "whereunto you have already attained by that same standard walk,"

[1] So, for instance, by PAULSEN, *Ethics*, Eng. trans., pp. 91 f., and THILLY, *Introduction to Ethics*, p. 190, note.

that there are distractions in marriage, and that since the Lord is soon to appear and to end the marriage relation, one had better choose a life in which he can more completely and easily devote himself to moral endeavor.[1] Asceticism would say that marriage is contaminating, or that there is merit in celibacy, and such opinions neither Paul nor any apostle to our knowledge ever held.[2] The insistence of Jesus upon the necessity of his disciples remaining in the world rather than becoming recluses or monks is echoed repeatedly in Paul. He is insistently opposed to anything that would detract from neigborliness or the legitimate enjoyments of those whose Master both in words and practice had rejected asceticism.

It is the same standard of values that explains the indifference of the earlier interpreters of Jesus to social evils like slavery and prostitution. Jesus had indeed said nothing directly against either evil, but it is clear that the man who would love his neighbor as himself could not long endure to see his neighbor either a slave or a prostitute, and, as Christian history shows abundantly, must endeavor to end both institutions by law. We should have expected that an apostle would have been as eager for such reforms as a modern philanthropist, and, as will presently appear, within the limits of the Christian community itself equality and social purity were unceasingly, passionately urged; but in all the apostolic literature both slavery and prostitution are accepted as abiding elements in a wicked world. They would perish only with the age. There is no more striking picture of a radical submitting to a social evil he saw was incompatible with his own ideals than that furnished in the little letter of Paul to Philemon in which the apostle

---

[1] 1 Cor. 7: 29, 31, 32.

[2] While we cannot deny that Paul regards the unmarried state as superior to the married, the entire discussion contained in 1 Cor., chap. 7, will dispossess a fair mind of any predisposition to discover within it genuine asceticism.

recounts how, as one result of having converted his friend's runaway slave Onesimus, he was sending him back "a brother beloved"[1] to a slavery from which he had safely escaped. The apostles have, indeed, many words of counsel and exhortation for both master and slaves. The master is not to threaten his slaves, since they both have one Master with whom there is no respect of persons,[2] and he is to treat them with justice and equality.[3] Directions for the conduct of slaves are also numerous, as one might expect, but all to the same effect. Slaves are to be obedient,[4] as servants of Christ. A position in which a man was both a slave and a brother was certainly anomalous, and, had it not been for the hope that the new age with its readjustments was close at hand, unendurable. Some slaves must have seen this, as possibly the runaway Onesimus; but more certainly those Christian slaves who, as we know from 1 Tim. 6:1, were tempted to look with contempt upon a Christian master who did not emancipate them.

That, notwithstanding his refusal even to hint at emancipation, Paul could also write that "*in Christ* there is neither bond nor free"[5] shows the difference between the standards when applied to the coming kingdom and when applied to the age that was to end within the lifetime, possibly, of the slave himself. That the two conceptions did not affect one another is the clearest possible evidence of the failure of Paul to see the social bearing of Christianity.

The attitude of the apostle toward prostitution and other evils which depended upon sin rather than upon misfortune and law is not radically different from that displayed by them toward slavery, though no fornicator or otherwise licentious person was to be permitted to live within the Christian community or could hope to enter the kingdom of

---

[1] Philem. 16.   [2] Eph. 6:9.   [3] Col. 4:1.
[4] Eph. 6:5; Col. 3:22; Tit. 2:9; 1 Pet. 2:18–25.   [5] Gal. 3:28.

God.[1] Yet, so far as we know, no effort was made by the apostolic church to reduce or control prostitution and other vices by law, or in any way except by the conversion of the evil-doers themselves. Apostolic Christianity at this point was thoroughly individualistic. The Christian as such was to be chaste; society would always be licentious. Paul expressly implies that prostitution is a permanent factor of un-Christian society, and that it is impossible for the Christian, in Corinth at least, to avoid associating with fornicators. In such a case he must needs go out of the world— a saying which marks the nearest approach to cynicism contained in apostolic literature.

In matters which involved neither the distinction between the flesh and the spirit, nor the liability to charges of revolution, Paul's attitude is singularly moderate. The majority of the members of his churches had been heathen. Before their acceptance of Jesus as Christ they had shared in the beliefs which characterized the masses of the Græco-Roman world. Few of them had been cultured,[2] and can hardly have been possessed of that indifference to the minutiæ of conventional religion which marked the freethinkers of the empire. Idolatry and the mass of customs which it engendered had been the real forces in their lives. Now they had abandoned idols and turned to the worship of the living God. But they had no more withdrawn from their world than had the primitive Christians withdrawn from the Jewish world. But their situation was far more perplexing than that of the Jerusalem community. They were still living in the environment of the innumerable customs which pagan society had inherited with its cults. First of all was the idol itself. What should be the attitude of the Christian toward it? The answer which the apostolic church made is very simple and to be expected. Idolatry was radi-

1 1 Cor. 5:9, 10; 6:9; Eph. 5:5; Heb. 12:16; 13:4; 1 Tim. 1:10; Rev. 21:8; 22:15.
2 1 Cor. 1:26, 28.

cally different from Judaism, and Christians were to keep from all worship of idols.[1] The reasons for such an attitude seem patent enough, but they are not those of Paul. He argues at length to show that while an idol, as every Christian would realize, was nothing at all,[2] since there was no God but one, at the same time the things which the millions of the empire sacrificed to idols they sacrificed to demons. Idolatry was, therefore, impossible for the Christian. How could he drink the cup of Christ at the Lord's Supper and the cup of demons? That would be to provoke the Lord to jealousy.[3] But such general instruction, even if literally followed, could not prevent a complication of social life. Much of the meat which had been offered for sale in the shops had been previously dedicated to some idol. Should the Christian eat it and so far recognize the idol as an existing fact? The Corinthian church divided on the question: There were the "weak brethren," and the "strong brethren." The Pauline position was distinctly that of the latter.[4] The Christian could eat anything, provided he did not make it a matter of conscience. Even when at a dinner he was not to ask questions of his host for conscience' sake, but was to eat what was set before him without attempting to discover whether or not his meat had been dedicated at some heathen shrine. If, however, some "weak" brother was troubled by this superiority to moral casuistry, the brother who was "strong" was not to eat. His self-denial,

---

[1] 1 Cor. 10:14; 1 John 5:21. The hatred of idolatry shown by the early church is seen in such passages as 1 Cor. 5:11; 6:9; 2 Cor. 6:16; Gal. 5:20; Eph. 5:5; Col. 3:5; 1 Pet. 4:3; Rev. 2:14, 20; 21:8; 22:15. The degeneration that followed idolatry is realistically traced in the first chapter of Romans. A somewhat less severe picture is given in Acts 14:8-18. Whether Paul would actually identify idols and demons we may well doubt, but the *worship* of idols was not of them (for they were nothing), but of the demons with whom the Christian was always at war.

[2] 1 Cor. 8:4.

[3] 1 Cor. 10:20, 22. More fundamental is Paul's classification of idolatry with the works of the σάρξ, Gal. 5:20; but this conception is not exploited, although a hint of it may be found in Eph. 5:5; Phil. 3:19. In this connection also see Rev. 9:30.

[4] 1 Cor. 8:1 f.; 10:19; *cf.* Rev. 2:14, 20.

however, is clearly declared by Paul, not to be for his own advantage, but for that of the "weak brother,"[1] and an expression of Christian love. Knowledge (γνῶσις) was indeed desirable, but, unless controlled by love, it might lead to unchristian arrogance.[2]

For love was the fruit of the Spirit.[3] Faith itself was energized by it,[4] and love alone gave value to the "gifts" the Christian might expect to possess.[5] Nor was there to be any limitation in the expression of the virtue. If apostolic Christianity felt no responsibility for establishing a Christian civilization, it most emphatically did feel the responsibility of treating all men, whether or not of the household of faith, with self-sacrificing love. The apostolic literature abounds in exhortations to treat all men in the spirit of Christ. "Avenge not yourselves, beloved," says Paul to the Romans,[6] "but give place unto the wrath of God; for it is written, Vengeance belongeth unto me; I will recompense, saith the Lord. But if thine enemy hunger, feed him; if he thirst, give him to drink. Be not overcome of evil, but overcome evil with good." And to the Galatians[7] he wrote: "Let us work that which is good toward all men." With humanity once possessed of such a spirit, the new age would indeed have dawned.

III

The fact is, however, that the apostolic thought does not carry this great principle of Jesus to its logical conclusion. Apostolic teaching regarding social relations concerns the

---

[1] The issue here is not that of Rom. 14:13-22, but the underlying and controlling principle is the same. *Cf.* 1 Cor. 10:23, 33; 11:1. On vegetarianism in the ancient world see VON DOBSCHÜTZ, *Die urchristliche Gemeinde*, pp. 274-76.

[2] 1 Cor. 8:1f.   [3] Gal. 5:22.

[4] Gal. 5:6.   [5] 1 Cor., chap. 13.

[6] Rom. 12:19-21. Note the recurrence of the judgment *motif*.

[7] 6:10. *Cf.* Rom. 15:2; Heb. 12:14; 13:2.

church and its members rather than society at large. The ethical and social teachings of Peter and Paul would have been almost meaningless to any but those who shared in their faith. A Christian society was evidently expected by them to result from the segregation of Christians, rather than from the transformation of an empire. Christian civilization, paradoxically enough, was a by-product of apostolic Christianity.

The reasons for this surprising fact do not lie in any indifference of the early Christians to others. Where could one find more devoted servants of their time than the humble men who faced all the perils of their time, rejoicing in opposition, nay death itself, if only Christ were preached and so the "time be redeemed" by bringing to others the news of the possibility of their salvation? Or where more noble directions to do good to all men? Or where can we find a more passionate lament than that of Paul over the indifference of the Jews to his gospel? He is ready even to be accursed for their sakes, and, what is more, out of his sorrow and his belief in the divine absolution, constructs a prophecy, not yet fulfilled, that at last, moved with envy at the sight of gentiles enjoying the blessings properly their own, the Jews as a people will repent and join the Christian community. Indeed, he is even ready to postpone the second coming of Christ until this glorious consummation is attained.[1]

No, the reasons are quite other, and in the explanation do we see again the fundamental contrast recognized by the apostle between Christian life and Christian messianism. In the first place, the division of labor, so to speak, within the church was wholly dependent upon the Spirit. If he gave some person the gift of apostleship or of evangelization, such a one attempted, not to reform society, but to induce

[1] See Rom. 10:1—11:32.

individuals to accept Jesus as the Christ and join the church. The entire process, therefore, was neither of man's choosing nor centrifugal. A man might be as passionately devoted to the preaching of the gospel as Paul, and yet be of almost no significance as an influence upon the society of the empire at large; while, on the other hand, the church had been redeemed from a present evil age, and it was to have as little as possible to do with that age.

The second, and far more important, ground for the indifference of apostolic Christianity to the establishment of a Christian civilization that would replace the heathen, lay in its conception of an eschatological kingdom. It believed implicitly and explicitly that civilization, as it existed in the empire, had not long to survive. Across the entire horizon of the future the early Christians saw the messianic judgment and the beginning of a new age in which men were to live only in the bodies of the resurrection. So far from planning for posterity, they could hardly believe that there was to be any posterity. The Lord was to return shortly,[1] even during the lifetime of their own generation;[2] believers if dead were to be raised, if alive were to be changed in the twinkling of an eye; the judgment was to be set, the kingdom established, the wicked destroyed. The time was short, and ever growing shorter.[3] *Maran atha.* The Lord comes. The end of all things was at hand.[4] The judge stood before the doors.[5] Why, then, plan social revolutions, or even social ameliorations? The Christian's wrestling was not with flesh and blood, but with rank upon rank of angels, the powers of the air.[6] It was better to endure patiently the days of waiting, for in the Day that was to come all earthly differences would be effaced.

[1] Rom. 13:11, 12; 16:20; 1 Cor. 7:29: Phil. 4:5.

[2] 1 Thes. 4:15–17; 5:1, 23, 24; 2 Thess. 1:7; Rom. 13:11, 12; 1 Cor. 1:7, 8; 7:29; 11:26; 15:51, 52.

[3] Rom. 13:11, 12; 1 Cor. 16:22; Phil. 4:5; Isa. 5:8 Heb. 10:25, 37.

[4] 1 Peter 4:7.   [5] James 5:9.   [6] Eph. 6:12.

The perception of the hopelessness of attempting to convert all individuals before this awful day of Jehovah awoke not only thankfulness that there were those who were already saved as brands from the burning, but profound sorrow, amounting in some cases to pessimism. "All that is in the world, the lust of the flesh and the lust of the eye, and the vainglory of life, is not of the Father, but is of the world, and the world passeth away and the lust thereof,"[1] says 1 John, and a little later,[2] "we know that the whole world lieth in the evil one." The wild joy over the destruction of sinners that runs through the Apocalypse of John is but the natural outcome of the recognition of an inherent hostility between the new groups of God's elect and the wicked, persecuting empire in the midst of which they lived. And long after, when the delay of the coming of Jesus was beginning to cause doubt and scorn, the unknown person who wrote in the name of Peter[3] could hold to the Enochian belief that the present heavens and earth had survived the Noachian flood, stored with fire reserved against the day of judgment and destruction of ungodly men.

But again the writers of the apostolic age were unable to bring their hopes born of their new life quite into subjection to this narrowing eschatology. At least Paul could not. The salvation to which his passionate heart looked was something too great to be limited to the few men of lowly calling he found at Corinth and the other cities he had evangelized. The rulers of this age might pass away unsaved, but in moments when his heart rather than his logic spoke, he could see all creation groaning and travailing together in pain, waiting for the adoption — the resurrection of the believer;[4] he could see all creation brought into subjection to Jesus Christ, every knee bowing to his great name.[5] Just how he

---

[1] 1 John 1:17.　　[2] 1 John 5:19.　　[3] 2 Peter 3:7.
[4] Rom. 8:19-22.　　[5] Phil. 2:10.

would co-ordinate this thought with his general teachings it is impossible at this distance to say. Perhaps, as he was a very great man, he would not try to co-ordinate them. At any rate, there they are a tribute not only to a masterly imagination, but to the power of the new life the social capacities of which, because of his own historical limitations, he could not fully appreciate. Yet, with him as with Jesus, Christian life must be social in order to be true to itself. Strip from his teaching its enswathing eschatology, and we have the non-messianic elements in the teaching of Jesus. God and men had found each other. The divine life complemented the human. Each man was made alive and was to be kept alive by the Spirit of God. This body of Christ, what is it, if one ceases to believe it but a temporary thing, but the beginning of a redeemed humanity? And this new life that is drawn from the Spirit, what is it but the eternal life of which Jesus speaks, which will refuse to look merely to the rescue of individuals from an evil age, and as soon as it discovers that its hope for the immediate return of the Christ is a disappointment will go out to the rescue of institutions and the conquest of the empire itself?

Christian civilization was the inevitable result of the new life taught by Jesus, experienced by individual Christians, organized by the Christian communities, and interpreted by the apostles in the vocabulary and concepts of Pharisaism. The interpretation was transitory; the divinely imparted life, eternal. He who would see the heart of apostolic Christianity must find it in this work of the Spirit in the lives of those who believed Jesus to be the Christ and accepted his teachings as the everlasting principles of ethical and religious living. With the apostles, as with their Master, the essentials of Christianity lie in personality, and not in formula; in the Spirit and not in the letter.

CHAPTER III

THE FAMILY AND THE AGE

THIS conception of the church as a fraternity within the Roman empire makes it easy to appreciate the effect of the messianic hope upon the Christian conceptions of life. The apostles were not social philosophers, but they did set forth what the members of the church should consider proper customs for themselves. Thus in each department of social life their teaching is affected both by practical considerations resulting from the actual environment of the Christian, and also by the regulative conceptions of their eschatology. Eternal life was being lived, but it was not to be without its ethical formulas. And these formulas were in part derived from the conventionalities of the civilization in which the messianic fraternities found themselves.

I

The family did not originate with Christianity. So far as we know, apostolic Christianity did not attempt any change in its form or ceremonies in the different countries into which it spread. Yet this by no means is to be interpreted as arguing that Paul approved of the Græco-Roman moralists in matters relating to the sexes. On the contrary, it is patent that he found in heathen society a distinct danger to the pure life which the Christian should attempt to live. In fact, the greatest danger that threatened the new communities lay in the social ideals and customs that prevailed throughout the Græco-Roman world.

Thanks to the over-zealous efforts of certain apologetes, we have grown so accustomed to the portrayals of the depravity of the heathen society of the first century that it is difficult to realize that an empire that had yet hundreds of years to live, and was not to reach its greatest prosperity for a century, was neither decrepit nor rotten. Especially hard is it to realize the simple distinction between the capital and the provinces, and to believe that throughout the provinces there was a sturdy, self-respecting middle class which, however its members may have enjoyed occasional gladiatorial sports, was yet maintaining a conventional domestic morality by no means greatly inferior to that of any modern nation. Just as the letters of Pliny tell of beautiful home life among the official class in the capital, the gravestones are noble defenders of *bourgeois* morals. Men were not all like the heroes of Petronious and Apuleius, and women were not all like that notorious matron who counted years by her husbands rather than by the consuls. Throughout the empire there was developing a new conception of the rights of married women. Gradually they had passed out from the restrictions of the old *in manu* marriage and were permitted to study, if not to practice, learned professions, to control their own property, and in many other ways to break from the restraints set by the old conceptions of the subjection of the wife to the husband. All this disturbed the minds of conservatives of those days, just as similar tendencies disturb conservatives in the present day. For those who were admirers of old Roman ideals, as many of the fashionable writers profess themselves, there was indeed sufficient ground for lamentation; yet, nevertheless, the emancipation of women advanced steadily. It even possibly aided the Christian conception of the ideal position of women as one of equality with men. But, unfortunately, the abolition of restraints seems to have been followed by no moral uplift. Alongside of this emancipation of women of the wealthier classes there persisted the old ideas of the veniality of sexual impurity on the part of men, as well as a growing tendency to divorce. The upper classes were not marrying, and the number of children in case of marriage was growing less, notwithstanding the government's effort to check the evil by the establishment of privileges for those who had three children. What was worse, there was springing up a sort of legalized concubinage that was neither prostitution nor marriage.

In addition to these tendencies in the Græco-Roman family, there was also the recognition of prostitution as an element in the social life of all cities. It is impossible to go into this matter in detail, but the readers of the polite literature of the empire know only too well how heathen society regarded the matter. If few Roman philosophers would take the position of Cato, they seldom censured the practices he advised. The other and nameless form of licentiousness, which played such havoc in the moral system even of a Socrates, was not only prevalent, but actually a matter of academic debate. Plutarch has a lengthy dialogue as to the relative merits of the love of boys and the love of women.[1] Such a fact as this makes very evident the public opinion in the midst of which the first gentile churches sprang up. Practices like these, abhorrent though they were to Jewish and Christian morality, were sharply distinguished by the ethical writers of the day from lust and ignoble passion of all sorts. No one would accuse Plutarch, for instance, of favoring orgies or debauchery. Temperance, or self-control, was the greatest of personal virtues both for him and for all men of his type. But chastity on the part of men was a matter of preference—a practice of a semi-ascetic morality. Confusing as are the implications of such a statement, the historical student must admit that the great and good men of the Greek and Roman type distinguished marital faithlessness from prostitution, and regarded

[1] *Morals* (Eng. trans.), "On Love."

what today would be considered licentiousness as morally neutral. That such a conception ever was outgrown must be laid largely to the credit of the Christian teaching we are considering. Chastity of both men and women, not merely the maintenance of the married vow, was an ideal of all Christian teachers. The triumph of this ideal is a tribute to the wisdom of those called to confront a problem which at the outset must have appeared all but insoluble.

A second fact that gave the early Christians difficulty as regards marriage was the Christian teaching itself. Jesus himself had taught that in the approaching kingdom men were neither to marry nor to give in marriage, but were to be like the angels.[1] Indeed, he had even said that unless a man hated his father and mother he could not be his disciple.[2] Paul, with his persistent emphasis upon the "flesh" as the point of attack of sin, must have deepened the uncertainty of his converts as to the rightfulness of maintaining, much more entering upon, matrimony. The matter became so vital that the Corinthian church wrote to the apostle for light.[3] Should Christians marry, and, if married, should they live together as husband and wife? If one of the married pair were not a Christian, should the marriage be broken?

These were the questions forced upon the church by both its social environment and its own teachings. The answer that Paul makes to them is clearly determined by its general conception of the relation of the Christian to the world and the kingdom, and by his belief in the shortness of the time to elapse before Christ returned. It will be found *in extenso* in 1 Cor., chap. 7. His positions may thus be stated: (*a*)

---

[1] Mark 12: 24. "The sons of God, children of the resurrection," Luke 20: 36.

[2] Luke 14: 26.

[3] The suggestion of RAMSAY, *Historical Commentary on Corinthians*, *in loco*, that the Corinthians were considering universal marriage as a panacea for the prevalent morality, can hardly be considered seriously. See MASSIE, *Journal of Theological Studies*, July, 1901, pp. 527, 528.

marriage is a lawful thing for a Christian; (*b*) it is to be justified wholly from the side of physical appetite, as a sort of prophylactic against licentiousness;[1] (*c*) for those who are able to withstand appetite, celibacy is preferable, since, if married, they will be likely to be more devoted to their husbands or wives than to the Lord; (*d*) the general position governing his teaching, he frankly says,[2] was not obtained from any teaching of Jesus, but is given as his own opinion (γνώμη), as one who had received mercy from the Lord to be trustworthy. How far he was governed in this teaching by his eschatology is evident.[3] "By reason of the present distress [*i. e.*, in the storm and stress period before the reappearance of the Christ] it is good for a man to be as he is.[4] Art thou loosed from a wife? seek not a wife. But and if thou marry, thou hast not sinned." Thus, again, it appears that Paul does not regard it as any part of his work as an apostle to develop a philosophy of marriage, or, in fact, any social program, for persons who are so soon to be living in conditions in which only the spiritual elements of life are to survive. Marriage he regards as a temporary institution, to pass away with the age.[5]

Yet it would be a serious injustice to the apostolic thought to leave the matter here. One must consider, also, the closely

---

[1] Yet even in marriage the husband and wife are to live apart occasionally for religious growth, 1 Cor. 7:5.

[2] 1 Cor. 7:25.   [3] 1 Cor. 7:26.

[4] TEICHMANN, *Die paulinische Vorstellung von Auferstehung und Gericht*, p. 20, holds, on the basis of *4 Esdr.*, 5:8, that Paul advises against marriage because of the general belief that childbirth would be especially dangerous during the period preceding the advent of the Christ. So, too, THACKERAY, *St. Paul and Contemporary Jewish Thought*, 76. Such a view is by no means impossible, and becomes the more probable when one recalls that there was no persecution or other specific danger threatening the church at Corinth at the time Paul wrote these words. For reference to Jewish literature see p. 166, n. 3, above.

[5] Yet it is temporary only as the age itself is temporary. The society in which it is abolished is not earthly, but heavenly. As an institution it is as permanent as the age. Of that hallucination which has often overtaken good men and induced them to attack marriage, as an unjustifiable conventionality to be outgrown in the progress of civilization, he happily has no trace. Apostolic Christianity is no champion of free love, no matter under what euphemisms it may masquerade.

allied theme of chastity, so unavoidably forced into notice by any study of the social conditions in which apostolic Christianity developed. As we should expect, here is no mere balancing of two possible goods; far less a recognition of the moral possibility of any such question as that debated by Plutarch. No moralist ever struck out more boldly at that laxity which, to modern eyes, is the worst feature of the Roman civilization. The doctrine of the Nicolaitans, which was the same as that of Balaam,[1] leading directly to licentiousness—how anxiously is it censured in the Apocalypse of John.[2] The most superficial reader of the opening chapter of Romans feels the heat of Paul's hatred of heathen vice. The matter in his treatment becomes again one of contrast between σάρξ and πνεῦμα—of the supremacy of the spiritual life, and the supremacy of the moral imperative found in the nature of that life. Brushing aside all casuistry, he puts the case frankly: it is a choice between living after the flesh and reaping corruption, or of living after the Spirit and reaping eternal life.[3] The fornicator cannot enter the kingdom of God.[4] Thus even here there is no appeal to law, either of Moses or of Jesus. The Christian must be pure because he is a Christian. He is to live in the flesh the sort of life that is to be his after the resurrection. Social ethics were never more directly based upon religion. No man could appeal to higher motives. As Marcus Aurelius might summon the thought of Nature to assist him in early rising, Paul made the Christian's union with God's spirit the basis for personal purity. "As for fornication, let it not so much as be named

---

[1] Numb. 31:16, cf. 25:1-15.

[2] Rev. 2:6, 15, cf. the teaching of the woman Jezebel, Rev. 2:20.

[3] Gal. 5:16—6:10; 1 Cor. 5:9.

[4] Eph. 5:5; cf. 1 Thess. 4:4 f. WERNLE, Christ und Sünde bei Paulus, pp. 129 f., compares the various catalogues of sins given by the apostle in Rom. 1:29; 13:13; 1 Cor. 5:10, 11; 6:9; 2 Cor. 12:20, 21; Gal. 5:19 f.; Col. 3:5, 8; Eph. 4:31; 5:3, 5. In all but two reference is made to licentiousness. See also VON DOBSCHÜTZ, Die urchristliche Gemeinde, p. 283.

among you!¹ Know ye not that your body is a temple of
the Holy Ghost which is in you, which ye have from God?
Glorify God therefore in your body."² Only thus could the
resurrection of the body and the achievement of the life of
complete triumph over the flesh be guaranteed. Nothing gave
him more anxiety concerning the churches in Thessalonica and
Corinth than the danger that threatened in this regard from
heathen society; and the great struggle in which the apostle
engaged with the Corinthian church seems to have had one of
its main roots in the unwillingness of the church to discipline
a member who had broken even the lax conventionalities of
heathen society. And it may well be noticed that the apostle
demands this chastity of men quite as much as of women.
Possibly one might say he was even more insistent upon it
because of the attitude of the Græco-Roman mind to which
reference has already been made.

Thus the family in the apostolic teachings appears a secondary good. On the whole it was wise, Paul thought, not
to establish one for oneself. It is true, to be able to live
unmarried was evidence of a special divine charism,³ but he
himself had a right to be married as well as Peter, yet preferred celibacy (or shall we say widowerhood?) and could
wish that all men were of the same mind.⁴ And this applied
to women quite as truly as to men.⁵ Similarly, the Seer of
Patmos saw the 144,000 who had not defiled themselves
with women standing with the Lamb, the first fruits unto
God and the Lamb.⁶ It is not difficult to see how such a
disparagement of marriage would lead to the aceticism of
the next century after the apostles.

---

¹ Eph. 5:3. So, too, Heb. 13:4.   ² 1 Cor. 6:19, 20.

³ 1 Cor. 7:7. JACOBY, *Neutestamentliche Ethik*, p. 34, note, refuses to classify the
χάρισμα of this text with χαρίσματα in general. His position seems hardly justifiable
in view of the general position of Paul concerning the "gifts." It would seem as if he
meant by them special and characteristic powers possessed by various believers, which
in accordance with his usual tendency he explained as resulting from the working of
the Holy Spirit.

⁴ 1 Cor. 9:5 f.   ⁵ 1 Cor. 7:39, 40.   ⁶ Rev. 14:4.

II

If now we pass from the apostles' treatment of the relation of the sexes to that accorded the family as an institution, we discover at once that they are true children of this age. Paul's conception of marriage as a purely physical matter, advisable as a means of preventing irregular alliances, could hardly fail to be accompanied by frank and unquestioning statements concerning the inferiority of woman in the family. It is true that "in Christ" there was to be no distinction, but not so in the church. There the women were to be silent.[1] They were to remember that the woman was made from man, and not man from the woman;[2] that veils were necessary still on account of the angels.[3] The husband was the head of the wife[4] and, supposedly at least, capable of giving her all such instruction as was needed by the weaker vessel.[5] The wife, finally, was to be subject to her husband.[6] And all the apostolic teaching is to the same effect.[7]

In Paul's eyes, also, the unmarried woman was subject to her father. He could prevent her marriage, and as a lesser good he could permit it. After becoming a widow, however, the same woman was, in accordance with the spirit of the age, given new rights. She could marry whom she chose, only ἐν κυρίῳ, i. e., probably, within the circle of believers.[8] Later advice given in his name makes remarriage obligatory on young widows.[9]

Yet though he might thus treat the family as a secondary good, and though he might thus insist upon Christians conforming to the social conventions of their day, Paul's teaching concerning divorce is that of Jesus himself. The question

[1] 1 Cor. 14:34, 36. [2] 1 Cor. 11:12.

[3] 1 Cor. 11:10. The meaning of this enigmatic saying is probably to be found in Gen. 6:2-4 and the evil which sprang from the union with angels mentioned there.

[4] 1 Cor. 11:1-16; Eph. 5:23. [5] 1 Cor. 14:35.

[6] Eph. 5:22; Col. 3:18; cf. 1 Cor. 7:39. [7] 1 Pet. 3:1, 7.

[8] 1 Cor. 7:36-40; 9:5; 2 Cor. 6:14. [9] 1 Tim. 5:14.

as to the separation of married persons from unbelieving partners was a very natural one for Christians of the type of those in Corinth, and the matter was treated by Paul explicitly.   Again he works from a general principle that is far more important than its particular application.   Christians thus married are certainly to maintain the home for the benefit of each other and their children; for the unbelieving husband is sanctified in the wife, and the unbelieving wife is sanctified in the brother; else were their children unclean.[1]   Whatever else this last clause may mean, it certainly exhibits strikingly Paul's regard for the unity of the home, and especially for the children.[2]

Brought face to face with an actual separation of husband and wife, Paul speaks in the name of Jesus: "the wife shall not depart from her husband, but and if she depart, let her remain unmarried or else be reconciled to her husband; and let the husband leave not his wife."[3]   Here is the one clear instance in which the apostles quote Jesus as an authority in ethical matters, and it is worth attention that it is at the one point at which the social content of Christianity cannot change except for the worse.   If there is anything in all the specific social teaching of Paul that may be said to have transcended the historical situation in which it was uttered, it was this concerning the family: the union of a man and woman in marriage is a primal fact of humanity; it is not a matter of contract, it is an actual status.   Separation may be permitted, but not remarriage to other persons.   Divorce is neither instituted nor permitted by New Testament ethics.[4]

[1] 1 Cor. 7:14.

[2] On this latter point see also the position taken as to the saving quality of child-bearing; 1 Tim. 2:15; cf. 5:14.

[3] 1 Cor. 7:10, 11; cf. Mk. 10:12.

[4] It is worth noticing that this use of the saying of Jesus by Paul furnishes a critical control of the saying itself. In Matt. 5:32; 19:9 the exception clause παρεκτὸς λόγου πορνείας or μὴ ἐπὶ πορνείᾳ is found, but not in Mark 10:11 or Luke 16:18. On general critical principles, therefore, the clause would likely be dropped, but the decision is strengthened by the absence of any such exception in the teaching of Paul. Cf. JACOBY, Neutestamentliche Ethik, p. 356. To the contrary (mistakenly), MATHEWS, Social Teaching of Jesus, p. 87,

There remains the matter of apostolic directions for the control of the inner relations of the Christian family. These are given so repeatedly as to indicate that the matter was regarded as of first importance. They are not in accord with modern ideas in some points, but are clearly such as would have made the Christian family ideal in the society of the first century. In general they are the outcome of the positions already described. Wives were to be in subjection to their husbands;[1] children were to obey their parents; fathers were not to provoke their children to wrath, but to nurture them in the chastening and admonition of the Lord.[2] It is not difficult to see in these directions a modification, but not a destruction, of the parental authority so universally recognized in both Jewish and Roman civilization.

To make these essentially local and historical applications of Christianity universal and authoritative in matters of the family is to check the growth of the Christian spirit in social affairs at the limit reached by these civilizations. Such a check, however, so clearly possible only as long as one lived under the control of an eschatological conception soon to be made untenable by the failure of the Christ to return to usher in the expected messianic age, Christian history shows was short-lived. In the family, as in all things, it was the ideal element of Paulinism, not its specific application, that proved permanent. And in these matters, at least, most Christians are agreed. He would be a rare man who would today attempt to make the Pauline teaching as to Corinthian women operative in western Christendom.

But to understand Paul completely one must also consider his attitude toward the family as a social unit, wholly apart from its basis as a union of persons of opposite sexes. It is here that the apostle comes nearest to the thought of Jesus.

[1] Eph. 5:22 f.; 1 Pet. 3:1.   [2] Eph. 6:1 f.; Col. 3:18-25.

It will be recalled that with the Master the family became the formal concept of the kingdom. God was Father, disciples sons and therefore brothers, and all who entered the kingdom were to become like little children. Paul, in his less practical moments, when he is dealing with ideals and not with questions of church discipline, has similar expressions. God is a loving Father[1] quite as much as a dread sovereign,[2] and most beautiful of all the Pauline expressions is that in the Ephesian letter, "I bow my knees unto the Father from whom every fatherhood in heaven and on earth is named."[3] Other figures fall hardly below this. The church is sometimes conceived of as the bride of Christ; sometimes as a virgin to be kept spotless till the coming of her lord. The man who could so use a social institution can hardly be said to have disparaged it, however much he may have regarded it as a secondary good.[4]

III

Thus if one were to summarize the apostles' teaching as to the family, it would be something like this: Except in the case of divorce, and then under the direct influence of Jesus, they did not attempt to introduce any new conception of the family. They rather treated the Jewish and the heathen marriage from the Christian point of view, as an institution to be preserved. As a result they held up ideals for families in the Græco-Roman life of the first century. Only in so far as these ideals involve universal principles are they of importance to today's life. The new Christian life, possessed as it is by the very genius of corporate expression, has worked out, within the limits set by these general principles, such particular social institutions as it has judged necessary and human imperfections have permitted.

Thus again the application of historical criteria enables

---

[1] Rom. 8:14–17.   [2] *Cf.* Eph. 4:6.   [3] Eph. 3:14, 15.

[4] As a matter of curiosity, it might be added that there is no evidence that the Christian pastors performed wedding ceremonies.

us to distinguish the essential and the pedagogic elements of the apostle's thought. Long hair and veils, silence in religious meetings, subjection to their husbands—these are but elements in the apostle's adjustment of the external life to a Græco-Roman civilization. So, too, his treatment of marriage as a purely animal survival. Under the domination of a formal and ethnic thought, he undertook to prepare men for another world. In his estimation the present age was hopelessly evil, its surviving animalism and such of its members as did not live according to the spirit, doomed to certain destruction. From this point of view, it was idle to attempt reform or to assist social evolution. Christians, though not to abandon this world, were to live as citizens of another. Thus the family was a matter of but secondary importance, and women, though ideally equal with men, were in point of fact treated as inferior.

In so far apostolic Christianity was temporal. But in this social teaching Paul was giving but an interpretation of something that he knew and preached as neither Jewish nor temporal; and that something was life, born of an actual faith in God. This life it was that formed the basis of his moral teachings, and which, he urged, should be allowed to express itself in acts of love to men. Those who held God as Father would treat men and women as equal members of the new fraternity. And it was this essential Christianity that outgrew the specific social directions of the apostle. In Paul's noble conception of the religious worth and responsibilities of a man's body with all its passions, in his insistence upon love between man and wife, in his refusal to regard marriage as a mere contract capable of dissolution, in his recognition of the rights of children—in a word, in his recognition of the domestic implications of the new moral and religious life, Paul was opening up the permanent force and ideals of subsequent social evolution.

CHAPTER IV

THE ECONOMIC AND POLITICAL BEARING OF ETERNAL LIFE

THE years in which Christianity first began its history were years of prodigious economic and political change. The growth of the Roman republic had of necessity broken down and established trade routes quite as truly as it had recombined kingdoms into the first empire. Commercial intercourse between Asia and Africa was supplemented by the enormous traffic between cities like Alexandria, Antioch, Tarsus, Ephesus, Corinth, Marseilles, and Rome. Industries were developed to the very limits allowed by slavery. Enormous banking houses sprang up all over the empire; Judea itself, after having for centuries shared but little in the economic life of its neighbors, then sought its place in the world-commerce. At the same time there was an extraordinary redistribution of wealth. The enormous booty of the eastern wars at first had fallen into the hands of a few wealthy Romans. The standard of living set by them had controlled the habits of the wealthy classes throughout the provinces, and in consequence there, as in the capital itself, ruinous prodigality was soon epidemic. Uninvested wealth is pretty certain to find its way into the hands of middlemen, and the Roman empire offered no exception to the rule. Shopkeepers grew into capitalists; slaves into freedmen; freedmen into millionaires. The entire age grew commercial.

At the same time it grew imperial. The multitude of small kingdoms and city-states that had composed the ancient world had become things of the past, and in their stead there had arisen the ever-developing empire. For the first time in human history the civilized world was at peace with itself, and united against the barbarians of the forests of Europe, the steppes of Asia, and the plains of Arabia and Africa. It was impossible for the imagination of any thoughtful man to rest unstirred. So it was that there seems to have arisen throughout the empire bands of men who sought either to carry the political transformation still farther, or to check the progress of a movement toward the complete centralization of power in an irresponsible monarch. So much, at least, looks out upon us through the stern regulations of the age against all sorts of sodalities. "Societies of this sort," wrote Trajan to the younger Pliny who had recommended forming a fire company in Nicomedia,[1] "have greatly disturbed the peace of the province. Whatever name we give them, and for whatever purposes they may be founded, they will not fail to form themselves into factious assemblies, however short their meetings may be." The same danger Trajan discovered in large meetings called to receive contributions of money.[2] Throughout the entire legislative and imperial rescripts a similar fear of political disturbance is evident. To speak against Cæsar was the worst of crimes.

Into this commercial empire Christianity came, with a message that from the point of view of the empire itself must have been suspicious. It taught another king, Jesus,[3] and it sought to make its followers live as if citizens of another kingdom. As long as such teachings were seen through the medium of a highly protected Judaism, they might very well pass among the Romans as a part of the impossible religion of the Jews; but when once Christians left the synagogues and made devotion to their king and kingdom the supreme test of loyalty to their own fraternities, it is clear that Roman officialism could not fail to be alarmed.

[1] PLINY, *Letters*, bk. x, 43   [2] *Ibid.*, bk. x, 94   [3] Acts 17:7.

To adjust the new life of the church to an aggressive commercialism, and at the same time to preserve it from being misconceived as a political movement, were problems requiring no small sagacity.

Yet, after all, from the point of view occupied by Paul, its solution was not difficult. The new value given life by eschatological messianism, the spirit of *laissez-faire* in politics which obtained in his pharisaic training, suggested at once the conduct to be advised. How opposed to anything savoring of revolution this conduct should be has already appeared. We have now to examine the positive teachings of the apostles concerning the ethical principles obtaining in economic and political matters.

I

The teaching of Jesus upon wealth was set forth in language which might be easily misunderstood to indicate hostility to wealth as such. He realized the moral difficulties which lie in the possession of property, and, above all, the constant temptation of the rich man to grow independent and superior to his fellows. It was because of this that he so insisted upon the fraternal use of property. Wealth was a small good for a man face to face with eternity. It is true that his teaching is not strictly economic. Doubtless because of the circumstances of the time in which he lived, beyond saying that one cannot serve both it and God, and that one is to seek first God's kingdom and his righteousness, he has left no utterance concerning the matter of the production or, strictly speaking, the distribution of wealth. He was rather concerned with its consumption. But even here his words are not those of the economist, but of the moralist. Indeed, he has left no economic program. In the case of wealth, as in the case of all human matters, he is concerned with moral relations, and it is from this point of view that his words have permanent value. With Jesus wealth is a good, but a secondary good. By being used in the spirit of love, and for the purpose of building up a fraternal humanity, it gains its only worth.[1] And this means that it should be given freely and as one is confronted with others' needs.[2] In fact, so strong are his expressions concerning the duty of charity that, were it not for the corrective of his other and more general teachings concerning love, one might be justified in adopting the interpretation of his words so often championed, that Jesus taught that all wealth should be given away. Interpreted in their genetic relations with the fundamental principles of his teaching, however, these injunctions to charity appear in their true light. They are the one application of such principles to the historical conditions in which Jesus found himself.

And as such charity reappeared in the apostolic fraternity.

For one cannot be far from the truth in holding that it was the recollection of their manner of life with Jesus a few months previous that led the apostles in the early days of the Jerusalem church to favor the continuance of an arrangement in which no limits were set upon the devotion of wealth to the needs of the community. And thence resulted the outgush of Christian love which led to the sale of land and other property, and the devotion of the proceeds to the maintenance of a common fund which was devoted to supplying the needs of poor Christians.[3]

Many[4] have seen in this spontaneous κοινωνία, in which,

---

[1] Luke 16:1 ff.

[2] For instance, Luke 6:30; 12:33; Mark 10:21. In general see MATHEWS, *Social Teaching of Jesus*, chap. 6; PEABODY, *Jesus Christ and the Social Question*, chap. 4; ROGGE, *Der irdische Besitz im Neuen Testament;* CONE, *Rich and Poor in the New Testament*, chaps. 1–5; HEUVER, *Jesus' Teaching concerning Wealth*.

[3] There is no need of supposing that the entire membership of the church sat down to a common meal. The numbers, as well as Acts 2:46, preclude this.

[4] For instance, NITTI, *Catholic Socialism*, p. 62. A number of quotations are given in PEABODY, *op. cit.*, p. 26, note.

as one of the two accounts of Acts says, no one thought of his own property as his own,[1] a form of communism.   It is very difficult for one who would use words accurately to assent to such an opinion.   Communism consists in something more than self-sacrificing ·charity.   If words mean anything, to give one's coat to a tramp is not to constitute oneself a disciple of Fourier.   No more were the Christians at Jerusalem communists because they ministered to their poor.   There is not the slightest indication that they ever united in a common productive effort, ever uttered a word against the institution of private property, or gave their assent to any peculiar theory of the distribution of wealth. The situation was much simpler.   These Christian messianists expected that their Lord was soon to come to establish his heavenly kingdom.   This faith constituted a bond of union both with Jesus and with each other.   They were brethren.   Some of their number were in need of assistance. It was but an expression of the fraternal love which characterized the new life when those who had property should minister to their less fortunate brothers.   The time in which property would be of use was rapidly shortening, and for that reason, if for no other, wealth might well be put to its best use.   Such an explanation so satisfies all the conditions that it seems almost supererogation to call attention to the fact that the mother of Mark seems to have owned her house,[2] and that in the story of Ananias and Sapphira, whatever may be its historical value, there is no evidence that its writer supposed that in the Christian church there was ever any compulsory charity.[3]   The two wretches die as liars, not as breakers of a communistic compact.

But even such consistent, if indeed, under the belief of his speedy return, too literal, following of the teaching of

---

[1] Acts 4:32; *cf.* 3:44, 45.   In the *Didache*, 4:8, and in the *Epistle of Barnabas*, 19:8, this statement becomes a command.

[2] Acts 12:12.   [3] Acts 5:1-11.

Jesus was but short-lived in the church. His words were interpreted to refer to charity rather than to general economic life, and charity became throughout the different Christian communities what it has since become—a giving of a certain portion of one's income to the poor, chiefly those, doubtless, at Jerusalem. Wherever one can trace Paul there one can also discover his indefatigable effort to raise money for poor Christians.[1] However much this effort may have depended upon some politic motive, like maintaining the good-will of otherwise proselyting Jewish Christians,[2] there can be no question as to the importance he accords charity as a Christian virtue. Even the common meals furnished the poor of the Jerusalem church were perpetuated in the meals of the Græco-Roman churches like Corinth.[3] It is true that this meal soon became symbolical[4] rather than eleemosynary, the expression of a fraternal unity rather than of charity; but even thus its origin does not seem to have been quite forgotten, for alongside of the memorial supper there seems also to have been a more substantial meal. In other ways, also, the teachings of Jesus upon charity seem to have received especial attention. Paul admonishes the elders of Ephesus not to forget their Lord's word, "It is more blessed to give than to receive[5] and the poor-fund raised in his churches seems to have been sufficiently large to warrant a system of treasurers like Tychicus and Trophimus.[6]

Yet there is no suggestion that Paul thought it necessary

[1] 1 Thess. 4:11; Rom. 15:26-33; 1 Cor. 16:1-4; 2 Cor. 1:8 ff.; 8:4; 9:1 ff.; Gal. 2:10.

[2] Cf. 1 Cor. 16:1, 3; 2 Cor. 9:1.   [3] 1 Cor. 10:16; 11:24.

[4] The influence of the Greek mysteries may here be traced, but it is easy to give undue importance to this element in the universalizing of early Christianity. Cf. HATCH, Influence of Greek Ideas and Usages upon the Christian Church, chap. 10; CHEETAM, Mysteries, Pagan and Christian; WERNLE, Beginnings of Christianity, Vol. II, pp. 123 f.

[5] Acts 20:34, 35.

[6] Acts 20:4, 5; cf. Acts 24:17; Rom. 15:25, 26; Gal. 2:10. See RENDALL, Expositor, 1893, p. 321. The technical word for this contribution was διακονία.

for all his converts to beggar themselves in order to assist others from beggary. "Let thine alms sweat within thy hands until thou knowest to whom thou art giving it," says the *Didache*,[1] and Paul was quite as much opposed to indiscriminate charity. He insisted that the Christian should keep within the ranks of the wealth-producers. "We hear," he wrote the Thessalonians, "of some that walk among you disorderly, that work not at all, but are busybodies. Now them that are such we command and exhort in the Lord Jesus that with quietness they work and eat their own bread." "If any will not work, neither let him eat,"[2] he also commanded the Thessalonians, as if in the very spirit of modern philanthropy. In several of his letters[3] he recalls to the mind of his converts his own habit of life, how he worked daily in order that he might not become a burden to any, and that, too, while he distinctly recognizes his right along with other religious teachers to be supported by the community to which he ministered in spiritual things.[4] Perhaps at this point we find Paul in his most interesting position. The custom of the rabbis, and far more of the philosophers, favored the giving of presents to teachers. Thus, as a teacher, to say nothing of his being an apostle, he might have claimed the privilege of being supported by his disciples. This, as has already been said, he declined to do, but his declination was made in such form as really to strengthen the right of other teachers to be paid. Whether or not such persons had abandoned their ordinary vocations we cannot surely say, but probably they had. Only on this supposition can we account for Paul's anxiety that those who were over his converts in the Lord and who ministered to them in spiritual things should be cared for in material

[1] 1:6.   [2] 2 Thess. 3:10.

[3] 1 Thess. 2:9; 2 Thess. 3:7, 8; 1 Cor. 9:1-18; 2 Cor. 11:7; 12:13

[4] 1 Thess. 5:12, 13; 2 Thess. 3:9; 1 Cor. 9:1-14.

things. The very Scriptures taught the lesson, he insisted, when they taught that a man was not to muzzle the ox that trod out his grain.[1]

This insistence upon charity and self-support, as well as upon the payment of teachers, by others as well as Paul[2] argues strongly for the presence in the early churches of others than those who were poor or essentially proletarian. And this conclusion is corroborated by many hints in the apostolic and subsequent literature, not to mention the archæological testimony of the second and third centuries. Poor there were, but also those who were well to do; possibly, since there seems to have been a city treasurer, even a few rich.

To appreciate, however, the general social status of the churches outside of Judea, at least, one must think of communities composed of small shopkeepers, artisans, slaves, all being kept by the influence of their leaders steadily at their daily toil, doing heartily whatever they undertook, as unto the Lord, and all contributing to some fund which was applied to the needs of the other "saints." It is certainly a charming picture of simplicity and generosity—the farthest possible removed, on the one side, from any communistic propaganda, and, on the other, from mere commercialism.

But the leaders of the early church, if devoted to sobriety, industry, and charity, were none the less suspicious of the rich. In Paul's later letters he repeatedly warns his converts against covetousness, likening it to idolatry,[3] and rigorously excluding the covetous, with fornicators and thieves and drunkards, from the heavenly kingdom.[4] And it is worth noticing that this suspicion of the rich did not pass away. The epistle to Timothy declares[5] that the love of money is the root of all evils, and the author of He-

---

[1] 1 Cor. 5:9.   [2] Heb. 13:17.   [3] Col. 3:5.
[4] 1 Cor. 5:10, 11: 6:11; Eph. 5:5.   [5] 1 Tim. 6:10.

brews[1] bids Christians to be free from the love of money. Far more severe is the author of the epistle of James, which, whether it represents pre-Pauline Christianity or not, certainly represents the un-Pauline point of view. In all folk-literature there is no sterner denunciation of wealth or of that obsequiousness which even in the brotherhood of Christ gives special honors to the well-dressed and wealthy man. "Go to now, ye rich, weep and wail for your miseries that are coming upon you. Ye have laid up your treasure in the last days. Behold the hire of the laborers who mowed your fields, which is of you kept back by fraud crieth out."[2] In these stern words we see, however, not merely a hostility to wealth as such, but to the un-righteous and oppressing rich; and it is noticeable that even here there is no word of revolution, but a trust in the retribution to come in the day of judgment.

Despite the progress of Christianity among the wealthier classes, confidence in the poor man as over against the rich man, and the desire that all men should give to charity, may be said to characterize the first century of the life of the church. Once we even seem to catch some echo of the old communal charity of the ancient church, when in the *Two Ways* we read:[3] "Thou shalt communicate in all things with thy neighbor; thou shalt not call things thine own: for if ye be partakers in common of things that are incorruptible, how much more should ye be of those things that are corruptible;" but the context makes it likely that the words urge only charity.

The church as a whole seems never to have committed itself to other than the Pauline view of industry, private property, and charity in proportion to God's prospering. By the time we reach the second century we find the church

---

[1] Heb. 13:5. A reason for the minimizing of economic ambitions is almost a paraphrase of Matt. 6:31-34.

[2] Jas. 5:4.   [3] *Epistle of Barnabas*, 19.

fathers discussing the paradoxical teachings of Jesus with much the spirit, and oftentimes with the same casuistry, as the writers of today, while a little later Chrysostom urges an academic communism on the ground that all money put into the common fund would be divinely increased!

If now we seek for the motives that induced the apostles thus to inveigh against wealth while urging industry and charity, they will all be found either within the traditions of those who had lived with Jesus, or else within the general messianic expectations of the early church. It is hardly possible to suppose that the churches which preserved the records of Jesus' teaching that go to make up our gospels should have been utterly indifferent to the repeated injunction of Jesus to make wealth a secondary good and to practice charity. Just as impossible is it not to perceive that the expectation of a speedy return of Jesus to establish an ideal but unearthly society would have tended inevitably to minimize the value set upon wealth. The leaders of the church, with remarkable exceptions like Augustine, have always seen a Christian use of property in the endowment of ecclesiastical institutions. But an endowment presupposes a permanent institution, and this was just what the eschatology of the apostles made impossible. Their charity funds were for immediate consumption, not for permanent investments. Even the apostolic injunction to industry was primarily called out by an indifference to earthly conditions born of the eschatological hope. To erect the apostolic teaching into legislation is therefore impossible. As a whole, it is not even the expression of fundamental principles. Yet none the less—perhaps one should say all the more—is it valuable, for it discloses one fundamental fact, viz.: *Christianity has no economic program.* And another great fact emerges from the apostolic treatment of a commercial age: Economics, like all other aspects of life, is to be controlled by love—love that helps the less fortunate; love that refuses to judge a man by his possession or lack of wealth; love that refuses to make its possessor become through idleness a burden upon society.

But these are not rules. They are the elements of a Christianity that is dependent upon no theory of the second coming of Christ, or upon any formal messianism. Essential Christianity needs no such motives, and may even thrive better without them, for it is an expression of the *new life that is born from the contact of a soul with its God, and is nourished and directed by the teaching of Jesus.*

II

The influence of eschatological hopes in producing the conservative spirit shown by the apostles in the matter of wealth is even more marked in their words concerning politics. Jesus had left no teaching regarding the state. The nearest approach he made to the matter was his general reply to the Jews, to render unto Cæsar the things that are Cæsar's;[1] and to Pilate: "Thou couldest have no power except it were given thee from above."[2] Any man who attempts to erect a theory of politics upon two such statements will need considerable imagination, and deserves small credence. The fact is that in politics Jesus adopted a thoroughgoing policy of *laissez-faire*, refusing to complicate his real purpose in life with any consideration of political difficulties or reforms.

The same general attitude seems to have characterized the teaching of the primitive church. It is true that, as far as one can judge from the early sections of Acts, the first Christians judged that they were free to disobey the commands of the authorities whenever they interfered with

[1] Matt. 22:18-22.

[2] John 19:11. In general see MATHEWS, *Social Teaching of Jesus*, chap. 5.

what seemed to them to be clearly Christian duty,[1] but Jesus himself may be said by implication to have countenanced the same view, when he told to his disciples that they would be brought before kings and governors, for his sake, and promised them the aid of the Spirit in making their defense.[2] But the persecutions which came upon the church at Jerusalem were not so severe as to lead to any distinct attitude of hostility on the part of the Christians, either to the Roman or to the Jewish officials.

Paul seems to have had a good knowledge of law, both imperial and, if one may judge from the niceties of his references in his letter to the Galatians, local. He also, doubtless, realized the difficulties which beset the man who could be represented as in any way dangerous to the Roman empire. Yet he knew the advantage of Roman citizenship, and, from one point of view, the entire book of Acts is an argument for the legitimacy of Christianity because of the repeated protection shown Paul by various Roman officials. Perhaps it is in part for this reason that he seems to have been remarkably courteous in his references to the imperial power. He tells the Romans that the state is of divine origin,[3] and that it is to be obeyed implicitly under fear of just punishment: "Let every soul be in subjection to the higher powers: for there is no power but of God; and the powers that be are ordained of God." "For for this cause ye pay tribute also; for they are ministers of God's service, attending continually upon this very thing." And this of an emperor like Nero! Similarly Peter in addressing the Christians scattered throughout the empire bade them beware of being arrested for disorderly conduct, and to "honor the emperor."[4] At the same time Paul believed that all governments were but temporary, and that the rulers

---

[1] See the words of Peter and John, in Acts 4:19.

[2] Mark 13:9–11. [3] Rom. 13:1–7. [4] 1 Pet. 2:17.

of this age, both Jewish and Roman,[1] were to come to nought.[2] His attitude in general was not in the least, therefore, that of co-operation with the state, but that of submission to its requirements. In fact, he does not, apparently, think that the state is a matter in which the Christian has any particular share. This appears clearly in his strong words to the Corinthians against going into heathen courts, with their interfraternal troubles. The state might be appealed to for protection, but never to decide the differences of Christians.[3] It was bad enough that there should be dissensions within the Christian brotherhood, but they should be settled within the Christian community "by some wise man able to judge between brothers." Christians should never appear before the heathen judges to plead their difficulties with each other. "Do you not know," he asks indignantly, as he recalls them to their messianic hopes, "that the saints are to judge angels?"[4] and that "men who are unjust cannot inherit the kingdom of God?"

Here again we evidently have teaching that can be adjusted only to certain distinct historical conditions. Neither Peter nor Paul is drawing out a theory of the state. Each is endeavoring to show his converts how to live in an existing empire while waiting for the coming of the Christ. To elevate this work into lasting doctrine is to be untrue to historical conditions. It was not that all government was *right;* it was simply a divinely ordered element of a period of waiting. The true Christian citizenship was not in earth, but in heaven. The heavenly kingdom was not to be set up on the earth by any transformation of the Roman empire.

[1] 1 Thess. 2:16; Rom. 9:22; 11:1-36.

[2] 1 Cor. 2:6; 15:24; *cf.* Acts 17:7.

[3] Acts 28:19.

[4] 1 Cor. 6:1 ff. *Cf.* the saying attributed to Jesus, according to which the Twelve were to sit on thrones judging the twelve tribes of Israel, Matt. 19:8; Luke 22:30.

It was to come suddenly, miraculously. Had Paul returned to life at the beginning of the fourth century, there could have been no more surprised man than he upon reading the proclamation of Constantine. Persecution he could understand, for it was to be expected that an evil age would pursue the followers of the Christ it had killed;[1] but an earthly government gradually recognizing the civil rights of both Christians and heathen, with Christian officials and Christian legislation, was something of which he never dreamed. It was, in fact, something of which few Christians dreamed for two centuries after the apostle's death.

It is obvious, therefore, that we cannot regard the apostolic teaching concerning the state as of lasting significance. So to treat it would be to end political evolution. To submit to governmental oppression has been often the most unChristian of acts, and Paul himself was to fall a victim to his own refusal to allow his rule of passive obedience to extend over matters of conscience. The paradox of the political significance of Christianity never was more striking. On the one hand stand these directions of the apostle to submit to the imperial power, and on the other is the manifest fact that Christianity, in the same degree as it has been unaffected by tradition and authority, has always made toward political change. How may the paradox be resolved? By a resort to the facts which condition the teaching. It is inconceivable that Paul should have thus taught, had he perceived a social and political future before Christianity. It was because he believed in the cataclysm attending the return of the Christ that he urged the Christians to hold aloof from the state. Once free a man from this belief, and the apostolic teaching is impracticable. And this is precisely what happened in the process of time. The Christ did not return; Christianity could not hold itself from politics. It

[1] 1 Thess. 1:6; 2:14, 15.

remade the Roman empire; it has remade every state in which it has been allowed free scope.

Has, then, apostolic Christianity no political significance? Before a categorical answer is given one may well decide as to which apostolic Christianity is meant: that which deals with a religious ethic, or that which deals with a specific application of such ethic to an age believed to be rapidly moving toward its end? If the latter is meant, apostolic Christianity had a political message for its own day; but that message passed with its day. To enforce it again would mean to sanction tyranny. If the former is meant, then apostolic Christianity has no specific political message. Christianity in the teaching of its great apostles as in that of its Founder, is a life and not a political system. It may have political effects; it cannot have a political program. A government is Christian, not when it is a republic rather than a monarchy, or a monarchy rather than a republic; or when its subjects are either indifferents or martyrs. It is Christian when its institutions embody the spirit and are regulated by the principles of Jesus. And that this may be true, revolutions, despite Paul's word to the Roman church, may sometimes be the most sacred of Christian duties.

Thus again by a resolution of its historical form it is easy to discover the fundamental ethic of apostolic Christianity. Its highest good is the living of the eternal life of the Spirit, and its highest imperative is born of the need of living according to the measure of that spiritual life already possessed.

Although, therefore, formally the apostolic ethic was dominated by apocalyptic and eschatological concepts, essentially it was the life of Spirit—a moral life based upon religion. Formally, therefore, the church was a group of messianists awaiting a kingdom that never came and indifferent to all customs of society except those that were evil;

essentially the church was a group of men and women endeavoring to let the new religious and ethical life that had come to them from God through accepting Jesus as Christ express itself in social relations.

And the life lived. Jesus was greater than the men who interpreted him, even when they interpreted him aright, and it is he and his work, and the life with God he revealed, that formed the strength of historical Christianity. The new life must needs be expressed in temporary vocabularies and concepts, but it could not be restrained by them. It conquered them—the mighty systems of an Augustine, an Origen, a Justin, even of a Paul. And thus inevitably, because it was the social expression of a life, the church became the parent of a Christian civilization; the Christian woman of a Græco-Roman civilization became the Christian woman of a Christian civilization; the Christian family of the first century grew into the Christian family of today; the Christian fraternity, loyal to an imperial tyranny, became the champion of a Christian democracy that, with all its revolutionary power, even as yet has not come to its own in either politics or economics.

SUMMARY

The results of our investigation may now be summarized with a view to their use in constructive processes which lie outside our present purpose.[1]

1. An impartial comparison of the New Testament literature with the contemporaneous and immediately preceding literature of Judaism shows an essential identity in the general scheme of the messianic hope. In the New Testament as in the Jewish literature we find that the general scheme of deliverance by God involves the two ages, the two kingdoms of Satan and God, the coming of the kingdom in the future by cataclysm, the establishment of the day of judgment, the resurrection of the dead, and the personal Christ.

2. The New Testament literature modifies this general scheme of Judaism only as it is compelled so to do by the actual facts connected with the life of Jesus. Thus it recognizes that the Christ has suffered and died, and that his death is vicarious. Its belief in the resurrection is no longer a theory, but a generalization of the fact in Jesus' own career. Its understanding of a personal Christ is now supplemented by a knowledge of the historical career of Jesus as a preacher and exponent of divine love as well as sovereignty. The new Christianity also magnifies the Spirit —the actual interpenetration of the divine and human personalities. At the same time such elements of the older hope as are not affected by these facts appear in the New Testament as a part of the hope of the coming kingdom to be established by Jesus. The new messianism of the New Testament is essentially eschatological, a matter of hope.

[1] This constructive work has been sketched by me in various numbers of *Christendom*, Vol. I (1903), and will be found further developed in my forthcoming book, *The Gospel and the Modern Man*.

3. This identity between an older and a later expectation shows that, in so far as the Christian messianism is not controlled by the actual facts of the career of Jesus, it is an inheritance from Judaism. It is therefore an interpretative concept which, like the cosmological concepts of the time, is without a basis of experience—the means of expressing and interpreting facts of experience and of history. This interpretation as used by Jesus of himself becomes the exposition of a consciousness of a divine personality, and as used of Jesus by his disciples is the ultimate valuation of a personality they recognized as the exponent of God. This personality rather than its interpretation is, especially in its two-fold historical revelation of God-in-man and of the resurrection, the first great essential of the Christian gospel.

4. In the case of those Jews who could see in Jesus such a personality as would warrant their interpreting him in messianic—i. e., in ultimate—terms, there followed a genuinely moral adjustment with God which resulted in a radical experience of the divine Spirit. This spiritual life, which was correlated with the expected messianic future and the immortal life, is an indisputable matter of experience, and one that is regarded (with varying emphasis) by the New Testament writers generally as the evidence of the credibility of their messianic hope: in particular as the basis for their confidence in their acquittal in the coming judgment, and for their assurance of their participation in a resurrection similar to that of Jesus, and in the joys of the expected glory. This new life, rather than its interpretation, is the second essential verity of the Christian gospel.

5. For constructive purposes it is necessary to distinguish between the facts of the life of Jesus and of Christian experience, on the one side, and their interpretation and exposition in the formulas of messianism, on the other. The latter are seen to be pedagogic in the sense that messianism

was the great channel by which the fundamental verities
were valued and brought to a generation under the control
of the messianic expectation.   We should not be justified in
saying that the interpretation was necessarily incorrect.   It
will be efficient, however, only with those in whose apperception it already exists, and the New Testament itself contains abundant evidence of a process of redefinition of the
messianic interpretation of Jesus for the sake of those who
needed some more philosophical valuation of his divine personality.   A definition is thus at once the result, the expression, and the cause of an ever increasing vital faith.

6. The history of the Christian community as found in
the New Testament indicates clearly that the new life resulting from faith in Jesus and the consequent actual interpenetration of the human and divine personalities, was
checked in its expression by the survivals of Jewish messianism in the Christian communities.   But it could not be
and was not destroyed.   The fundamental impulse of that
life is one of self-sacrificing love like that of God, and this,
rather than an inherited eschatology, turned out to be the
dominant element of the new religion.   Its history modified
the messianic expectation and gave to some of its terms
new definitions born of the philosophical apperception of
western peoples.   Such redefinition, so far from being a
loss, was inevitable and beneficent to believers who were not
Jews.   It furnished mediating concepts and valuations
which enabled the new converts to bring themselves into the
same relationship with God that the Jewish messianic concept had enabled the Jews to attain.   But the Christian life
itself, and the real nature of faith, were not changed.   Both
grew in the same proportion as men came to God through a
supreme definition of Jesus.

7. We have thus suggested the method presupposed by
any theological reconstruction that in any true sense is loyal

to the historic Gospel. The theologian must be a historian. There must be, first, a precise interpretation of the Gospel as it stands in the New Testament, in its own terms and from its own point of view. Second, there must be a discrimination between the messianic and kindred interpretative formulas and concepts, on the one hand, and, on the other, the facts in the records of the life of Christ and of Christian experience which fair-minded criticism, psychology, and sociology will regard as assured. Then, third, there will be the presentation of these facts, through the use of such interpretative and pedagogical concepts as will do for today what the various concepts of the New Testament did for their day.

Such a method judges historical facts by genuinely historical criteria, and therefore distinguishes between the essential and purely economic elements of Christianity without abandoning scientific limitations. From it there must result a new confidence and appreciation of that historical gospel which gave rise to faith rather than was caused by faith. For while the method will recognize to the full the fundamental verities of Christian experience, it also will give full value to historical facts. In these it will find data for the same moral stimulus and the same religious hope they have always aroused during the centuries of Christian history. On the one side, this method avoids that assertion of the perpetual authority of interpretative concepts and that dogmatism which have always proved fatal to the spontaneous and persuasive expression of the Christian spirit; and, on the other hand, it avoids that mysticism which belittles the historical facts which really have made Christian assurance possible. Such an historical method prepares the way for religious psychology and leads to a theology at once scientifically positive in its reliance upon objective facts, consonant with the known laws of personality and historical criticism; it conserves every essential fact and implication of the gospel as it was preached by Jesus and Paul, and revitalizes that Christian hope of deliverance from sin and death that has been the great power of historical orthodoxy.

Unless we mistake greatly, there is room for such a theology, at once critical, experiential, historical, revering Jesus as the divine Way rather than the divine End, dominated by a conviction of immortality, and insistent that humanity needs to be saved from sin and suffering, and that, by sharing in the divine life revealed in Jesus, humanity can be carried, both generically and individually, to the next and, because spiritual, higher stage of that process which is the expression of the eternal will of God. Not an interpretative concept born of an abandoned cosmology and a persistently political conception of God, but the eternal life born of God through the mediation of faith in Jesus as his revelation—that is the eternal element in Christianity. And such a life is possible for the man of any age who will allow the facts of the gospel to control his estimate of himself and his possible destiny, his conduct toward others, his faith in Jesus, and his trust in a revealed God. To make these facts dynamic in reason and will, he may use whatever worldview he may regard as the modern equivalent of messianism, or whatever terms he may regard as supreme definition of that divine Personality whom the first Jewish believers called the Messiah.

In a word, to remove or to allow for messianism is not to destroy the essentials of the gospel—the personality, the teaching, and the resurrection of Jesus; a rational faith in God as Father; a certainty of divine forgiveness; an experience of the eternal life; an assurance of a complete life beyond and because of death. It is rather to make them more intelligible, more convincing, more certain, and more dynamic.

INDICES

INDEX OF SUBJECTS

INDEX OF REFERENCES

I. OLD TESTAMENT

329

IV. MISCELLANEOUS

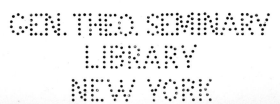

THE DECENNIAL PUBLICATIONS OF
THE UNIVERSITY OF CHICAGO

THE DECENNIAL PUBLICATIONS

ISSUED IN COMMEMORATION OF THE COMPLETION OF THE FIRST TEN
YEARS OF THE UNIVERSITY'S EXISTENCE

AUTHORIZED BY THE BOARD OF TRUSTEES ON THE RECOMMENDATION
OF THE PRESIDENT AND SENATE

EDITED BY A COMMITTEE APPOINTED BY THE SENATE